Jefferson's Vendetta

JOSEPH WHEELAN

Jefferson's Vendetta

THE PURSUIT

of

AARON BURR

and the

JUDICIARY

CARROLL & GRAF PUBLISHERS
NEW YORK

JEFFERSON'S VENDETTA
The Pursuit of Aaron Burr and the Judiciary

Carroll & Graf Publishers
An Imprint of Avalon Publishing Group Inc.
245 West 17th Street ✦ 11th Floor
New York, NY 10011

AVALON
publishing group incorporated

Copyright © 2005 by Joseph Wheelan

Library of Congress Cataloging-in-Publication Data is available.

ISBN: 0-7867-1437-9

9 8 7 6 5 4 3 2 1

Designed by Pauline Neuwirth, Neuwirth & Associates, Inc.

Printed in the United States of America
Distributed by Publishers Group West

Contents

Come not between the dragon and his wrath.
—King Lear

Prologue

There was exactly as much right to shoot the persons in question as to do what has been done.
—Congressman John Randolph of Virginia,
protesting the Senate's suspension of
habeas corpus for treason suspects

[Burr's] guilt is placed beyond question.
—President Thomas Jefferson

RICHMOND, MARCH 26, 1807

Eight dusty riders and a shuttered carriage threaded their way through the Virginia capital's crowded streets, entering the retail and business district at the foot of Capitol Hill. With a clatter of hooves, the little convoy pulled up at a hostelry, advertised by a large sign with a painted golden eagle. It was the Eagle Tavern, their destination. A small, lithe, middle-aged man emerged from the carriage, stretched his legs, and filled his lungs with the damp, spring-scented air. Blinking in the bright afternoon sunlight, he took in the sights around him: the knots of staring men, the shops and business, the budding dogwoods, and the sun dipping toward the west.

The riders dismounted, their eyes never leaving the passenger. Over the past twenty days, they and their prisoner had traveled eleven hundred miles together over muddy trails and roads, through the dangerous Alabama Indian country and the crossroads towns of Georgia and the Carolinas. The captive wore the same clothing in which he had been arrested: a floppy dirty-white hat, and an old blanket coat that a river man might put on to keep warm. The onlookers' interest sharpened when they noted the stranger's fine boots and his quick, dark eyes—eyes that blazed like stars in a midnight sky.

Soon the news was all over Richmond: Aaron Burr, America's most-wanted man, had arrived under a heavy guard—Aaron Burr, the former vice president, slayer of Alexander Hamilton; Aaron Burr, who had supposedly plotted to seize New Orleans, capture its shipping and cannons, loot its banks, and then invade Mexico and Spain's Southwestern territories.

In the Alabama backwoods, they had caught the infamous Aaron Burr, whose wicked schemes, while never carried out, had caused the Army to march into New Orleans, militias to be activated, and the Navy to be placed on alert. It mattered little that Burr's expedition, when captured on the Mississippi River above New Orleans seven weeks earlier, had turned out to be pathetically small—just sixty men, women, and children. Aaron Burr was going to be charged with treason. If convicted, he could hang for it.

—⚏—

Burr, rather than Thomas Jefferson, had nearly become the third U.S. president in 1801. If Jefferson had not already known it, that election had informed him in no uncertain terms that Burr could upset his Republican Party leadership, his plans for a second term, and his dream of establishing a Virginia dynasty in the President's House.

Over a snowy, bone-chilling week in February 1801, U.S. House members, in their Constitutional role of electoral tie-breakers, had steamed up their drafty chamber during thirty-five futile roll-call votes while trying to break the unforeseen 73–73 electoral-vote deadlock between Burr and Jefferson. On the thirty-sixth ballot, after Jefferson had secretly acquiesced to a brokered deal for Federalist votes, the House elected him, and Burr became vice president. Jefferson, appearing serene as always but in reality badly shaken by Burr's surprising showing, immediately took steps to ensure that it would never happen again. He unleashed the wolfish Republican press on Burr; denied patronage appointments to Burr loyalists, thereby eroding Burr's political base; pushed through a Constitutional amendment that changed the rules for electing vice presidents; and thwarted Burr when he ran for New York governor, denying him any chance for a political comeback. In that April 1804 gubernatorial election, all of Burr's enemies—the Livingston and Clinton clans and Alexander Hamilton, as well as Jefferson—had coalesced to assure his defeat. Burr's duel with Hamilton beside the Hudson River at Weehawken three months later had ended his political career as surely as it ended Hamilton's life, and he had turned to fabulous schemes of conquest and empire in the Spanish Southwest, Mexico, and, some said, even in trans-Appalachian America. Now he was the most famous fugitive of his age, and his name, like Benedict Arnold's, was a byword for treason.

—m—

About 10 P.M. on February 18, 1807, lawyers Nicholas Perkins and Thomas Malone were playing backgammon in their cabin in Wakefield, Alabama, when two plainly dressed horsemen stepped out of the darkness and knocked on their door. The strangers asked for directions to the local tavern and to the home of a Colonel Hinson.

As they conversed, Perkins, who was also a militia officer, observed some interesting details about the smaller horseman, who was letting his companion do most of the talking. Clad in an ordinary blanket coat, crossed by a leather strap from which hung a tin cup and a hunting knife, the man wore unusually fine boots and rode an excellent horse equipped with a quality saddle and new holsters. Examining the man more closely, Perkins was struck by his eyes: they "sparkled like diamonds." It suddenly came to him that this might very well be the former vice president, Aaron Burr, for whom a $2,000 reward had been offered. The instant that the men departed, Perkins rode to Sheriff Theodore Brightwell's home and rousted him from bed. Together, they set out through the woods to

Colonel Hinson's home. Because the travelers had not seen Brightwell, Perkins sent the sheriff inside to join them by the kitchen fire, while Perkins shivered in the freezing woods, waiting for daybreak.

Early in the morning, Brightwell, Burr, and Burr's traveling companion, Robert Ashley, rode away from the Hinson home. Learning from Mrs. Hinson that they had sought directions to Pensacola, Perkins borrowed a canoe and paddled to Fort Stoddert, located on the Mobile River a few miles from Spanish West Florida, and alerted the garrison commander, Lt. Edmund P. Gaines. Gaines organized a mounted patrol and it quickly overtook the three travelers. The young lieutenant, who would serve with distinction in the War of 1812, placed Burr under arrest, ignoring Burr's protests that he had no authority to do so.

Gaines soon began to hear unsettling reports that Burr's supporters in the nearby settlements were plotting to free him. The settlers' own implacable hatred of the colonial Spanish, who prevented them from trading on the Gulf Coast, made them natural allies of Burr, who had schemed to invade the Spanish Southwest. Inside Fort Stoddert, Burr, companionable and charming as ever, had made friends of members of Gaines's immediate family. He played chess with Gaines's wife, and shared his medical supplies with Gaines's ill brother, George S. Gaines, an Indian trader. But then Lieutenant Gaines learned that Burr had supposedly tried to bribe two sentinels to help him escape. At about the same time, a Spanish naval officer from Mobile asked to see Burr. Told that that was impossible, the Spaniard immediately returned to Mobile. While his intentions were opaque, it was the last straw for the jittery Gaines. Fearing that Spanish troops might show up next, Gaines decided to send Burr to Washington.

—◊—

Between Fort Stoddert and Washington lay eleven hundred miles of dangerous Indian country, and settled regions where Burr might find allies. Gaines picked nine reliable, sturdy men: Nicholas

Perkins, who would be the leader; Thomas Malone, Perkins's roommate; and seven soldiers. Worried that Burr might try to persuade one of the guards to help him escape, Perkins made his men swear that they would speak to the prisoner only when necessary.

Burr, Perkins, and the eight guards rode out of Fort Stoddert on March 6, 1807, as Burr's new friends watched sadly. Some women wept, and a mother-to-be later named her child Aaron Burr; neither age nor misfortune had diminished Burr's gift for making friends.

The riders followed "Via Dolorosa," a well-traveled Indian pathway, encountering hundreds of Indians, who permitted the heavily armed men to pass unmolested. Day after day, cold rain fell. The men forded flooded creeks and rode single-file on muddy paths through the hardwood forests where the bare tree trunks were black from the rain. Averaging forty miles per day, they avoided settlements and camped in the woods at night, where they were sometimes serenaded by the howling of wolves. Burr slept alone in the only tent. Although he was fifty-one years old, he possessed the stamina of a man half his age, and never complained about the hard traveling. The ten men passed through the soggy Alabama and Georgia backcountry mostly in silence.

At Chester, South Carolina, not far from one of the homes of Burr's only child, Theodosia, and her planter husband, Joseph Alston, the travelers approached a tavern where people were gathered outside.

To everyone's astonishment, Burr leaped from his horse and announced, "I am Aaron Burr, under military arrest, and claim the protection of the civil authorities." Perkins and the guards jumped to the ground, and Perkins ordered Burr to re-mount his horse. Burr refused.

Flinging down his pistols, the powerfully built Perkins looped an arm around Burr's waist and one-handedly slung him back onto his horse. Malone snatched Burr's reins, other guards whipped his horse's flanks, and the party galloped away, as the townspeople gaped. The entire episode had taken less than a minute.

For the first time, Burr's stoicism failed him, and he burst into tears. Malone, young and impressionable, wept with him.

After they had gotten some distance away, Perkins returned to Chester, where he bought a closed carriage to discourage Burr from again seeking civil protection, now that they were in a more populous region. Burr rode inside the carriage through North Carolina and Virginia. Forty miles from Washington, in Fredericksburg, Virginia, Perkins received instructions from President Thomas Jefferson to turn back to Richmond.

Jefferson, Secretary of State James Madison, and Attorney General Caesar A. Rodney had decided to prosecute Burr for treason in Virginia, in whose farthest jurisdiction, a remote Ohio River island owned by Irish émigré Harman Blennerhassett, a disturbance had occurred three months earlier.

RICHMOND, MARCH 30, 1807

The Eagle Tavern wasn't the best lodging house in Richmond—the White Swan Tavern atop Capitol Hill was more highly regarded—but over a period of twenty years the Eagle had attracted a loyal clientele of planters, sportsmen, and state legislators. The Eagle sprawled over an entire city block, and, should anyone still overlook it, an 8-by-5-foot sign displaying a splendidly painted golden eagle announced its presence. Thomas Sully had earned $50 for his eagle, a pittance compared with his future earnings as a renowned portraitist, best known for his painting of young Queen Victoria.

At midday, John Marshall, chief justice of the U.S. Supreme Court and one of Richmond's leading citizens, strode through the tavern's crowded public room and entered a private room. Marshall, fifty-one, tall and loose-jointed like his political arch-enemy and third cousin once removed, Thomas Jefferson, normally liked to stop at the tables of friends and neighbors to exchange pleasantries. But his manner on this day was brisk; clearly, he was on judicial business. Marshall, his wife Polly, and their many children occupied a brick home a short distance away, and Marshall's lithe, somewhat shambling figure could be seen about town when he was not kept away by his Supreme Court responsibilities in Washington, or his federal circuit-riding duties in Virginia and North Carolina. In the early mornings, he liked to roam the City Market along the James River, stowing his purchases in a basket looped over his arm. Marshall's presence in the Eagle Tavern might have gone unremarked except for the fact that he and the city's judges and lawyers usually patronized the White Swan Tavern, where they enjoyed Colonel John Moss's fine wine cellar and bar, and his well-laid table, always covered with crisp linen.

The men who thronged the Eagle Tavern knew something important was going to happen, and they wanted to witness it. The news was all over town that Aaron Burr, being kept under guard in a room somewhere on the premises, was due to make a formal appearance before Marshall.

—∾—

Five weeks earlier in Washington, the chief justice had written what would turn out to be a critical decision involving two alleged Burr co-conspirators: Dr. Justus Erich Bollman and Samuel Swartwout. Bollman, a thirty-seven-year-old German-trained medical doctor and adventurer, was renowned for his daring rescue of the Marquis de Lafayette, the Revolutionary War hero, from the Austrian prison where he had been banished by leaders of the French Revolution. Swartwout was a Burr devotee whose older brothers, John and Robert, had belonged to Burr's "Little Band" during Burr's heyday as a New York political operator.

Bollman and Swartwout had been arrested in New Orleans by order of General of the Army James Wilkinson after they had delivered coded letters to him from Burr. Wilkinson had reacted with shock—whether it was genuine or not remained to be seen—upon reading the letters' contents: a proposed joint expedition by Wilkinson and Burr against New Orleans and the Spanish Southwest. In short order, Wilkinson had fired off urgent warnings to Jefferson, and then marched his troops into New Orleans, which he declared to be imperiled by Burr and his minions and needing martial law. Wilkinson had promptly arrested Bollman, Swartwout, and three other men for treason. Denying them their Constitutional rights to legal representation and a court hearing, the general had sent the prisoners on naval ships to Washington (Bollman and Swartwout) and Baltimore (the three other men).

Events reached a boil on Washington's Capitol Hill in late January, just as Bollman and Swartwout were being locked in the brig at the Marine Barracks, where they were guarded, day and night, by an officer and fifteen Marines. Urged by congressional leaders to reveal what he knew about the Burr conspiracy, President Jefferson had issued a special message, describing a dangerous conspiracy to separate the western states from the Union and conquer Mexico. "The prime mover in these was Aaron Burr," the president declared. While Jefferson acknowledged that Burr had also spoken of colonizing the Ouachita River Valley in northeastern Louisiana, this enterprise was only a "pretext for all his preparations." When the West resisted secession, the president said, Burr had decided to instead seize New Orleans, empty the banks and the military stores, and to then embark for Mexico. Burr's "guilt is placed beyond question," said the president.

Jefferson's emphatic condemnation of Burr without a hearing or trial might not have concerned the president's fellow Republicans, but it troubled Federalists. John Adams complained that "the first magistrate ought not to have pronounced it before a jury had tried him," adding that Burr "must be an Idiot or a Lunatick [sic] if he has really planned and attempted to execute such a Project as imputed to him. . . ." Federalist Senator William Plumer of New Hampshire also doubted that Burr was capable of "all the absurdity that is ascribed to him. He is a man of first-rate talents. He may be capable of much wickedness, but not of folly."

Adams and Plumer were in a decided minority. With Jefferson maneuvering behind the scenes through his Senate floor manager, William Branch Giles of Virginia, the Senate the next day, January

23, suspended habeas corpus. That venerable "Great Writ" requires every arrestee to be brought before a judge so that the reason for his detention can be formally declared; it is one of the Constitutional safeguards that sets the United States apart from tyrannical regimes where prisoners can be held indefinitely without being charged. Article I, Section 9 of the Constitution states that habeas corpus may be suspended only when, "in Cases of Rebellion, or Invasion the public Safety may require it."

The Senate's approval of Giles's proposal proved to be highly unpopular. Amid a hurricane of criticism, the House indignantly rejected it, 113–19, with Congressman John Randolph of Virginia asserting, "There was exactly as much right to shoot the persons in question as to do what has been done."

—m—

While the debate over habeas corpus raged at the Capitol, Dr. Justus Bollman sent a note from his Marine Barracks cell to the President's House: Bollman wanted to tell Jefferson everything that he knew of Burr's plans.

Eager to hear the real story behind the Burr conspiracy, Jefferson had Bollman brought to Secretary of State Madison's office to meet with Jefferson and Madison. Bollman extracted a promise from Jefferson to guard the confidentiality of what he was about to say. "The P. assured him that nothing which he might say or acknowledge, should be made use of against himself," said Madison's notes of the January 23 meeting. Jefferson and Madison also assured Bollman that it was "a settled rule" that no such statement made to a government official "could be extorted from him as a witness" in court. Although he would later discover this to be untrue, Bollman believed at the time that he was safe from self-incrimination, and proceeded to tell his story.

Burr's sole purpose was to lead an expedition against Mexico, said Bollman. In New Orleans, Burr intended to seize French artillery and enough shipping—unless Britain responded to Burr's overtures and supplied naval ships—to transport his expeditioners to Vera Cruz, the jumping-off point for his march to Mexico City, where Burr planned to make himself king. Burr did not intend to plunder New Orleans's banks, Bollman said, or to detach the West and unite it with Mexico; Burr believed that the two regions were too distant geographically and mismatched culturally.

Jefferson and Madison were skeptical. In his notes, Madison dryly observed that Bollman wished to explain his own conduct and Burr's in a favorable light. At Jefferson's request, Bollman wrote a twenty-page statement in his prison cell.

Even though Bollman and Swartwout had not been charged with any crimes, the federal circuit court in Washington refused to release them. The evidence against them consisted of affidavits from General James Wilkinson and from William Eaton, the Barbary War hero whom Burr allegedly tried to recruit; and Burr's encrypted letter to Wilkinson. However, while the evidence brimmed with allegations about Burr's supposed intentions, it failed to implicate Bollman and Swartwout. Yet, by 2–1, the court rejected the men's request to go free, with the two Jefferson appointees overruling their Federalist colleague. The defendants' lawyers, Charles Lee and Robert Goodloe Harper, promptly appealed to the Supreme Court.

If there was an overture to the Burr proceedings in Richmond a month later, it was the Supreme Court's February 21 ruling, written by Marshall, in *Ex Parte Bollman and Ex Parte Swartwout*. The decision reversed the circuit court's ruling, and set Bollman and Swartwout free. And it forcefully stated what treason is, and what it isn't: "To conspire to levy war, and actually to levy war, are distinct offenses," and "conspiracy is not treason."

That said, Marshall went on to write words that he would later regret and upon which grand juries would predicate their indictments. "It is not the intention of the court to say that no individual can be guilty of this crime who has not appeared in arms against his country. On the contrary, if war be actually levied, that is, if a body of men be actually assembled for the purpose of effecting by force, a treasonable purpose, all those who perform any part, *however minute or however remote from the scene of the action* [author's italics], and who are actually leagued in the general conspiracy, are to be considered as traitors. But there must be an actual assembling of men for the treasonable purpose, to constitute a levying of war." Marshall clouded the issue further by adding, ". . . the crime of treason should not be extended by construction to doubtful cases. . . ."

Other judges released the three prisoners whom Wilkinson had sent from New Orleans to Baltimore: Kentucky Senator John Adair, a general and veteran of the Revolutionary War; Peter V. Ogden, the nephew of former New Jersey Senator Jonathan Dayton; and attorney James Alexander, arrested for representing the other detainees.

—m—

A hush fell over the Eagle Tavern's public room as Aaron Burr, flanked by U.S. Marshal Joseph Scott and two deputies, was led to the private room where Marshall awaited him. Pale and weary-looking, but washed, shaven, and wearing clean clothing, Burr stepped into the room with the three guards, and the door closed behind them.

Burr and Marshall were distant colleagues from rival political, geographical, and social worlds. Both had served as Continental Army officers at Valley Forge during the punishing winter of 1777–1778. If they had not become acquainted then, they surely did in Philadelphia during the 1790s, when Burr was a senator from New York and Marshall was a Virginia Congressman. At the U.S. Capitol in Washington on March 4, 1801, Chief Justice Marshall had administered the oath of office to President Jefferson, with Vice President Burr standing at his side. And in 1805, Associate Justice Samuel Chase's impeachment trial in the Senate brought the men together again; Vice President Burr was the presiding judge, while Marshall was a defense witness.

At the brief hearing in the Eagle Tavern, U.S. Attorney George Hay asked that Burr be held on charges of treason and for the high misdemeanor crime of violating Spain's neutrality. Burr and his lawyers contested the motion.

In no hurry to rule on such important motions, Marshall instead asked Nicholas Perkins to describe his long journey with Burr from Alabama to Richmond. Then, before adjourning, the chief justice adopted a suggestion made by Hay—that the hearing should be reconvened the next day in the state Capitol's second-floor courtroom, to accommodate the large crowd that was expected.

The idea was actually Jefferson's; he wanted a great audience to witness Aaron Burr's final degradation.

[I]

The "Hand of Malignity"

This wandering meteor . . . which now has suddenly fallen among us, as if
from the skies.
                        —U.S. Attorney General Caesar Rodney
                                on Aaron Burr

The Virginia Capitol's federal courtroom clearly would not hold
everyone who wished to witness Burr's battle for his life, so
Chief Justice John Marshall moved the proceedings downstairs to
the Virginia House of Delegates. Forty feet wide and eighty-six feet
long, the House chamber was the largest indoor public meeting
place in Virginia. But before long, it, too, had reached its capacity.

The prosecution team was led by U.S. Attorney General Caesar
Rodney, in what would be his only appearance at the proceedings,
and Virginia U.S. Attorney George Hay, who was mourning the
death just a week earlier of his twenty-five-year-old wife, Rebecca.
Representing Burr were John Wickham, the gregarious leader of
the Virginia bar, and a friend and neighbor of Marshall; Edmund
Randolph, a former Virginia governor who had been Attorney
General and Secretary of State under George Washington; and

Burr himself, one of the most respected trial lawyers of his day. It was said that Burr had never lost in the courtroom.

Hay, not known for flowery oratory, succinctly stated the government's grave allegations: that Aaron Burr had conspired to lead an uprising in the western states and territories and separate them from the United States—an act of treason, punishable by death—and also to invade the Spanish Southwest and Mexico, a violation of the 1794 Neutrality Act, for which he could be sent to prison for three years. Burr had intended to rule his conquered empire from New Orleans, charged Hay. "Hating a people whose confidence he had once enjoyed, but which had been indignantly withdrawn, he resolved to usurp territory and dominion, and to establish a monarchy within a territory of the United States, without regard to the incalculable evils, the bloodshed and desolation which a civil war never fails to produce. . . ."

For Burr to be held for treason, Hay believed that he needed only to convince Marshall that the government had good reason, or "probable cause," to *suspect* that Burr had committed treason. Hay reasoned that, at this early stage, he needn't *prove* it; that would happen at the treason trial. Citing Sir William Blackstone, the English jurist and legal writer, Hay said that a suspect could be held on a charge so long as prosecutors met the relatively low threshold of proof required of probable cause. Only if it were "manifestly apparent" that no crime whatsoever had occurred—say, in the unlikely event that a supposed murder victim turned up alive—could a judge countenance releasing a suspect without bond, with no charge filed.

Burr, said Hay, had assembled an armed force on Blennerhassett Island, near Marietta, Ohio, and led it down the Ohio and Mississippi rivers, intending to seize New Orleans, where reports of their approach caused "great alarm and consternation."

While New Orleans had undoubtedly been thrown into confusion, it was not so much due to the approach of Burr and his sixty expeditioners as to the harsh measures imposed by General James Wilkinson, the commander of all U.S. Army forces, ostensibly in response to Burr's scheme. Wilkinson had subjected the United States' chief southern port to martial law and had suspended habeas corpus. As time would show, however, Wilkinson's motives had little to do with the threat from Burr; they were more sinister.

Prosecutors read from Barbary War hero William Eaton's affidavit and submitted General Wilkinson's deposition and Burr's coded letter to him—the very evidence with which the government had unsuccessfully attempted to commit Dr. Justus Bollman and Samuel Swartwout for treason. The Burr letter, as interpreted by Wilkinson, exhorted Wilkinson to join his army to Burr's Mexico invasion force. This letter, with Wilkinson's ensuing letters to Jefferson, had been the trip wire for the events that ended in Burr's flight into the Southern backwoods, an act as damning as were the affidavits and letter, the prosecutors said; Burr's flight was no less than an admission of guilt, as was his desperate attempt, while in federal custody, to seek sanctuary in Chester, South Carolina, a "mere mockery and evasion. He knew that there the law would do nothing with him."

Burr and his attorneys, however, asserted that the government was *persecuting*, not prosecuting, Burr. "My designs were honorable and would have been useful to the United States," said Burr. "I fled, it is true, not from an investigation into my conduct, but from military despotism." The affidavits of Eaton and Wilkinson, he said, were "abounding in crudities and absurdities."

Burr and his followers intended to clear and settle 400,000 acres of the Ouachita River Valley (near present-day Monroe, Louisiana), not start a war. "We confess we had boats, but such boats only as were calculated to accommodate families removing to form settlements," said Edmund Randolph. "Yet are they suddenly, by magic art, to be converted into Mississippi men-of-war? Where were the arms with which they were equipped? There were no guns, no swords, not a particle of ammunition."

Attorney General Rodney protested that the government did not wish to persecute Burr; its aims were honorable. Prosecutors would demonstrate by their conduct that they were "not influenced by malicious or vindictive passions to persecute him, as it has been supposed." Burr, said Rodney, was "this wandering meteor . . . which now has suddenly fallen among us, as if from the skies."

John Wickham derided Hay's interpretation of probable cause, innocence, and guilt as a perversion of the presumption of innocence until guilt is proved: "He is to be presumed guilty, 'til his innocence shall be established. Is this correct? Is this law?" He mocked the government's decision to bring Burr to Virginia to face the charges—"Was there no law, no justice in South Carolina or Georgia?"—and said Eaton's affidavit claiming that Burr *intended* to seize American territory and Mexico did not add up to evidence of an actual insurrection. "What kind of an invisible army must this have been, when in the course of three months not an individual could be found to testify to its existence?"

Knowing that Marshall would never commit Burr for treason if this dangerous insistence on proof were not quashed, Rodney complained that the government had only known of Burr's arrest for five weeks. "There has been no possibility of getting the proof which his counsel contend is necessary."

The prosecution, declared Wickham, was confusing intentions with actions. Furthermore, he said, revealing what would become the keystone of Burr's defense: "Overt acts should be first established, and then an intention proved, which would constitute treason. General Eaton's testimony has no weight, because it does not establish an overt act." Wilkinson's affidavit and the uproar in New Orleans also failed to prove an overt act. "Has that place [New Orleans] been attacked?" asked Wickham. "The conduct of Wilkinson was enough to frighten them. They knew nothing but what he chose to disclose." The government's contention notwithstanding, flight is not evidence of guilt. If it were, said Wickham, "I fear then the people of New Orleans would all have been guilty of treason, if it had been in their power. They would all have fled from military despotism to a land of liberty."

If the government was unready to prosecute Burr, declared Edmund Randolph, it should discharge him. "If a contrary doctrine should prevail, we should want nothing, to have a complete star-chamber mode of proceeding established among us, but such a precedent as this."

When the attorneys had finished, Marshall announced that he would issue a written ruling the next day, April 1.

George Hay sent his notes of the day's proceedings to the President's House, as he had the previous evening. Jefferson, suffering from a blinding headache that had prevented him from riding to Monticello when Congress adjourned three weeks earlier, was bedridden in a darkened room of the President's House, able to work for only an hour or two a day. But there can be no doubt that even so incapacitated, Jefferson managed to study Hay's notes; one can picture the president's long, freckled face, illuminated by a dim light, bent attentively over Hay's reports.

—⁓—

To say that Jefferson was highly interested in the Burr case would be a colossal understatement; Aaron Burr had become a lightning rod for the president's many frustrations. At the moment, most of them revolved around James Monroe, the U.S. Minister to Great Britain. To Jefferson's vast irritation, Monroe had signed a treaty with England that notably did not forbid the impressments of American seamen. Now Monroe was insisting on returning to America to challenge Secretary of State James Madison for the presidency in 1808, thereby disrupting Jefferson's carefully mapped plan of Virginian succession, which was supposed to be Madison, *then* Monroe. Not helping matters any, Virginia Congressman John Randolph, a leader of the Republican dissidents who called themselves "Old Republicans," was endorsing Monroe over Madison. Jefferson was also trying to tone down the embarrassing outbursts of his son-in-law, Virginia Congressman Thomas Mann Randolph—who, time would show, was mentally ill—over Jefferson's supposed preference for his other son-in-law, Virginia Congressman John W. Eppes.

Compared with these sticky problems, the Burr case appeared blessedly straightforward to Jefferson, and offered the delightful possibility that his former political nemesis might be convicted and hanged for treason. Yet, only five months earlier, General Wilkinson's conduct had been a far graver concern. On October 22, 1806, Jefferson had asked his cabinet whether Wilkinson should be dismissed as General of the Army, for having "engaged with [Burr] in this design as his lieutenant, or first in command, and suspicion of infidelity," and for disobeying orders to leave St. Louis to organize New Orleans's defenses against the Spanish. The cabinet members did not agree on a course of action.

While trying to divine Wilkinson's loyalties, Jefferson had virtually ignored eight letters from the Kentucky U.S. Attorney, Joseph Hamilton Daviess, sent between January and July 1806, warning of Burr's supposed plans for an expedition against Spain and for separating the western states from the Eastern Seaboard states. Disgusted with Jefferson's apparent indifference, Daviess had begun his own newspaper, *The Western World*, to disseminate his conspiracy theories and those of former Senator Humphrey Marshall—Daviess and Marshall, by pure coincidence, were both Federalists and brothers-in-law of the chief justice—as well as numerous stories implicating Wilkinson. The articles were widely reprinted in the Eastern papers.

Only when General James Wilkinson's warning letters arrived in Washington in November 1806 did Jefferson act against Burr— and thereafter become Wilkinson's staunch champion. Brushing aside the reports, buzzing like clouds of mosquitoes, that Wilkinson had been in league with Burr, and with Spain too, the president issued a nationwide proclamation denouncing the purported Burr conspiracy. Strangely, only two months later, in early January 1807, Jefferson had confessed to William Plumer, the Federalist senator from New Hampshire, that he did not believe there was sufficient evidence to convict Burr of either treason or high misdemeanor.

Candor, doubt, and angry frustration all coexist uneasily in Jefferson's letters and papers throughout 1807, the year in which the president used all of his considerable power to destroy his enemies.

From the shadows, Jefferson had orchestrated Burr's political downfall; now he was embarked on an open crusade to destroy the man himself, publicly proclaiming Burr to be a menace, while privately acknowledging that there was not enough evidence to convict him of treason.

Why? Possibly, he was concerned that the Federalists might ally themselves with Burr to damage the Republicans' seemingly unassailable position as the dominant party. Whether his actions were motivated by political contingency or personal spite, Jefferson appeared to take inordinate pleasure in his former vice president's capture. In a letter to George Morgan, Jefferson gloated over the fact that when he was arrested, the usually dapper Burr was wearing "an old white hat, a pair of Virginia cloth pantaloons, and old Virginia leggins, and an old Virginia cloth coat."

APRIL 1, 1807

Chief Justice Marshall's eyes swept the crowded chamber and then dropped to the handwritten pages spread before him. Burr, he declared, could be held for allegedly violating Spain's neutrality, a high misdemeanor, but he could not be held for treason. He announced that a grand jury would meet May 22 to consider the misdemeanor charge, and, if the government insisted on continuing to press for a treason charge, whether to charge Burr with that crime as well.

Prosecutors had neither proved that an overt act of treason *might* have been committed, nor had they convincingly implicated Burr, Marshall said. Thus, they had failed the test of probable cause, although this did not preclude prosecutors—when they had obtained more evidence—from attempting to persuade a grand jury to indict Burr for treason. Marshall had not expected the government to present overwhelming proof of Burr's guilt, but only to meet the lower threshold of probable cause. It had not. Treason, said the chief justice, citing Article III, Section 3 of the Constitution, "consists of overt acts which must be proved by two witnesses or by the confession of the party in open court." The government's evidence indicated Burr might have discussed separating the western states, and might have planned to invade Spain's North American territories, but "an intention to commit treason is an offence entirely distinct from the actual commission of that crime. War can only be levied by the employment of *actual force*. Troops must be embodied, men must be assembled in order to levy war. . . . Treason may be machinated in secret, but it can be perpetrated only in open day and in the eye of the world."

Why, Marshall asked, had the government not yet produced any evidence that Burr had raised an army in order to commit treason?

"Several months have elapsed since this fact did occur, if it ever occurred," Marshall said. "More than five weeks have elapsed, since the opinion of the Supreme Court [in Bollman and Swartwout] has declared the necessity of proving the fact, if it exists. Why is it not proved? . . . It is impossible to suppose that affidavits establishing the fact could not have been obtained by the last of March."

An audible sigh arose from the courtroom when Marshall uttered these words, by themselves sufficiently inflammatory to infuriate Jefferson and his advisers.

But Marshall did not stop there. Troubled by George Hay's attempt to apply Blackstone's rather Draconian view of probable cause—that a suspect could be discharged only when suspicions were proved utterly groundless—Marshall continued:

"I do not understand him [Blackstone] as meaning to say that the hand of malignity may grasp any individual against whom its hate may be directed, or whom it may capriciously seize, charge him with some secret crime, and put him on the proof of his innocence."

Government lawyers, naturally enough, assumed that the "hand of malignity" was a disparaging reference to the Jefferson administration. Whether or not this was his purpose, Marshall, upon learning that his words had been so interpreted, issued a rare clarification to the press. He had intended "only an elucidation of the general doctrine laid down by Blackstone," the chief justice said.

Marshall set a $10,000 bond for Burr on the high misdemeanor charge. The government lawyers argued for a higher sum, while Burr's attorneys claimed that he probably would be unable to raise even $10,000. Marshall let the bond stand, and that very afternoon five men—Thomas Taylor, John G. Gamble, John Hopkins, Henry Heth, and M. Langhorne—pledged the amount, and Burr went free.

In a letter to James Bowdoin, the American minister to Spain, Jefferson complained bitterly about Marshall's decision. "The judges here have decided that conclusive evidence of guilt must be ready in the moment of arrest, or they will discharge the malefactor. If this is still insisted on, Burr will be discharged, because his crimes having been sown from Maine thro' the whole line of the Western waters to N. Orleans, we cannot bring witnesses here under 4. months."

For weeks, Jefferson brooded over Marshall's taunting question, "Why is it not proved?" "As if an express could go to Natchez, or the mouth of Cumberland, & return in 5 weeks, to do which has never taken less than twelve," he fumed to William Branch Giles. "But all the principles of law are to be perverted which would bear on the favorite offenders who endeavor to overrun this odious Republic." In Jefferson's view, the Judiciary was rapidly becoming as great a menace as Burr. He condemned "the tricks of the judges to force trials before it is possible to collect the evidence, dispersed through a line of 2,000 miles from Maine to Orleans."

Yet Jefferson had begun this very task weeks earlier. In his self-appointed role as Burr's chief prosecutor, he had bypassed normal procedures and instructed his cabinet to canvass the countryside "from New York to New Orleans" for witnesses and evidence that could be used against Burr. Government agents were fanning out across the land with questionnaires Jefferson himself had helped prepare. It would be nearly two hundred years before the nation would see another federal dragnet of this magnitude.

Marshall's disparagement of the government's evidence and his refusal to hold Burr for treason prompted Jefferson to refocus his battle plan. The Judiciary had overreached, he firmly believed—not only in the Burr case, but in its rulings dating back several years. In fact, since John Adams's "midnight appointments" of judges in the last hours of his administration, the Judicial Branch had needed reining in. Not only had it placed itself over the Executive and Legislative branches, but the Judiciary "proclaims impunity to that class of offenders which endeavors to overturn the Constitution, and are themselves protected in it by the Constitution itself." John Marshall was the apotheosis of the Judiciary's power grab. Remove Marshall and, like an organ freed of a malignant tumor, the body politic would heal itself.

Impeachment had proved to be a dull scalpel; Jefferson's attempted removal of Associate Justice Samuel Chase from the Supreme Court in 1804–1805 had ultimately failed. The president now had a better remedy: a Constitutional amendment curbing the Judiciary's powers. Burr's trial would give the people an opportunity to "judge both the offender & judges for themselves. . . . They will see then & amend the error in our Constitution, which makes any branch independent of the nation."

If Burr went free, but, as a consequence, the Constitution was amended to limit the Judiciary's power, Jefferson was convinced that "it will do more good than his condemnation would have done."

Thomas Jefferson, who would be celebrated as a benevolent philosopher–statesman, architect, inventor, farmer, and gifted writer—and rarely remembered as a vindictive man—had already declared Burr guilty "beyond question," had attempted to suspend habeas corpus, and had unleashed an army of federal agents on the nation. Now, he had also commenced an all-out war on the Judiciary.

[2]

The Political Maestro

[He had] no confidence in the Virginians; they once deceived him, and they were not to be trusted.

—AARON BURR'S REASON FOR INITIALLY DECLINING TO BE
THOMAS JEFFERSON'S RUNNING MATE IN 1800

WASHINGTON, MARCH 4, 1801

Three hundred people, bundled up against the damp chill of late winter, crowded into the half-finished Capitol, with its catwalks and piled lumber, to witness the first presidential inauguration ever held in the United States' new seat of government. The disordered setting amplified the distinct impression that Washington remained little more than a jumbled encampment, rather than the capital of a dynamic new republic. It strained the sensibilities to picture Major Pierre L'Enfant's design of grand avenues radiating from a series of circles amid grids of lettered and numbered streets while contemplating the raw buildings jutting from the woodland clearing near the Potomac and Anacostia rivers.

L'Enfant had haughtily withdrawn from his own project rather than surrender any authority over it. Thereafter, the task of carrying it through to completion had fallen to an assortment of men;

Secretary of State Thomas Jefferson, for example, had personally selected the locations of the Capitol and the President's House. For all that had been accomplished in a decade of planning and building, the city's bleakness had inspired a visiting diplomat to nickname it "The city of magnificent distances." In the wintertime, the cold dampness emanating from the Potomac and Anacostia rivers sank deep into the bones. In the summertime, the city was sulfurously hot and plagued with mosquitoes. Its red clay turned to greasy mud in wet weather, and to choking dust in dry.

But on this day, Washington's many drawbacks were forgotten in the contagious excitement investing Jefferson's inauguration as the third president of the United States. Change was in the air. George Washington had been dead fifteen months, and the first Republican president in the nation's history was about to take office.

—m—

President-elect Jefferson entered the Senate at noon sharp. Disdaining the tradition followed by John Adams and George Washington of riding to their inaugurations in fancy carriages, Jefferson had walked to the Capitol from his boarding house, Conrad & McMunn's, with an escort of Republican supporters and a Maryland artillery unit. He strode into the Senate chamber with members of the House of Representatives and John Marshall, who had been appointed Chief Justice of the U.S. Supreme Court just five weeks earlier. Awaiting them in the packed Senate was Vice President Aaron Burr, sworn in earlier by James Hillhouse of Connecticut. Burr had already administered oaths of office to the newly elected senators.

Notably absent was President Adams, who had left Washington before dawn for his home in Braintree, Massachusetts, rather than witness Jefferson's moment of triumph; the bruising 1800 election that had resulted in Adams's defeat would rankle for years. It would also mark the beginning of the Federalists' journey to extinction. The victors, Jefferson and the ascendant Republicans, were calling their triumph the "Revolution of 1800," believing that it signaled the realization of their cherished, but antiquated, ideal of a small federal government benignly presiding over a happy people who enjoyed broad personal liberties.

When Jefferson arrived, Burr stood on Jefferson's right as Marshall swore him in as the new president. Marshall then stepped to Jefferson's left side, and Jefferson, the fifty-seven-year-old Founder, faced his audience with the two forty-five-year-old leaders from the younger branch of the Revolutionary War generation flanking him. Burr and Marshall were barely out of their teens when Jefferson wrote the Declaration of Independence in 1776, though they were already serving as combat officers in the Continental Army. Their recent elevation to national prominence had come through singular service to their respective parties, Burr for his political wizardry in placing New York in Jefferson's vote column, and Marshall for having defied Talleyrand's arrogant ministers X, Y, and Z in 1798—thereby supplying the Federalists with a good reason to lead the nation into an undeclared, two-year naval war with France, the so-called Quasi-War.

Nothing in Jefferson's almost inaudible inaugural address—his soft voice scarcely carried beyond the first row—foreshadowed his attempts six years in the future to destroy the men on either side of him. Nor did anything in the ceremony suggest the astonishing chain of events that had thrust the three men together on the Senate dais to begin with—three men who distrusted and disliked one another.

The amazing journeys of Burr and Jefferson to the Senate platform, fraught with potholes and detours, had begun fourteen months earlier, in January 1800 in Philadelphia. There, Burr had met with Vice President Jefferson and probably also with his campaign managers, James Madison and Albert Gallatin, to discuss the fall presidential election. Jefferson hoped to accomplish what had not yet been seriously attempted in the United States—defeat a sitting president.

There was no question that Jefferson would be the Republican presidential candidate; but in order to unseat President Adams,

Jefferson knew that he needed New York's twelve electoral votes. The South was safely Republican, and the Northeast would vote for Adams and the Federalists. That left the middle states in play. New York's importance became magnified by the likelihood that Pennsylvania, which had delivered fourteen electoral votes to Jefferson in 1796, would deadlock. To win New York and, thus, win the election, Jefferson and his managers needed as their ally Aaron Burr, the Empire State's brilliant political operator.

—∽∾—

Smart and energetic, Burr was descended from two unusually distinguished bloodlines of outstanding scholars, educators, and clerics. His earliest American ancestor, Jehue Burr, reached the Massachusetts Colony in 1630 with Governor John Winthrop's Puritan fleet. Jehue's descendants distinguished themselves as soldiers and religious men. Aaron Burr's father and namesake, the Rev. Aaron Burr, became the famous second president of the College of New Jersey, in Princeton.

Jonathan Edwards, colonial America's great theologian, was Aaron Burr Jr.'s grandfather. Edwards was one of the fountainheads of "The Great Awakening," the religious revival that swept the East in the 1730s and 1740s. The Calvinist Edwards was severe and passionate: One of his most famous sermons, "Sinners in the Hands of an Angry God," became a staple of literary anthologies. The Rev. Aaron Burr Sr. met and married one of Edwards's eleven children, Esther, on June 29, 1752, in Newark, New Jersey. He was thirty-seven; she was twenty-one. Their first child, Sarah, was born on May 5, 1754. On February 6, 1756, Esther bore a son, Aaron Jr.

And then, as though the Burr family had become a personification of one of Edwards's blood-curdling sermons about God's wrath, a whirlwind of disaster enveloped it. The Rev. Aaron Burr Sr. died of fever on September 24, 1757. Jonathan Edwards, summoned by the Princeton college's trustees to succeed his son-in-law as the college president, died six months later, in March 1758, after receiving a smallpox inoculation. Two weeks after her father's death, Esther Burr, twenty-seven, died of smallpox. A family friend, a Dr. Shippen, packed off the orphaned children, Sarah, four, and Aaron Jr., two, to Philadelphia. The children's grandmother, Sarah Edwards, went to Philadelphia in September 1758 to bring them home, but she died of dysentery. In just one year, two generations of Aaron Burr's family had perished.

The Rev. Timothy Edwards, the children's uncle, eventually took charge of them and hired tutors for his nephew. Young Burr disliked his uncle's strict household and ran away several times, once signing on as a cabin boy on a merchant ship; but before the ship sailed, he was found and brought home. It is no wonder that the boy studied so hard to get into college at Princeton.

At eleven years of age, Burr met all of the entrance requirements, but his small stature persuaded the fathers of the College of New Jersey (now Princeton University) to delay his matriculation until he was thirteen, when he was admitted as a sophomore. As if to make up for the two years of waiting, Burr studied sixteen to eighteen hours a day, displaying his lifelong indifference to food and drink and, in the process, nearly wrecked his health. Moderating his severe study habits, he joined the American Whig Society, one of the college's two literary societies, whose members included James Madison and Lighthorse Harry Lee, the future father of Robert E. Lee.

For whatever reason—perhaps it was a harbinger of the problems Burr would have with Virginians—Burr switched to the American Whig Society's rival group, the Cliosophic Society, and there found a lifelong home. Burr's society fellows would form a distinguished company in later years: Tapping Reeve, his one-time tutor, future brother-in-law, Connecticut Supreme Court justice, and founder of the nation's first law school, at Yale; two U.S. Supreme Court justices, Henry Brockholst Livingston and William Paterson; Jonathan Dayton, a future New Jersey senator and lifelong Burr confidante; and Luther Martin, the future "Bulldog of Federalism" and famous trial lawyer, who would be of invaluable service during Burr's hour of greatest need.

Graduating at age sixteen, Burr, because of his ancestry, was expected to enter the Presbyterian ministry. But religious studies didn't suit him, and he quit them to study law. The outbreak of the Revolutionary War in 1775 pushed him in yet another direction—the Continental Army.

—∿—

In September 1775, five months after Lexington and Concord, Colonel Benedict Arnold, with eleven hundred men, including young Captain Aaron Burr, and two fellow officers who would prominently figure in Burr's life thirty years later, James Wilkinson and Jonathan Dayton, struck out into the Maine wilderness hoping to surprise the British at Quebec and capture Canada. The Maine woods, however, nearly undid them. A bone-chilling rain fell without letup as the Americans hacked their way through dense thickets and poled up the dark, swollen rivers that threaded the gloomy forests. Floods carried off boats, food, and supplies, and the surprise maneuver on Quebec became a harrowing ordeal. Fording icy rivers, sleeping on the wet ground, devouring dogs and even their own moccasins when there was nothing else to eat, the ragged soldiers began to drop from hunger, pneumonia, exposure, and exhaustion. On November 7, 1775, only half the men who had begun the trek reached Quebec.

Sixteen years earlier, during the French and Indian War, General James Wolfe had led British troops up the forbidding cliffs along the St. Lawrence River to the Plains of Abraham before the city, and had there defeated the French. Wolfe and the French commander, the Marquis de Montcalm, both died in the battle that made Canada British. But Wolfe had attacked in September, and boats had carried his army up the St. Lawrence; the Americans stood before Quebec in November after a draining, six-week march. And while Wolfe had commanded four thousand officers and men, Arnold now mustered only five hundred.

At Quebec, though, good news reached Arnold: General Richard Montgomery had captured Montreal and was now free to assist him. Arnold sent Burr to Montgomery to arrange a rendezvous of their forces at Quebec for a combined assault on the British. His note to Montgomery said of Burr, "He is a young gentleman of much life and activity, and has acted with great spirit and resolution on our fatiguing march."

When Montgomery arrived in Quebec, however, he brought only three hundred men with him, which increased the American force to just eight hundred. In a swirling snowstorm on New Year's Eve, 1775, rightly believing the British would have their guard down, Montgomery launched the assault. Burr was in the vanguard. It might have succeeded but for a lone sentry who rousted a crew of gunners. As the British cannons opened fire, Arnold fell, wounded in the leg. Montgomery shouted, "Push on, brave boys; Quebec is ours!" just before grapeshot swept the vanguard, instantly killing Montgomery and ten others—in fact, everyone except Burr. Burr exhorted the Americans to follow him, and set out, but found himself alone. As it turned out, without his knowledge, Montgomery's second-in-command had ordered a retreat. With shot and shell flying around him, Burr tried to lift the general's body onto his shoulders, but Montgomery was too heavy, and Burr had to leave him on the field.

Burnished in the nineteenth-century American consciousness would be the lone, diminutive figure in the romantic painting "Little Burr," a reference to Burr's small stature—a wiry 5-feet-6 when fully grown. In the painting, nineteen-year-old Captain Burr, under enemy fire before the walls of Quebec, snow falling on his tricorner hat, stoically bears the body of his fallen commander, General Richard Montgomery, through deep snow back to American lines. The painting is a paean to courage, loyalty, and the indomitable human will. And, while Burr undoubtedly was one of the Revolutionary War's heroes, the painting was not altogether accurate, as was true of much of what passed as fact regarding Burr. It was strange that a man so vilified through the years would be portrayed so heroically on the walls of American schoolrooms.

Promoted to major at the age of twenty, Burr joined George Washington's staff in June 1776 at the general's Richmond Hill headquarters outside New York City. The convergence of Burr and Washington at Richmond Hill, while lasting just ten days, was portentous in two respects: Some historians would believe that Washington then formed his dislike for Burr, and Burr would one day live in Richmond Hill. Perhaps Washington's antipathy toward Burr was no more than the resentment of a slow, silent, and deliberate man toward one more nimble-minded and articulate. But a more likely source of Washington's later coolness toward Burr was his alliance with Washington's detractors, as defeat followed disheartening defeat for the hapless general. Burr believed, as did many Continental Army officers, that Washington was an incompetent commander who should be replaced—by either General Horatio Gates or General Charles Lee. Washington, as adept politically as he was unlucky militarily, quashed the nascent insurrection by blaming Lee for the Continental Army's failure to win a smashing victory at Monmouth, New Jersey, in June 1778, and then court-martialing him. Washington, not known for being thick-skinned, undoubtedly remembered the names of every Lee supporter—such as Burr, who wrote a letter on Lee's behalf. Burr was soon watching contemporaries with little or no combat experience reach general rank, while he remained becalmed at the rank of colonel.

A satisfying assignment for Burr, who had wanted combat duty and not staff work, was as General Israel Putnam's aide-de-camp. While with Putnam, the field commander in New York, Burr witnessed the Continental Army's defeats at Long Island and New York. During the rebels' dash north through Manhattan with the British at their heels, when he encountered a brigade hunkered down in a fort without entrenchments, Burr urged the commander, General Henry Knox, a future Secretary of War, to withdraw. If he stayed, Burr warned him, his men would be wiped out or captured. Knox spurned Burr's advice. Unwilling to abandon the brigade to annihilation or captivity, Burr boldly addressed Knox's men, exhorting them to follow him; they did, re-establishing a line on Harlem Heights, where the Continental Army won a victory the next day, September 16, 1776.

Burr's excellent reputation as a combat officer led to his appointment as commander of "Malcolm's Regiment," which, under his command, became a crack unit. At Valley Forge during the bittercold winter of 1777–1778, the "Malcolms" so impressed his superiors that Burr was asked to restore discipline to a troubled unit there. Malcontent ringleaders had plotted a mutiny, and Burr, when he discovered the plan, secretly unloaded the mutineers' weapons; then, at midnight, he ordered the unit into formation. Unaware that his musket was empty, the mutiny's leader raised his weapon to shoot his commander. Burr's sword flashed, and the mutineer's bloody arm dangled at his side, later to be amputated.

In Westchester County, Connecticut, when Burr was given the thankless assignment of putting a stop to looting by renegade Continental Army troops, he established around-the-clock patrols, which he personally supervised at all hours. The looting stopped. But the long hours on horseback, combined with years of exposure in all weather and the consistently poor food, caused Burr's health to fail. In the hundred-degree heat of the Battle of Monmouth, he had suffered the first of his lifelong migraine headaches, which he nicknamed "the torment." Now, beset by a variety of other ailments as well, his constitution unraveled. Unable to continue military service, on March 10, 1779, he resigned his commission, which he had held for nearly four years. He was twenty-three.

Burr resumed his legal studies, completing them in just two years, and the New York Bar waived its rule requiring three years of study, so long as he passed the bar examination, which he did in April 1782. Poised to begin a legal career, Burr met with a pleasant complication. He got married.

The bride was Theodosia Bartow Prevost, the sharp-witted widow of a British Army officer. During the war, her home near Paramus, New Jersey, was an urbane oasis for Continental Army officers weary of the banality of camp life. In gratitude, they made sure she was spared the harsh measures usually aimed at Tories.

James Monroe once interceded on her behalf with New Jersey officials, as did Burr, who became her friend. In December 1781, he
learned that Theodosia's husband, Colonel James Mark Prevost,
had died of wounds while serving in Jamaica. On July 2, 1782,
Theodosia became Mrs. Aaron Burr, despite their ten-year age difference and her five children.

Burr joined other young Patriot lawyers who were establishing
themselves in New York City—among them John Jay, Rufus King,
and Alexander Hamilton. Burr and Hamilton often worked
together on cases, and together they won what at the time was the
largest monetary award in America, in a case against two New York
merchants on behalf of Frenchman Louis Le Guen. Burr's meticu-
lous preparation became his hallmark, and enabled him to put
together an impressive string of courtroom victories. When arguing
a case, he was known for cogency, precision, and quiet sarcasm
rather than for oratory, the favored style of many lawyers, including
Hamilton.

But it wasn't long before ambition and partisanship turned the
occasional law partners, Burr and Hamilton, into rivals. Governor
George Clinton, an anti-Federalist, named Burr New York Attorney
General in 1789, just as Hamilton was becoming a political strategist
for the Federalists, the party of Washington and John Adams. Their
rivalry blossomed into enmity in 1791 when the State Assembly
passed over General Philip Schuyler, Hamilton's father-in-law, for
another U.S. Senate term, and elected Burr in Schuyler's place.
(U.S. senators were not elected by popular vote until after the 17th
Amendment's ratification in 1913.)

In October 1791, Burr moved into a rented room in
Philadelphia and took his seat in the Second Congress. He had
found his true vocation. It wasn't law; it was politics.

—◊◊◊—

Theodosia was already suffering from the cancer that would kill her
in three years. Although ill for much of their marriage, she had
borne Burr two daughters—Theodosia, in June 1783, and Sally,

who lived just three years—followed by two stillbirths. Theodosia's two sons from her first marriage, Frederick and John Bartow Prevost, served as law clerks in Burr's office while her three daughters from that marriage had left the scene. While Burr was away, the two Theodosias—the forty-five-year-old mother and her precocious eight-year-old daughter—were on their own at Richmond Hill, the thirty-year-old New York mansion on twenty-six acres whose lease Burr had taken over early in 1791. Not only had Richmond Hill served as George Washington's military headquarters, it had also been the home of Vice President John Adams and his family in 1790, when New York was the nation's capital. The grounds of the six thousand-square-foot mansion, two miles outside the city, ran down to the Hudson River. (It no longer stands at what today is the intersection of Charlton and Varick streets.)

Burr went into debt furnishing Richmond Hill and stocking its wine cellar and library. Among the books on his library shelves were Edward Gibbon's *Decline and Fall of the Roman Empire*, Jeremy Bentham's works, and *Vindication of the Rights of Women*, the protofeminist work by Mary Wollstonecraft, mother of Mary Shelley, the author of *Frankenstein*.

Wollstonecraft's 1792 book made such an impression on Burr that he obtained an oil portrait of her. It was one of the few possessions that he managed to keep throughout his tumultuous life. Even before he discovered Wollstonecraft and began touting her book to anyone who would listen, Burr's reputation as a progressive thinker was secure. As a state assemblyman, he had tried unsuccessfully to ban slavery in New York, and represented blacks on behalf of the New York Manumission Society, which crusaded against the re-enslavement of free blacks and established the African Free School in New York. He also held the startling belief that the government should *negotiate* with Indian tribes—at odds with nearly everyone else, including Thomas Jefferson, who advocated the Indians' removal or extermination. Virtually alone among the American leaders of his time, Burr could claim to have an Indian friend, Joseph Brant of the Mohawks.

But Burr's daughter, Theodosia, was his greatest project, especially after his wife's death in May 1794. Believing that she was the equal of any man, Burr educated her as he would have a son. His advocacy of women's education was rare in an age when girls were taught little beyond simple reading and writing. As he once declared to his wife, Burr wished to "convince the world what neither sex appear to believe—that women have souls!" Burr believed that women's education was of paramount importance because children received their first impressions almost exclusively from their mothers, the "repositories of all the moral virtues" that went into the making of men of "excellence."

Burr personally supervised Theodosia's upbringing and education. To inculcate self-sufficiency, he made sure that she slept alone at an early age—an unusual practice at the time—and encouraged her to walk through unlit rooms at night to conquer her fear of the dark. He also supervised her tutors. At age nine, Theodosia read Latin and Greek, and was able to read French so rapidly that her father had trouble keeping her in French-language books. Starting at 5 A.M. daily, she studied mathematics, literature, pianoforte and harpsichord, and dancing. She fenced, was a respectable pistol markswoman, and became an expert horsewoman in an era when few women rode.

After her mother's death in 1794, Theodosia, at the age of eleven, became mistress of Richmond Hill. Nearly every distinguished dinner guest—and they included Charles Maurice de Talleyrand, Jerome Bonaparte, James Madison, Thomas Jefferson, and John Adams—came away dazzled by her wit, by her musical talent, by her ability to quote poetry by the hour, and by her flashing black eyes and aristocratic beauty. Throughout Theodosia's short life, even after marriage and motherhood, Burr continued to encourage her to read and learn: "It will add greatly to my happiness to know that the cultivation of your mind is not neglected . . . I advise you, as soon as you have finished a play, novel, pamphlet, or book, immediately to write an account and criticism of it."

Theodosia's friends included Alexander Hamilton's daughter, Angelica, and the young widow, Dolley Todd, and her infant son. Burr had befriended the Todds while boarding with Dolley's mother, Mrs. John Payne, in Philadelphia. Playing matchmaker, he introduced Dolley to one of his former college classmates, Congressman James Madison of Virginia. It proved to be a lasting match.

—∽∾—

During the summer of 1791, Madison and Jefferson traveled through New York state, ostensibly to study nature, but really to examine the Republican flora and fauna; in other words, the reigning Clinton and Livingston families, and Aaron Burr. Political fault lines were deepening between the Federalists, the propertied party of the Constitution, and the rising anti-Federalists, or Republicans—the common-man party of the Declaration of Independence, and a forerunner of the modern Democratic Party. The Federalists were strong in the North, the Republicans in the South. Jefferson, the undisputed Republican leader, and Madison were seeking Northern allies, and undoubtedly saw a future party leader in Burr.

Aaron Burr, arguably America's first professional politician, was devoted to the nuts and bolts of politics but ideologically lukewarm. For Burr, politics, like the law, was more an intellectual exercise, a sport even, to be played "for fun and honor & profit." What Jefferson and Madison thought of Burr's lack of partisan rigor isn't known, but Jefferson wouldn't have understood; politics, he believed, was serious business, "a service to mankind." The visit to Burr by Jefferson and Madison was a watershed, proof that, at the age of thirty-five, Burr was an emerging political leader—but for which party?

Early in the 1792 New York governor's campaign, Federalists were considering Senator Burr as a possible challenger to incumbent Republican Governor George Clinton, and also looking at him as a credible vice presidential alternative to John Adams, who was disliked by some party members. Alexander Hamilton, however, was not convinced that Burr would truly represent the Federalists' interests. Burr's candidacy for governor ended when John Jay, the Federalist Chief Justice of the U.S. Supreme Court, decided to enter the race. The balloting during the April election was close, and the canvassing committee raised questions about results from three counties—Otsego, populous and pro-Jay; and Tioga and Clinton, smaller counties that leaned toward Clinton. If all three were counted, Jay most certainly would win. The canvassing committee's divided report showed the strain of its sharply delineated partisanship—the panel had seven Clintonians and four Jay partisans. New York's two senators, Burr and Federalist Rufus King, were asked to settle the issue.

Burr and King disagreed, too. Burr wanted to accept the Clinton County votes and reject Tioga's and Otsego's; King said all three counties should be counted. The seven Clintonians on the canvassing board adopted Burr's plan, announced Governor Clinton's re-election, and burned all the ballots, as the election law stipulated. A dispute raged for months: Newspapers exchanged broadsides, pro-Clinton and pro-Jay pamphlets were furiously produced, and there was a legislative investigation.

Burr fought to clear his name of the taint of partisanship, but the Federalists now knew he was not one of them. Warned by Rufus King that Burr might upstage John Adams, Hamilton quietly began writing letters designed to stain Burr's reputation. He was careful to send them only to acquaintances who did not know Burr personally. Burr was "unprincipled" and his conduct "equivocal," Hamilton wrote. "Mr. Burr's integrity as an individual is not unimpeached," he said. "As a public man, he is one of the worst sort." It was a campaign that Hamilton would wage fitfully for the next dozen years. Burr had made his first great enemy.

—— ⚭ ——

Devoting himself to his senatorial duties, Burr soon rose to Senate Republican leader. Nearly alone, he opposed sending John Jay to England to negotiate a new treaty. When his fears that Jay would be

too accommodating were borne out and Jay brought home his con-
troversial 1794 treaty, Burr led the doomed opposition to it. The Jay
Treaty inaugurated ten years of bitter partisanship between
Republicans and Federalists. Burr also championed Tennessee state-
hood, which made him many new friends in the West, including
Andrew Jackson, Tennessee's first congressman. In 1797, when the
New York General Assembly replaced Burr in the Senate with
Philip Schuyler, whom Burr had supplanted in 1791, Burr returned
to the State Assembly.

Hamilton continued trying to poison Burr's reputation with
Federalists and moderate Republicans. While serving as George
Washington's Secretary of the Treasury, he persuaded the president, who had little use for Burr anyway, to refuse to name him
Minister to France, even after Senate Republicans had nominated
him. (Republican James Monroe eventually got the position.) The
outbreak of the Quasi-War in 1798 opened another possible
avenue for Burr, a return to military life; President Adams recommended him for a brigadier generalship in the army being raised
by George Washington to fight the French. But Hamilton,
Washington's second-in-command, struck again, and Washington
did not appoint Burr.

Burr also made Virginia's Republican leaders uneasy. In 1796,
when Washington announced that he would not seek a third term,
Jefferson became the Republican presidential candidate who would
face Federalist John Adams and his running mate, Thomas
Pinckney. Senate Republicans selected Burr as Jefferson's running
mate, on the basis of his growing influence and the geographical
balance he would bring to the ticket. But Jefferson's obvious coolness toward Burr's candidacy signaled to Virginia's twenty-two
electors that, after casting their first ballots for Jefferson, they were
not bound to vote for Burr with their second ballots. (Until 1804,
the president and vice president were elected separately, with electors casting two equal votes; the candidate receiving the most electoral votes became president, and the runner-up was vice president,
no matter which party they represented.) Thus, just one Virginia

elector voted for Burr with his second ballot; the other twenty-one scattered their votes. Adams received seventy-one electoral votes to Vice President-elect Jefferson's sixty-eight. Pinckney got fifty-nine electoral votes and Burr, thirty.

Bruised by the Virginians' infidelity, Burr, in a rare display of pique, complained to Albert Gallatin that he had been "ill used by Virga. & No. Carolina" and had "no confidence in the Virginians; they once deceived him, and they were not to be trusted."

—∿—

As the election of 1800 approached, Burr was certain that he could deliver New York's electoral votes to Jefferson in the fall because in New York City he had painstakingly built what was arguably the first political machine in America. He had started with a core of politically connected men whose devotion would remain constant throughout Burr's long life: Matthew L. Davis, his future biographer; William P. Van Ness, who would one day defend Burr in a notorious pamphlet and serve as his second at a famous duel; John and Robert Swartwout, and in future years, their young brother, Samuel; and Burr's stepson, John Bartow Prevost. Burr's daughter, Theodosia, would call them "The Tenth Legion"—in antiquity, this was the name for Julius Caesar's most dependable troops—but they were better known as the "Little Band."

A keystone of the Burr organization was the Society of St. Tammany, a club of mechanics, laborers and artisans founded by a former Revolutionary War enlisted man, William Mooney. Tammany was formed as a protest against the exclusive Society of the Cincinnati, whose membership was restricted to former Continental Army officers. It became a political organization when Burr became its de facto "boss" in the late 1790s. (Tammany Hall, before its long association with the building by that name erected in 1812, was the executive arm of the Republican General Committee of New York County.)

As a state assemblyman during the late 1790s, Burr shepherded through a bill whose ostensible purpose was to create a municipal water system, The Manhattan Company, so that New York City could draw fresh water from the Bronx River and curb the spread of yellow fever in the city. But the water system charter, written by Burr, was really a Trojan horse for a seemingly innocuous provision that permitted surplus capital to be used to buy stock and for other vague financial transactions. Upon the launching of The Manhattan Company, this provision was swiftly invoked, and a Republican bank was established, breaking the Federalists' choke-hold on the city's banking. The Manhattan Company's bank was the ancestor of Chase Manhattan Bank.

During Burr's meeting with Jefferson and his managers in Philadelphia that January day in 1800, Burr laid out his plan for winning New York's electoral votes for the Republicans: First, capture New York City's twelve State Assembly seats, giving the party a sturdy majority in the state House. Then, when the House and Senate, with its thin Federalist margin, met to select electors, the House Republican majority would ensure selection of a solid-Republican slate of electors. Burr evidently impressed the Jeffersonians with his command of names and numbers, and his confident manner, for Jefferson wrote afterward that "at present there would be no doubt of our carrying our ticket there [in New York]; nor does there seem to be time for any events arising to change that disposition."

—◊—

Rather than campaign himself for a state assembly seat in the spring 1800 election, Burr concentrated on electing Republicans to New York City's twelve Assembly seats so that New York would vote for Jefferson in the fall. By persuading and arm-twisting, he put together a powerful Republican ticket that included former Governor George Clinton and Revolutionary War General Horatio Gates. Burr cagily kept the slate secret until the Federalist posted theirs—a lackluster lineup, as it turned out. Federalist leaders had trouble finding able candidates, much less well-known candidates who were willing to spend three months out of the year in

Albany, where the state capital had been moved from Manhattan in 1797. Even the Federalists conceded that the Republican ticket was superior. "The lamp of public spirit seems to have consumed all its oil," Robert Troup dolefully observed to Rufus King.

Bending over their maps, Burr and his lieutenants parsed the city into small, manageable districts. For each, they appointed a campaign committee to carefully record each resident's political preference and the likelihood of his donating time, services, or money, noting how much each could be expected to give. Burr was in his element, cajoling and encouraging, formulating grand strategy and attending to small details; he was a maestro coaxing sweet music from a ragged orchestra. He threw open his Richmond Hill home so that campaign workers would have a headquarters open at all hours, and, if needed, a place to eat and sleep, too—extra food and mattresses were kept on hand.

The law barred propertyless men from voting, but Burr found a loophole: He arranged for groups of them—in one instance, three dozen—to buy homes, thereby creating instant property owners, and instant voters. While there is no supporting documentation, it would be surprising if at least some of the money for the home purchases did not come from The Manhattan Company's bank.

Burr's organizational skills and his personal attention to matters large and small resulted in Matthew Davis jotting, on a bulletin sent to Albert Gallatin on the evening of May 1: "Republicanism Triumphant."

—∽∽—

Gallatin, in charge of evaluating potential vice presidents for Jefferson, looked no further than New York state and its three political power centers: the Clintons, the Livingstons, and Aaron Burr. He knew that Jefferson needed a New York running mate to had New York State's twelve Republican-leaning electoral votes. Gallatin drew up a short list: Burr; Robert R. Livingston, the long-time state chancellor and a Livingston patriarch; and former Governor George Clinton. Livingston was ruled out because he was unknown outside New York. Clinton agreed to run, but only if he could resign when he wished.

That left Burr, who bluntly told Gallatin that he distrusted the Southern Republicans after what had happened in 1796, and that he would not run. Jefferson and other Republican leaders quickly weighed in with promises that 1800 would be different; they would stand by him.

Burr reconsidered. After consulting the "Little Band," he agreed to be Jefferson's running mate, a decision that he would regret.

[3]

"The Man Whom His Country Delights to Honor"

I cannot bring myself to aid Mr. Jefferson . . . the Morals of the Author of the letter to Mazzei cannot be pure.
    —JOHN MARSHALL

WASHINGTON, MARCH 4, 1801

While swearing in Thomas Jefferson, his distant cousin, as president, Chief Justice John Marshall displayed a concord of spirit with the two Republicans on the platform that he did not feel. An ardent Federalist and recent appointee of President Adams, Marshall was decidedly unimpressed by the Republicans' so-called "Second American Revolution," the supposed return to the Declaration of Independence's principles of liberty and equality. That morning, in a letter to Charles Cotesworth Pinckney, Adams's running mate, Marshall had paid Jefferson a backhanded compliment: "The democrats [Republican Party] are divided into speculative theorists & absolute terrorists. With the latter I am not disposed to class Mr. Jefferson. If he arranges himself with them it is not difficult to foresee that much calamity is in store for our country—if he does not, they will soon become his enemies and calumniators."

The election had been a nightmare. Jefferson and Burr had tied with 73 electoral votes apiece; President Adams had received 65. As required by the Constitution, the task of breaking the Burr–Jefferson tie fell to the House of Representatives. But after nearly a week and thirty-five roll-call votes, neither candidate was able to claim the votes of a majority of the sixteen states. On the thirty-sixth House vote, there was movement; enough congressmen changed their votes that Jefferson was declared the victor. But the Capitol's halls and the city's boarding houses still buzzed with rumors of deal-cutting, rumors that soon would erupt in the press.

While Marshall admired neither Burr nor Jefferson, Alexander Hamilton discovered, when he asked Marshall to support Jefferson over Burr during the long deadlock, that the chief justice disliked Jefferson more. Pointing out to Hamilton that he no longer was a House member and therefore would not be voting, Marshall admitted that he harbored "almost insuperable objections" to Jefferson. "His foreign prejudices [Jefferson's fondness for France and antipathy toward England] seem to me totally to unfit him for the chief magistracy." He also feared that Jefferson, to increase his influence, would ally himself with the House of Representatives, thereby weakening the presidency. "I cannot bring myself to aid Mr. Jefferson," Marshall wrote, adding, "The Morals of the Author of the letter to Mazzei cannot be pure."

Federalists had not yet forgiven Jefferson for the Mazzei letter; four years later, it still aroused their indignation. Angry with George Washington because he had signed the Jay Treaty in 1796, Jefferson had unburdened himself to Philip Mazzei, a former Monticello neighbor who had returned to his native Italy. Jefferson's letter had referred to "men who were Samsons in the field & Solomons in the council, but who have had their heads shorn by harlot England"—an obvious allusion to Washington. Unfortunately for Jefferson, his blunt words had found their way into American newspapers in May 1797. Scalding criticism rained down on Jefferson, and he was quickly reminded that Washington had already become a secular American saint.

In this roundabout way, the Jay Treaty ended Vice President Jefferson's long friendship with Washington and made him even more of an outcast in the Adams administration. It had the opposite effect on Marshall, whose successful arguments for the treaty's ratification had elevated him to national prominence among Federalists.

—⁂—

Marshall's transformation into a rising Federalist leader was sealed by his integral role in the so-called "XYZ Affair." Had he not agreed to serve as one of Adams's three envoys to France in 1797, it is doubtful that Marshall would ever have been named to the Supreme Court—or that he would have been known outside of Virginia, for that matter. Unlike Jefferson and Burr, Marshall never aspired to a national reputation, and was content with his quiet, prosperous life as a Richmond attorney.

The Jay Treaty and the favorable terms that it granted Great Britain had not only angered Republicans, but also the French Directory, whose ostensible complaint—that it violated the French–American Treaty of Alliance of 1778—masked its belief that the United States was siding with France's great enemy, Britain. Incredibly, Republicans advised the French to send out their privateers to capture U.S. merchant ships, and thus punish Federalists for ratifying the Jay Treaty. The ensuing raids, some even launched from Charleston, South Carolina, and other U.S. ports, far surpassed Britain's fitful spoliation of American shipping; in a single year, the French seized three hundred U.S. merchant ships. President Washington discovered that it had been a mistake to name James Monroe, a Republican and a passionate Francophile, as Minister to France; Monroe was unwilling to get tough with the French. Yet, in attempting to rectify this error, Washington administration officials only made matters worse by recalling Monroe as he was trying to negotiate with the Directory in 1796. The Directory retaliated by rejecting Monroe's successor and curtailing relations with America.

Adams decided to try a different approach: He would send a team of diplomats to Paris. After naming Marshall as one of the three envoys, Adams then chose two Republicans—Elbridge Gerry of Massachusetts and James Madison. But Madison declined, which was just as well, because Federalists were pressuring Adams to include a second Federalist in the delegation. The president selected Charles Cotesworth Pinckney, a signer of the Constitution from South Carolina and Adams's future running mate.

The Directory, however, was uninterested in stopping the profitable depredations on U.S. merchantmen. When the envoys arrived in Paris in October 1797, the French foreign minister, Charles Maurice de Talleyrand, sent three low-level diplomats—identified in dispatches only as X, Y, and Z—to toy with the delegation. Before any negotiations on neutrality could begin, they told the Americans, the United States must pay Talleyrand a $250,000 bribe, and lend the French government ten million dollars to assuage French feelings, supposedly wounded by Adams's "insults." "Monsieur Y" hinted that the United States risked meeting the fate that had befallen some of the smaller, French-conquered European states; Napoleon Bonaparte and his army, for example, had just defeated Austria's army. Marshall shot back that the United States was unlike those nations. "They were unable to maintain their independence, and did not expect to do so. America is a great, and, so far as concerns her self-defense, a powerful nation."

After months of futile meetings, and no reciprocal French offers to discuss issues—even after Marshall delivered a magisterial, fifty-page statement of U.S. policy to Talleyrand—Marshall and Pinckney abandoned the mission and left France in 1798. Gerry hung on, in the vain hope that something might be accomplished.

Marshall's and Pinckney's reports of the "XYZ Affair," as it came to be called, had caused a national uproar when they were published in U.S. newspapers, and the envoys were hailed as heroes for refusing to bow to the French demands. Thus, when Marshall arrived in Philadelphia, the national capital, now throbbing with war fever, he received a tumultuous welcome. During endless rounds of dinners,

Marshall was pronounced "the man whom his country delights to honor." At a banquet at Oeller's Hotel attended by Federalist congressional leaders, Supreme Court justices, and members of President Adams's cabinet, an unnamed dignitary raised his glass and proposed a toast that became an instant slogan: "Millions for defense, but not a cent for tribute!" Marshall, who still believed he could return, like a Cincinnatus, to the comfortable grain of his old life in Richmond, would find out that there was no going back.

—m—

Born in 1755 in Virginia, Marshall was a contemporary of Burr's, but in background and lineage he was closer to Jefferson, twelve years his senior. Like Jefferson, Marshall was a great-great-grandson, through his mother's bloodline, of William Randolph and Mary Isham, the "Adam and Eve of Virginia." Sons of frontiersmen, Marshall and Jefferson both studied law at William and Mary College under George Wythe, Virginia's legal patriarch. When Marshall passed the Virginia bar in 1780, Virginia Governor Thomas Jefferson signed Marshall's license to practice law.

Besides sharing a certain history, Marshall and Jefferson also shared physical and personal traits peculiar to the Randolphs: Both were tall and lanky, and carelessly informal in their dress. But their differences were just as striking. Jefferson was blue-eyed, fair, and freckled; Marshall had black eyes and black hair. Unlike Jefferson, Marshall was a convivial man who enjoyed a large company of friends and a reputation as a storyteller. Marshall's popularity once caused Jefferson to grumble to Madison, during the height of the outcry over the Jay Treaty, that "his [Marshall's] lax lounging manners have made him popular with the bulk of the people in Richmond; and a profound hypocrisy with many thinking men of our own country. But having come forth in the plenitude of his English principles, the latter will see that it is high time to make him known."

The Revolutionary War was another divide between the two. Marshall had been a combat officer in the Continental Army, while

Jefferson had the misfortune to be Virginia's governor from 1779 to 1781, Virginia's most trying years, except for the Civil War.

Overwhelmed by impossible demands from the militia and leaders of the Continental Army's Southern command, and faced with Tory insurrections, Jefferson was also hobbled by the balky State Assembly, which could not muster a quorum during Virginia's days of greatest peril. Then, in January 1781, a British invasion fleet sailed up the James River, and the traitor Benedict Arnold, now a British general, force-marched nine hundred troops into Richmond, which had been hastily evacuated. The British blew up the powder magazine and burned and plundered public records. Unable to compel either the militia or the State Assembly to do his bidding, Jefferson resigned as governor on June 1, 1781, with no successor. Two days later, British Colonel Bonastre Tarleton and his marauding cavalry appeared in the foothills outside Charlottesville, hoping to capture Jefferson and some assemblymen. In the nick of time, Jefferson gathered up his family and sent them to a neighbor's home, then jumped on a horse and galloped into the woods as British dragoons swarmed over his property. To compound his humiliation that year, the Assembly, looking for a scapegoat, began an inquiry into Jefferson's conduct. Nothing came of it.

—◊◊◊—

Marshall received his baptism by fire at Great Bridge near Norfolk in December 1775. Six months later, he was with the Continental Army in Pennsylvania. In 1777, he fought at Brandywine Creek and Germantown, where he was wounded in the hand. Like Burr, Marshall was at Valley Forge during the unforgettable winter of 1777–1778. Unlike Burr, all of his time evidently was not taken up by military duties. Marshall was remembered by his new Valley Forge friends—and an old friend from childhood, James Monroe—for his stories, for his proficiency at quoits, a game like horseshoes, and for running footraces; his fleetness of foot earned him the nickname "Silver Heels." When the encampment broke up in the spring, Marshall was picked to help lead an elite light infantry unit. It fought in June 1778 at Monmouth Courthouse, the place where Burr commanded the Malcolms, and, in 1779, Marshall and his unit assaulted Stony Point and Paulus Hook on the Hudson. He then returned to Virginia to finish his law studies.

Elected to the Virginia House of Delegates, Marshall was a leader of the 1788 state Constitutional Convention, which met in an abandoned Richmond warehouse because the British had wrecked the state government buildings and the state Capitol was not yet completed. He lost a race for Virginia Attorney General, and declined invitations to go to Congress or to serve as U.S. Attorney. He was enjoying himself too much in private practice, where he was at his best handling appellate cases. His hallmark was a gift for focusing on the key issues during closing arguments.

In 1783, he married Polly Ambler, whose mother, the former Rebecca Burwell, had once been an infatuation of Jefferson's. The Marshalls built a home two and a half blocks from the Virginia Capitol and soon had ten children, six of them surviving to adulthood. The marriage had come within a hair's breadth of not happening at all. Polly had spurned Marshall's initial marriage proposal, and Marshall, despairing that she would ever accept him, had galloped away—possibly never to return. But a fast-riding cousin overtook Marshall with a lock of Polly's hair and the unspoken message that Marshall should not give up his courtship.

The life of a prosperous, well-connected Richmond lawyer was a banquet for a companionable man like Marshall, who loved good, leisurely conversation. There were the Saturday afternoon Quoits Club gatherings with Richmond's leading men at Buchanan's Spring, a resort on the edge of the city. In the shade of the oak trees, the thirty members talked and pitched quoits, trying to "ring the meg" with a discus. Then, when dinner was ready, they would gather around a long table in an open shed, washing down their meal with toddies, punch, and mint juleps. One Sunday a month, Marshall hosted a "lawyers' dinner" at his home for his attorney friends. And he was active in the Masons, the Society of the Cincinnati, and the Society of St. Tammany.

Marshall's devotion to the Federalists and to his commander-in-chief and friend, George Washington, continually threatened to pull him into national politics. But he steadily resisted. The Washington administration offered him appointments as U.S. Attorney General and Minister to France, and he turned them down. However, Marshall, like all Federalists, had been appalled by Citizen Edmond Charles Edouard Genet's warm reception in 1793 by Republican radicals as well as by his outrageous misbehavior—recruiting soldiers and fitting out privateers in U.S. ports to prey on British merchant ships. Revolutionary France and Napoleon, the Federalists believed, posed an imminent danger, and this seemed to be borne out when Marshall and his fellow envoys were snubbed in Paris.

—⁓—

To prepare for war with France, the Federalist-controlled Congress pushed a dense floe of legislation through to law—bills rushing to completion three Navy frigates whose construction had languished, and then adding more ships; formally establishing the U.S. Navy and reactivating the Marine Corps, which had been disbanded after the Revolutionary War; building Navy yards; and, on paper at least, expanding the U.S. Army from 3,500 officers and men to 50,000, with George Washington leaving retirement to lead them.

Reveling in their now-vindicated loathing of France, for so long held up by Republicans as a democratic ideal, the Federalists unwisely passed other measures that would boomerang on them: the Alien Bill, permitting the deportation or arrest of any alien; the Naturalization Act, which extended the residency requirement for citizenship from five to fourteen years; and, the most inflammatory of them all, the Sedition Act. Under the Sedition Act, any criticism of government, its officers, or its policies could be federally prosecuted as criminal acts. In other words, it sanctioned witch-hunts for "disloyal" speech. Republicans rightly feared that the measure would be aimed at their newspapers.

Nearly alone among Federalists, Marshall, too, worried about the effect of the Sedition Act, not so much its erosion of civil liberties as the harm that it might cause the Federalist Party—himself included. In the spring of 1799, Marshall was in a tough race to unseat an incumbent Republican congressman, and the Sedition Act, highly unpopular in Virginia, was hurting his campaign.

George Washington had persuaded Marshall, along with Washington's nephew, Bushrod Washington, to run for Congress during a memorable weekend at Mount Vernon. Concerned that just four of Virginia's nineteen House members were Federalists, Washington was trying to recruit new candidates. Bushrod succumbed first to his uncle's persuasion, but Marshall was determined to resume his private legal practice in Richmond so that he could pay off the debts he had accrued while in France for nine months. He stubbornly resisted Washington's blandishments, just as he had President Adams's when Adams, not long before, had offered him a seat on the U.S. Supreme Court. On the morning of his departure from Mount Vernon, Marshall rose early, hoping to slip out before Washington could resume his lobbying. But Washington was waiting for him on the veranda in his dress uniform, medals gleaming. One last time, the former president exhorted Marshall; disarmed by Washington's persistence, Marshall agreed to run for Congress. After a hard campaign, and with Patrick Henry's pivotal endorsement, Marshall defeated incumbent John Clopton in April 1799 by just 114 votes out of 1,500 cast in the election.

On December 14, 1799, Washington died of pneumonia at Mount Vernon. Marshall led the funeral procession in Philadelphia from Congress Hall to the German Lutheran Church. In the House of Representatives, Marshall paid the now-famous tribute, borrowed from Virginia Congressman "Light-Horse Harry" Lee: "First in war, first in peace, and first in the hearts of his country."

—∾∾—

Just as France had divided Federalists and Republicans, so it now fragmented the Federalist Party. Against his party's wishes, Adams dispatched William Vans Murray, Oliver Ellsworth, and William R. Davie to Paris to extend a peace overture to end the Quasi-War.

The result was the praiseworthy 1800 Treaty of Mortefontaine, in which France pledged to stop seizing U.S. merchant ships; the treaty also suspended the French–American alliance that had been so essential to American independence. Alexander Hamilton and other conservative Federalists—they would become known as "High Federalists"—indignantly branded the treaty a betrayal of Federalist ideals and a concession to the Republicans. They withdrew their support of Adams and made plans to support another Federalist in the 1800 election.

Marshall, however, stood by the president as his peace initiative and many of his other policies came under withering criticism from the High Federalists. When Adams sacked three cabinet members who had sided with Hamilton against him—War Secretary James McHenry, Secretary of State Timothy Pickering, and Treasury Secretary Oliver Wolcott—he turned to his loyal ally, Marshall, naming him Secretary of War, an appointment that Marshall declined even as the Senate was confirming him. Determined to have Marshall in his cabinet, Adams then named him Secretary of State. Marshall accepted, believing that the position better suited his talents.

In December 1800, about the time Adams realized that he had lost the election and that Jefferson or Burr would soon succeed him as president, Oliver Ellsworth resigned as Chief Justice of the Supreme Court. Adams cast about for a loyal Federalist.

The ten-year-old Supreme Court was a nonentity in 1800. Aside from the unpopular Sedition Act prosecutions—sometimes carried out by Supreme Court justices in their capacity as circuit judges—the high court had not yet made a mark. Its caseload was light, it addressed few Constitutional questions, and the press ignored its opinions. The Supreme Court was so inconsequential that when the Capitol was designed, no space was reserved for it; for years, it met in a cramped committee room in the basement.

Adams asked John Jay, the Supreme Court's first Chief Justice, to return to his former position. Jay, who was governor of New York, declined. The president briefly considered two Federalist associate justices, William Cushing and William Paterson, but they were favorites of the High Federalists whose disloyalty to him had cost him re-election.

For the third time in a year, Adams turned to John Marshall, his Secretary of State, and the loyal friend who had written Adams's final Address to Congress. Marshall accepted. With little debate, the Senate confirmed the appointment.

John Marshall, forty-five years old, who would become the most renowned chief justice in U.S. history, was sworn in with little fanfare on February 4, 1801, exactly one month before he, in turn, would administer the presidential oath of office to Thomas Jefferson.

Marshall served as both Chief Justice and Secretary of State during the often-chaotic last days of the Adams administration. As Secretary of State, he signed and sealed dozens of Adams's last-minute judicial appointments, the reviled "midnight appointments"—a Republican epithet that was not far off the mark. As Chief Justice, Marshall would be called upon to assay the validity of some of those same appointments.

—m—

In the thirty-four years as chief justice before him, Marshall, in small matters and large, would shape the Supreme Court and the Judiciary for the centuries that followed. He left his mark even in the prosaic matter of judicial attire. Before Marshall, U.S. judges wore whatever suited them—colorful academic robes, black robes, or crimson gowns like those of the British judiciary. Marshall's preference for the plain black robe, emblematic of the law's solemn neutrality, soon became the only acceptable garb for all American judges.

In larger matters, Marshall would broaden the Supreme Court's authority so that the Judiciary could become the equal of the Executive and Legislative branches. He would establish the Supreme Court's role as the protector and interpreter of the Constitution. All of these achievements would occur during Marshall's tumultuous first years as Chief Justice, when Thomas

Jefferson was president, sometimes in the face of daunting adversity conjured up by Jefferson himself.

John Adams would later describe his appointment of Marshall as Chief Justice as his "proudest act," a "gift" to the American people.

[4]

The Revolution's Inspired
Wordsmith

*Burr loves nothing but himself; thinks of nothing but his own aggrandize-
ment, and will be content with nothing, short of permanent power in his
hands.*

—Alexander Hamilton

WASHINGTON, MARCH 4, 1801

As he began reading his inaugural address, Thomas Jefferson
saw that his audience awaited his words with despair, anxiety,
or elation, depending on the listener's political orientation. Civility
had vanished from public debate during the past two years;
Republican resentment over the Quasi-War with France and over
the Federalists' use of the infamous Sedition Act to stifle criticism
of the Adams administration had seen to that. Then, Adams's willingness to parley with France had split his own Federalist Party
between himself and the radical High Federalists led by Alexander
Hamilton. In 1800, instead of supporting Adams, the High
Federalists had endorsed Charles Cotesworth Pinckney, Adams's
running mate, for president. The South Carolinian had siphoned
enough votes to deny Adams a second term. Republicans wanted to
hear Jefferson reaffirm his party's bedrock principles of states'

rights, agrarian ideals, and a benevolent but weak central government; Federalists prayed that Jefferson would not announce the wholesale dismantling of the federal government. Jefferson well knew that it was essential for him to strike the right note of conciliation and optimism in his first presidential speech.

"All will, of course, arrange themselves under the will of the law, and unite in common efforts for the common good," Jefferson said. "Let us restore to social intercourse that harmony and affection without which liberty and even life itself are but dreary things. . . . Every difference of opinion is not a difference of principle. We have called by different names brethren of the same principle. We are all republicans, we are all federalists." These healing words washed over the tense audience like a warm summer breeze; there was a light rustling of fabric as the listeners eased their stiff postures. Then Jefferson urged a common "attachment to union and representative government."

Marshall's relief upon hearing Jefferson's mild phrases leaked through the lines he added to the gloomy letter he had written to Pinckney before the inauguration: "It is in the general well judgd [sic] & conciliatory," he said of the address. "It is in direct terms giving the lie to the violent party declamation which has elected him, but it is strongly characteristic of the general cast of his political theory."

Burr's comparatively bland description of the ceremony noted that the day was "serene & temperate—The Concourse of people immense—all passed off handsomely—great joy but no riot."

Nowhere in the inaugural address appeared the metaphor that Jefferson liked to use in his private letters at that time, of America as a ship that has survived a terrific storm, but that now will be put on "her republican tack, & she will now show by the beauty of her motion the skill of her builders."

—◊◊◊—

The fierce backlash against the Alien and Sedition acts, the homely stepchildren of the Quasi-War with France, had been indispensable to Jefferson's election. And, as Marshall and the Judiciary would unhappily discover, the Sedition Act's usefulness to Jefferson did not end with his inauguration, when the act officially expired.

Understandably, Republicans saw both laws as aimed directly at them. The Alien Act gave the government the power to deport any alien, such as Republican leaders like Swiss-born Albert Gallatin. The Sedition Act, the Republicans believed, was designed to punish Republican editors who attacked the Adams administration's policies. Federalists did nothing to dispel this impression; on July 4, 1798, the day Congress approved the Sedition Act, Federalists toasted Adams with the words: "May he, like Samson, slay thousands of Frenchmen with the jawbone of Jefferson."

Unwilling to risk appearing unpatriotic by attempting to repeal the acts during wartime, Republicans had waged a guerrilla war, secretly led by Vice President Thomas Jefferson. The Southern states, wrote Jefferson indignantly, "are completely under the saddle of Massachusetts and Connecticut, and . . . they ride us very hard, cruelly insulting our feelings, as well as exhausting our strength and subsistence." Jefferson gloomily predicted that if the Alien and Sedition acts were permitted to stand, there would be "another act of Congress declaring that the President shall continue in office during life, reserving to another occasion the transfer of the succession to his heirs. . . ."

The Republicans' weapon was "nullification," with Jefferson as its most persuasive advocate. Nullification supporters reasoned that if the United States was indeed no more than a compact of individual states, the states retained all powers not explicitly assigned to the federal government by the Constitution. Thus, states could judge whether acts of Congress were Constitutional—and "nullify" them, if needed—since nowhere did the Constitution say they could not do so. At Monticello in September 1798, Jefferson shaped these ideas into nine resolutions that suggested that, as a last resort, states would be justified in forcibly resisting unconstitutional acts, and even leaving the union. These were shocking opinions, especially coming from the vice president; with popular feeling then running high against France, Jefferson's beliefs might even have been judged treasonous—that is, had his authorship become known.

John Breckenridge introduced the resolutions in the Kentucky legislature, after first deleting Jefferson's exhortation to forcible resistance and his call for immediate nullification. Breckenridge's additional revisions made the resolutions little more than requests that Congress repeal the Alien and Sedition acts. The Virginia legislature rewrote them so that they declared the Alien and Sedition acts to be unconstitutional—without prohibiting their enforcement in Virginia. Before the nullification movement could build up a head of steam, Federalists in Delaware, New York, Rhode Island, Massachusetts, Connecticut, New Hampshire, and Vermont pushed through resolutions denouncing nullification.

In the meantime, Federalist judges were already targeting Republican editors. The first major Sedition Act prosecution targeted Thomas Cooper, editor of the *Sunbury and Northumberland Gazette* in Pennsylvania, who was accused of maligning the president. After a jury convicted Cooper of sedition, in April 1800, Supreme Court Justice Samuel Chase, acting as a federal circuit judge, sentenced him to six months in jail and fined him $400. Benjamin Franklin Bache, who was editor of the Philadelphia *Aurora* and Benjamin Franklin's nephew, was arrested for seditious libel after penning a particularly venomous screed against President Adams. Bache died of yellow fever before he was tried, and his assistant, William Duane, who succeeded him both as editor and as Mrs. Bache's husband, also took his place as defendant.

Chase and District Judge Cyrus Griffin—Griffin would be Marshall's silent partner during Burr's trial—presided as U.S. circuit judges at the sedition trial of James Callender, a notorious Richmond editor and author, whose book, *The Prospect Before Us*, had stated, "Mr. Adams has only completed the scene [of] ignominy which Mr. Washington began." Callender was convicted in June 1800, fined $200, and sent to jail for nine months. From his cell, the unrepentant essayist wrote diatribes against Chase for the *Richmond Examiner* and *Virginia Argus*, while composing Volume 2 of *The Prospect,* partly underwritten by Vice President Jefferson, who contributed $100. Chase reportedly vowed to beat up the hack pamphleteer when he completed his jail sentence.

The harshest sedition penalty, also imposed by Chase, sent David Brown of Massachusetts to jail for eighteen months and fined him $480 for exhibiting "vicious industry" in circulating seditious statements. The Sedition Act prosecutions produced a total of twenty-five arrests and fourteen indictments; ten of the defendants, either Republican editors or their allies, were actually tried and convicted.

More than any other judge, Republicans despised Chase, the most aggressive of all the judges in prosecuting sedition. A popular Republican toast was: "Cursed of thy father, scum of all that's base. Thy sight is odious, and thy name is Chase." When Chase returned home to Baltimore after completing his full schedule of Sedition Act prosecutions, his traveling companion was John Marshall.

Soon after taking office, President Jefferson stopped the proceedings against Duane and pardoned Brown and Callender. He quickly regretted his clemency toward Callender, though. Upon failing to receive what Callender believed was a deserved federal job, the spiteful editor published a widely circulated broadside accusing the president of having fathered five children by his slave, Sally Hemings. In retaliation, Jefferson's loyal friend, the versatile George Hay, clubbed Callender to the ground on a Richmond street. In 1803, Callender drowned in three feet of water in the James River.

—◊◊◊—

January and February 1801 were anxious months for Republicans. For their part, Federalists had irretrievably lost control of Congress as well as the presidency, but the 73–73 Jefferson–Burr deadlock gave them a last chance to affect the election outcome, and, a few thought, even the possibility of retaining the presidency. The Federalists initially made overtures to Burr, although he, more than any other Republican, was responsible for the Federalist defeat.

Besides ensuring that New York would vote Republican, Burr had obtained a letter in which Alexander Hamilton had denounced John Adams. Intended for dissemination only in South Carolina, the Hamilton letter described Adams as a man of "disgusting egotism . . . liable to paroxysms of anger, which deprive him of self command and produce very outrageous behavior." The unstated message to South Carolinians was: Vote for Pinckney, and not Adams, for president. When Burr saw to it that the Hamilton letter appeared in major newspapers, however, Adams's re-election became an impossibility.

Burr spurned the Federalist overtures; Jefferson did not, and, as a consequence, Jefferson became president. This simple fact is often lost in the web of fiction that was spun around the election by Jefferson and his supporters, who made Burr out to be the shifty turncoat and Jefferson the man of principle—a reversal of their real roles.

Also nearly forgotten is Burr's cheerful willingness to step aside when a deadlock between him and Jefferson first appeared likely. "Know that I should utterly disclaim all competition—Be assured that the federal party can entertain no wish for such an exchange," Burr wrote to Jefferson's House floor manager, Congressman Samuel Smith of Maryland, on December 16, 1800. On December 23, he wrote to Jefferson: "My personal friends are perfectly informed of my Wishes on the subject and can never think of diverting a single Vote from you—On the contrary, they will be found among your most zealous adherents. As to myself, I will cheerfully abandon the office of V.P. if it shall be thought that I can be more useful in any Active station." This was followed by another note to Jefferson on December 26 expressing the hope that a Vermont elector would change his vote from Adams to Jefferson.

And then, something happened over the next three days to change Burr's attitude, from cheerful acquiescence to Jefferson's election to stubborn refusal to step aside. This new approach was evident in a December 29 note to Smith in which Burr complained about receiving letters—probably urging his withdrawal—in which "I perceived a degree of Jealousy and distrust *and* irritation by no Means pleasing or flattering." These letters grated so much on Burr that he fired off a second letter to Smith later the same day. "The question was unnecessary, unreasonable and impertinent, and I have therefore made no reply. If I had made any, I should have told that, as at present advised, I should not—What do you think of such a question? I was made a Candidate against my advice and against my Will: God Knows, never Contemplating or wishing the result which has appeared—and now I am insulted by those who use my Name for having suffered it to be used—this is what we call going on principle and not men. . . ." Pressure from the Republicans may not completely account for Burr's refusal to concede the election to Jefferson; pride and ambition may have swayed him, too. Or he may simply have believed that by stepping aside, he would be interfering with the people's will.

Amid their gloom over having lost the national leadership bequeathed to them by George Washington, Federalists saw two faint rays of hope. Rather than let the House decide the election, President Adams might declare a deadlock and name a new Senate president, whom he would then elevate to the presidency. Jefferson alerted Burr on December 15 to this rumored "usurpation," as Republicans called it. The Federalists' other recourse was to trade their votes in the House for concessions by Jefferson or Burr, which is exactly what they did.

A snowstorm enveloped Washington on February 11 as Congress met to count the electoral votes, creating the ideal atmosphere for intrigue. The outcome was as expected: Jefferson 73, Burr 73, Adams 65, and Pinckney 64. In the drafty House chamber, with snow and sleet tapping on the windows, the balloting then began. Each state cast one vote, decided by the majority of its representatives. If a delegation was deadlocked, no vote was cast by that state. To win, Jefferson or Burr needed to receive the support of nine of the sixteen states. After the first ballot, eight states favored Jefferson, six were for Burr, and two, Maryland and Vermont, were deadlocked. A shift to Jefferson by just one member of either

Maryland's or Vermont's delegation would decide the election. But through thirty-five rounds of balloting over five days, nothing changed.

The Capitol corridors and the rooms of Washington's boarding houses became hotbeds of politicking and speculation. Everyone had an opinion, but no one was more opinionated about Aaron Burr than Alexander Hamilton. "Burr loves nothing but himself; thinks of nothing but his own aggrandizement, and will be content with nothing, short of permanent power in his hands," Hamilton wrote to Gray Otis, a Massachusetts Federalist. Hamilton penned another, thousand-word-long, character assassination of Burr that was circulated among Federalists. President Adams, too, was appalled that Burr was so close to becoming president, but not for the reasons given by Hamilton. Adams objected to an outsider moving into the President's House. "All the old patriots, all the splendid talents, the long experience, both of federalists and antifederalists, must be subjected to the humiliation of seeing this dexterous gentleman [Burr] rise, like a balloon, filled with inflammable air, over their heads. . . ."

But other Federalists believed, as did Senator Gouverneur Morris of New York, that Burr, because he was not a doctrinaire Republican, "must be preferred" to Jefferson. "Burr is not a Democrat—He is not an enthusiastic theorist—He is not under the direction of the Virginian Jacobins," wrote Federalist Theodore Sedgwick of Massachusetts to his son in explaining why he reluctantly supported Burr. "He is not a *declared* infidel—He is not *publickly* [sic] committed against the great systems of the administration. . . ." And then Sedgwick adduced a clinching reason: "He [Burr] will not be able to administer the government without the aid of the federalists & this aid he cannot obtain unless his administration is federal."

But Burr refused to bargain for the Federalists' support. "Mr. Burr would not assist us," James A. Bayard of Delaware, then the House's Federalist leader, told a commission appointed in 1806 to investigate what became known as the 1801 election controversy. Bayard was even more explicit in a letter that he wrote to Hamilton in March 1801: "The means existed of electing Burr, but this required his co-operation. By deceiving one man (a great blockhead), and tempting two (not incorruptible), he might have secured a majority of the States. He will never have another chance of being President of the United States."

On Saturday, February 15, 1801, Jefferson told Congressman Samuel Smith that he would accept the Federalists' conditions and thus their support. The conditions to which he agreed were: to maintain the federal financial system; to preserve the Navy; and not to conduct a wholesale housecleaning of Federalist appointees, other than cabinet members. As Bayard explained it to Allan McLane, one of the Federalist officeholders on whose behalf Bayard had supposedly interceded with Jefferson, "Burr could not be brought in, and even if he could he meant to come in as a Democrat . . . [with plans to have] swept every [appointed Federalist] in the U. States. I have direct information that Mr. Jefferson will not pursue that plan." In fact, after Burr's rebuff, it was Bayard, as the ranking House Federalist, who had approached Smith, the ranking House Republican and Jefferson's ostensible representative, with the proposal. After consulting Jefferson, both Smith and Bayard would testify in 1806, Smith gave Bayard an affirmative response.

The very day that he made the deal with Federalists, Jefferson was writing to James Monroe—possibly laying the groundwork for his lifelong denial of having made any such pact—that he had made no promises to the Federalists. "I have declared to them unequivocally, that I would not receive the government on capitulation, that I would not go into it with my hands tied."

On Monday, February 17, 1801, the stalemate ended. Various Federalist congressmen from Maryland, Vermont, Delaware, and South Carolina either cast blank ballots or absented themselves. As a consequence, previously deadlocked Vermont and Maryland entered Jefferson's column. Delaware and South Carolina, which had voted for Burr, now reported their delegations evenly split. The final vote was 10 states for Jefferson, four for Burr, and two undecided.

If Jefferson had not known it before, the 1800 election informed him in no uncertain terms that Burr could jeopardize his cherished plans. Vice President Burr had to be stopped.

—~~~—

The new president was the shy, inspired wordsmith of the Revolutionary War generation. His gifted political leadership was matchless; he and his two Virginian successors, James Madison and James Monroe, would shape the presidency for fifty years. But Jefferson was not held in awe, nor did the United States' 5,308,000 inhabitants in 1801 regard any of the surviving Revolution generation members, still very much in control of the nation's affairs, with special reverence either. During the presidential campaign, for example, Jefferson had been accused of being a subversive atheist. The Revolution generation's leaders were not known for religious devotion, but atheism was a grave charge in the avowedly Christian republic. Jefferson took pains to point out that he was a deist, as were many of the founders, and no atheist. To his friend, Dr. Benjamin Rush, Jefferson declared that he believed in Divine Providence, the resurrection, future rewards and punishments, and in Christ's teachings, but not that Christ was the Son of God.

However, Jefferson's true religion was the Revolution and its ideals—as he saw them. In 1801, his vision of America encompassed a nation of farmers, landowners, craftsmen, and tradesmen loosely governed by a small federal government that delivered the mail, administered justice, conducted foreign affairs without—in Jefferson's words—"entangling alliances," and promoted and protected a robust trade, leaving everything else to individuals and their states. A confirmed Francophile from his days as Minister to Paris, Jefferson believed in the romantic, democratic ideals of the French Revolution, long after their betrayal by the despotism and slaughter that followed.

But those were Jefferson's tamer beliefs; on other subjects, he really *was* subversively radical—more so than the rest of his generation. Regarding Daniel Shays's 1786 tax rebellion, he had written,

"I like a little rebellion now and then. It is like a storm in the atmosphere." Although he had never fought on a battlefield, Jefferson believed that bloodshed had its uses: "The tree of liberty must be refreshed from time to time with the blood of patriots and tyrants." He once espoused what he called "generational sovereignty," the rebirth of the nation with each new generation—every nineteen years, by Jefferson's estimate—with a slate wiped clean of debts and laws. Jefferson's close friend Madison prevailed on him that this notion was best kept to himself.

By 1801, Jefferson's republican ideal was already superannuated. The booming United States had outgrown the old dream of a simple utopian society that had mesmerized Jefferson as he wrote the Declaration of Independence twenty-five years earlier. America had just concluded an undeclared war with France, with its new Navy having given a good account of itself. It now had a national bank and an Army, Navy, and Marine Corps; and the federal debt stood at $83 million. The "Second American Revolution" was a good slogan that had helped the Republicans to defeat the Federalists, but, as Jefferson would soon learn—aside from a consensus on chopping the federal debt and scaling back the Army and Navy—his party disagreed over how it should govern.

—∾—

Jefferson moved into the empty, half-finished President's House (one reached the second floor by climbing a rope ladder; there was no staircase) and promptly contracted severe diarrhea, which he blamed on fish that he had eaten, but which he probably got from drinking Washington's impure water. Although he tried to treat it by taking afternoon horseback rides and adopting a spartan diet, the diarrhea recurred sporadically for years, another chronic malady to go with his rheumatism and migraine headaches.

A widower, Jefferson lived alone in the President's House, except for his pet mockingbird, Dick, who liked to follow him around and perch on his shoulder as he worked. His late wife, Martha, herself a widow when she married Jefferson in 1772, had died in 1782, and now there were just their two daughters, Martha and Maria, both married and living in Virginia. Jefferson often wished that he were back in Virginia, too, at home in Monticello, his 5,682-acre farm a hundred and fifty miles southwest of Washington, or at 4,164-acre Poplar Grove in the Blue Ridge Mountains. At home, he could experiment with his crops and livestock, oversee his nail-making enterprise, and tinker with his gadgets. At the President's House, Jefferson mainly worked, humming and singing to himself while he sat at his desk for his usual ten to thirteen hours a day.

At fifty-seven, the president's reddish-blond hair was streaked with gray, but he had stayed lean, and he still stood a ramrod-straight six feet, two inches tall. Known as a good listener, he had a frank, amiable manner, although his red, freckled face was usually unreadable, making him seem unusually calm and unflappable. Reclusive and quiet, Jefferson liked working alone and hated public speaking. He dressed with conscious "republican" simplicity— shabbily, some would say—and in the mornings he received anyone who walked in the door of the President's House on public business. New Hampshire Senator William Plumer recalled the shock of his first meeting with Jefferson, who met him at the door dressed in an old brown coat, a red waistcoat, old corduroys, soiled woolen hose, and slippers without heels. "I thought this man was a servant; but Gen[era]l Varnum [a colleague from Massachusetts] surprised me by announcing that it was the President. . . ."

—∾—

Jefferson's father, Peter, was Welsh, and his mother, Jane Randolph of the ubiquitous Virginia Randolphs, was Scot-Irish. As a consequence, the Jefferson household never abounded in love for the Crown. Peter Jefferson, a surveyor, drew the Virginia–North Carolina boundary and the first map of Virginia. He died in 1757, when Thomas was fourteen. The oldest of the eight Jefferson children, Thomas was known as a quiet but amazingly devoted student during his two years at William and Mary, studying up to fifteen hours a day—as Burr later did at Princeton. After reading law under the legendary George Wythe, he entered the Virginia Bar in 1767. The following year, he reached the farsighted decision to build a home on Carter's Mountain, an 867-foot hill outside Charlottesville. In 1769, he entered public life as a member of the Virginia House of Burgesses.

His *A Summary View of the Rights of British America*, a denunciation of the British Parliament, attracted the attention of his House of Burgesses peers. Impressed by his facility with words, they sent Jefferson to the Continental Congress in 1775. In Philadelphia, he was remembered for being thin-skinned, self-conscious, and shy, and for never participating in a single congressional debate; John Adams, then Jefferson's friend, described him as "a silent member of Congress." But everyone agreed that Jefferson was Congress's most gifted writer, and it fell to him to set down the rebels' bold declaration of freedom from England. He wrote the Declaration of Independence in three days, while also working on Virginia's Constitution. The Declaration established Jefferson as his generation's best polemicist, utterly devoted to the revolutionary cause.

Now, twenty-five years later, Jefferson intended to establish a Virginia dynasty in the President's House. This was the same man who, just months earlier, had been so quick to condemn the Federalists for supposedly plotting to usurp his election and install a hereditary presidency. Jefferson's picked successors, Madison and Monroe, were kept close at hand for consultation; Madison as Secretary of State, and Monroe as Virginia's governor, but available for missions such as helping Robert Livingston negotiate the 1803 Louisiana Purchase.

Posterity-conscious even in 1801, Jefferson strove to cultivate a legacy as a wise, peace-loving president who bore no malice toward any man, even going so far as to revise potentially embarrassing passages in old letters. Yet, in March 1801, only nineteen days after taking office, he ordered the Navy to prepare a squadron to go to war on the Barbary Coast of North Africa, and, a month later, he began methodically destroying Burr's political power. Before a year had passed, Jefferson would embark on his crusade to humble the

Judiciary. Belying his carefully constructed image of benevolence was Jefferson's dark history of vindictiveness.

—∽—

In 1778, Jefferson wrote a "bill of attainder" convicting Tory Josiah Philips, whose guerrilla band had terrorized Virginia, of high treason and sentencing him to death. The attainder bill, employed by the English Stuarts to suppress rebels, pronounced a person's guilt and imposed a sentence without a trial. Jefferson's attainder bill, adopted by the Virginia legislature, stated: "It shall be lawful for any person, with or without orders, to pursue and slay the said Josiah Philips, and any others who have been of his associates." While Philips and several of his followers were captured before the bill took effect, the outcome was the same: The men were indicted, tried, convicted, and executed.

Virginia militia led by George Rogers Clark captured Colonel Henry Hamilton, the British commander in Kentucky and Ohio, in 1779 and brought him in chains to Richmond. Under wartime rules, Jefferson, as Virginia governor, normally would have paroled or exchanged a British officer such as Hamilton, but he refused to release him. Known as "the Hair Buyer" because he purchased scalps from Indians, Hamilton had also encouraged other Indian atrocities against Americans, and Jefferson was not about to let him go free. He ordered Hamilton kept in irons, and denied him writing materials. Even when George Washington asked Jefferson to release Hamilton, because British authorities had threatened retribution against American captives if he were not set free, Jefferson would not parole or exchange him. Nearly a year passed before Jefferson relented and agreed to Hamilton's parole, but only after Hamilton had signed a statement pledging not to criticize the patriots.

With independence and the advent of the constitutional government, Jefferson's new nemesis was another Hamilton, Alexander, whom Jefferson called "a colossus to the anti-republican party . . . an host within himself." Their enmity developed in the Washington cabinet of the early 1790s, when Treasury Secretary Hamilton was advocating a national bank, and Secretary of State Jefferson was arguing against it. It escalated with Hamilton's quiet undermining of Jefferson's attempts to foster a close relationship with France, Hamilton instead promoting closer ties to Great Britain. The respective leaders of the emerging Federalist and Republican parties battled one another in cabinet meetings and in the newspapers, with the Jefferson-subsidized *National Gazette*—whose editor, Philip Feneau, held a government sinecure supplied by Jefferson—lashing out at Hamilton, and the *Gazette of the United States*, edited by devoted Hamiltonian John Fenno, attacking Jefferson. Hamilton's personal ties to President George Washington, however, gave him a decisive advantage over Jefferson. Jefferson resigned his cabinet seat at the end of 1793, retreating to Monticello to enjoy a country retirement—but to also help Madison midwife the birth of the Republican Party.

—⚋⚋—

Immediately after his inauguration, President Jefferson set out to repeal the Judiciary Act. The Judiciary Act had created sixteen separate circuit courts with their own judges, a massive expansion of the three circuits then chaired by roving Supreme Court justices and local district judges. Adams selected new circuit judges, with lifetime tenure, for all sixteen positions before he left office; the new judges included Adams's nephew, William Cranch, and John Marshall's brother, James. Adams also named forty-two justices of the peace during the last hours of the last day of his presidency. Secretary of State John Marshall, who had helped draft the Judiciary Act as a member of the House Judiciary Committee, was in charge of sealing and delivering the judicial commissions.

Jefferson chopped seventeen of the justice of the peace positions—some because the appointments were sitting on a table in the Secretary of State's office and had never been delivered—and plotted the repeal of the Judiciary Act. Jefferson believed repeal would accomplish two praiseworthy goals: It would send the Federalists into further retreat, and appease the increasingly restive

"Old Republican" radicals, led by Jefferson's erratic cousin, Virginia Congressman John Randolph, who threatened to splinter the party.

Republicans had disliked the federal Judiciary even before the Sedition Act prosecutions and Adams's attempt to pack the courts. The Judiciary, Republicans were certain, was committed to advancing the Federalist Party's agenda, by siding with businessmen and bankers, large creditors, and large companies, and against small farmers and debtors. Moreover, the federal courts had the further drawback of being centralized—unlike the state courts—and of tending to cite English common law rather than ground their opinions upon statutes approved by legislative bodies. Federalists, of course, saw everything differently: The Judiciary was protecting the Union and private property rights.

Until Jefferson took personal charge of the effort, Republicans made little progress in attempting to repeal the Judiciary Act. But when a repeal bill known as "the president's measure" surfaced in Congress, it was shepherded to final approval on March 3, 1802. It eliminated ten of the sixteen circuit courts and shrank the Supreme Court from six justices to five. To prevent the Supreme Court from stopping the repeal from taking effect on July 1, a special Senate committee abolished the Court's new June and December terms, established by the Judiciary Act, and restored its former February session. As a result, the Supreme Court was unable to convene between December 1801 and February 1803. Jefferson had not only gone to war with the Judiciary, but had won the opening battle.

When the Supreme Court met in February 1803 for the first time in fourteen months, it shocked its enemies without really intending to. Charles Lee, the brother of "Lighthorse Harry" Lee and future uncle of Robert E. Lee, had challenged Jefferson's invalidation of four of Adams's justice of the peace appointments, his lawsuit taking its name from the lead plaintiff, William Marbury, a Georgetown businessman and Federalist, and from the defendant, Secretary of State James Madison. The case became that pillar of American Constitutional law, *Marbury v. Madison*. In his lawsuit, Lee asked that the Supreme Court demand that the Secretary of State explain why the judicial commissions signed by Adams and sealed by Marshall were not delivered. Lee contended that Congress had granted the Supreme Court the authority to require an explanation from Madison—in legal parlance, to issue Madison a writ of mandamus.

Marshall denied Lee's request, which must have briefly elated Republicans, until they read Marshall's reason in the opinion's last paragraphs. The law cited by Lee—Section 13 of the Judiciary Act of 1789, granting the Supreme Court the power to issue a writ of mandamus to Madison—was unconstitutional, the chief justice said. The Supreme Court is bound to enforce the Constitution, Marshall wrote, and the Constitution states that any law in conflict with it is void. In a few brief sentences, Marshall had established the Supreme Court's role as defender of the Constitution, and the Constitution's supremacy over laws passed by Congress.

A Republican newspaper shrewdly assayed *Marbury v. Madison's* import: "It seems to be no less than a commencement of war between the constituted departments. The Court must be defeated and retreat from the attack; or march on till they incur an impeachment and removal from office."

Jefferson could not have agreed more. Federalists, he said, "have retired into the judiciary as a stronghold, and from that battery all the works of Republicanism are to be beaten down and erased." Long departed were his initial high hopes for the Judiciary, which he described in 1789 as "a body, which if rendered independent, and kept strictly to their own department, merits great confidence for their learning and integrity." The president now intended to reduce the judicial stronghold to rubble.

Jefferson began pursuing judges whose conduct had especially outraged Republicans. With lifetime tenure, federal judges appeared to be impervious to attack, but Jefferson believed that he had found an effective weapon: impeachment, "the most formidable weapon for the purpose of dominant faction that ever was contrived," as he noted to Madison.

Impeachment's origins can be traced to 1376, when the British House of Commons removed two of Edward III's royal officers and four commoners with ties to the crown. In 1795, Britain's most famous impeachment trial, lasting seven years, had culminated in the acquittal of Warren Hastings, the Governor-General of British India, who had been charged with corruption and abuse of authority. Jefferson and Madison believed that Congress could similarly remove American judges who abused their authority. The time had come to test Congress's impeachment power.

The Republicans' first target was pitiable, sixty-five-year-old U.S. District Judge John Pickering of New Hampshire, who had suffered a breakdown in 1801 and thereafter displayed increasingly erratic behavior in court, ranging from profane outbursts to drunkenness. When Pickering, a patriot leader during the Revolution and author of New Hampshire's constitution, showed no inclination to step aside, the House impeached him. His trial in the Senate was a pathetic affair, with Pickering absent due to poor health, and his attorney, Robert Goodloe Harper, pleading with senators not to convict an insane man. But under pressure from Jefferson and Madison, the Senate found Pickering guilty of "high crimes and misdemeanors" and removed him. Republicans then tried unsuccessfully to expunge the record of Harper's references to Pickering's insanity (Pickering would die in 1805).

On the very day of Pickering's conviction, March 12, 1804, the House voted to impeach Supreme Court Justice Samuel Chase, the infamous Sedition Act crusader. Chase defiantly accused Jefferson of using impeachment to create vacancies on the Supreme Court that he could then fill with "timid and compliant judges." Federalist John Stephenson predicted that Chase's impeachment was just "the entering wedge to the complete annihilation of our wise and independent judiciary." Senator Timothy Pickering of Massachusetts believed it portended the destruction of "every man of considerable property who is not of the reigning sect." John Marshall, certain that if Chase were convicted, he would be impeached next, said, ". . . the present doctrine seems to be that a Judge giving a legal opinion contrary to the opinion of the legislature is liable to impeachment."

—⟋⟍—

Senators and congressmen murmured with pleasure and surprise when they entered the Senate chamber on January 2, 1805, to begin Justice Chase's impeachment trial. Vice President Burr, in his role as the Senate's presiding officer, had personally supervised the transformation of the chamber into a striking likeness of London's Westminster Hall as it appeared during Warren Hastings's famous trial. Carpenters had built a roomy new gallery. The senators' benches were covered in crimson cloth; blue cloth decorated the boxes designated for Chase's attorneys and for the House managers prosecuting Chase. Swathed in green cloth were the gallery benches, as well as the seats reserved for House members.

Shaky from a recent illness, Chase stood before Burr and the senators, without a chair to sit on, or a table on which to lay his papers. Burr ordered a chair brought for Chase when he requested one. Chase, sixty-four, was one of the four Maryland signers of the Declaration of Independence. George Washington had appointed him to the Supreme Court. White-haired and red-faced, Chase was called "Bacon Face" by Baltimore lawyers; fellow Associate Justice Joseph Story was kinder, describing him as "the living image of Dr. Johnson."

Justice Chase was charged with eight articles of impeachment— one article for misconduct at the treason trial of John Fries in Pennsylvania; five for misconduct during James Callender's sedition trial; and one for his unsuccessful attempt to prosecute a Republican newspaper editor in Delaware for sedition. The eighth article was for his diatribe to a Baltimore grand jury; in the grand jury's presence, Chase had denounced the repeal of the Judiciary Act, local and federal governments, and even democracy, warning that a Maryland General Assembly proposal to liberalize voting laws would reduce government to a "mobocracy." Upon reading newspaper accounts of Chase's remarks, Jefferson had immediately written to Congressman Joseph H. Nicholson, who had managed the Pickering impeachment: "Ought this seditious and official attack on the principles of our Constitution and on the proceedings of a State, to go unpunished?"

On February 4, when the trial reconvened after a weeks-long postponement, the capital shivered under a fresh snowfall, with temperatures hovering between zero and ten above. In the Senate, Vice President Burr enforced strict decorum as usual, not permitting congressmen or senators to snack or walk around the chamber. For nearly four years, Burr had been mainly relegated to his functionary position in the Senate, and kept at arms' length by Jefferson and his inner circle. But in the weeks before the trial, a transformation had occurred; he had become a sought-after dinner guest at the President's House, and he was even asked to suggest appointees to positions in the new Louisiana Territory. His three nominations were all appointed: J. B. Prevost, Burr's stepson, as New Orleans judge; James Brown, a Burr brother-in-law, as secretary of the Louisiana Territory; and, most portentously, Burr's friend, General of the Army James Wilkinson, as the new governor of the Louisiana Territory. But if Jefferson and his officials believed that their new solicitude toward Burr would prejudice him against Chase, they were mistaken. The vice president presided with what one newspaper described as the "dignity and impartiality of an angel, but with the rigour of a devil."

Remarkably, nearly every principal figure in Justice Chase's trial would resurface two years later at Burr's treason trial, but all in different capacities. Congressman John Randolph of Virginia took the lead in Chase's prosecution. Although he had no legal training and was notoriously eccentric, Randolph had become the de facto prosecutor because he had introduced the impeachment resolution. Aided by Congressmen Joseph Nicholson and Caesar Rodney, and others, Randolph faced a formidable defense team led by Luther Martin of Baltimore, Burr's former college classmate and arguably the best courtroom lawyer in America. Charles Lee, who had filed the *Marbury* lawsuit, assisted Martin, as did Philip Barton Key, the uncle of Francis Scott Key, who would one day write the lyrics for "The Star-Spangled Banner."

Martin argued that Chase's impeachment was not based on an indictable offense and, therefore, was invalid. Rodney and Nicholson insisted that this was not a prerequisite for impeachment. Chief Justice John Marshall testified on Chase's behalf. George Hay, who had defended and then beaten the late James Callender and was now U.S. Attorney for Virginia, testified as a prosecution witness about Chase's conduct during the Callender trial. Randolph's bizarre, disjointed closing argument—with frequent pauses while he gnawed on an orange or sipped watered wine—dealt the prosecution a sharp blow, especially when, at one point, he began sobbing.

On March 1, three days before Jefferson's second inauguration, the Senate voted. It failed to muster the two-thirds majority required to win conviction on any of the eight impeachment articles. Justice Chase remained on the Supreme Court.

Later that day in the House, Randolph proposed an amendment to the Constitution that would permit the president to remove any federal judge, with Congress's approval. Nicholson introduced a second amendment permitting state legislatures to vote at any time to remove their U.S. senators. The House did not act on either measure.

The Senate's failure to convict Chase dashed Jefferson's hopes of using impeachment to tether the Judiciary. Impeachment, he now believed, was "an impracticable thing, a mere scarecrow."

[5]

The Embattled Vice President

Jefferson hates him [Burr] as much as one demagogue can possibly hate
another who is aiming to rival him, yet Burr does not come forward in an
open and manly way against him . . . Burr is ruined in politics as well as in
fortune.

—FEDERALIST ROBERT TROUP OF NEW YORK

1801

Soon after Jefferson won the presidency on the thirty-sixth House
ballot, the Jeffersonian-controlled newspapers leveled their guns at
Burr. They accused him of seeking an under-the-table quid pro quo
with the Federalists. The Republican press carefully ignored the
obvious fact that if any deal had been made, Jefferson, and not Burr,
was the clear beneficiary. Fairness and accuracy played no part in
the process that now commenced; its purpose was to damage Burr's
reputation so irreparably that he could never again jeopardize the
Jeffersonians' dynastic dreams.

Aware that the controversy could undo his legacy if not managed properly, Jefferson took pains to record his version in his journal for posterity. In an entry dated February 12, 1801, he reported
that Edward Livingston had told him that House Federalist leader
James Bayard of Delaware had approached Republican leader

Samuel Smith on *Burr's* behalf, offering him the position of Secretary of the Navy if he switched to Burr. (Interestingly, Jefferson named Smith to this position temporarily, until Smith's brother Robert was free to take it over.) Jefferson restated Burr's supposed treachery in journal entries in December 1803 and January 1804, when the president was busy keeping Burr off the Republican ticket for the fall 1804 election. In April 1806, Jefferson reiterated in his journal that he had refused to make any concessions when approached by Gouverneur Morris, Dwight Foster of Massachusetts, and even President John Adams. This entry coincided with the filing of a "wager lawsuit" by members of Burr's "Little Band" in New York City Superior Court for the express purpose of taking depositions from Bayard and Smith, the men who had supposedly brokered the tie-breaking vote in the House on February 17, 1801. Bayard and Smith both testified that Burr had rejected the Federalists' offer and that Jefferson had taken it. Perhaps because of Jefferson's intercession or that of his ally, New York City Mayor DeWitt Clinton, the depositions of Bayard and Smith were not published during Jefferson's lifetime. In 1830, four years after Jefferson's death, James Bayard's sons made them public to clear their father's name.

Jefferson also began undermining Burr's New York City political base—the keystone of Jefferson's own election victory—by cutting Burr off from political patronage. Of seven major appointments requested by Burr in New York City, Jefferson granted just two—Edward Livingston as U.S. District Attorney, and John Swartwout as U.S. Marshal—and only after consulting Governor-elect George Clinton, DeWitt Clinton's uncle. Making the most of his opportunity to damage his major rival, Clinton rejected most of Burr's suggested appointees, while helping Jefferson fill an estimated six thousand jobs with loyal supporters of Jefferson and the Clinton and Livingston clans. In Connecticut and South Carolina, none of Burr's proposed appointees was named.

One of the snubbed New York City office-seekers—Matthew L. Davis, Burr's future biographer—traveled all the way to Monticello to confront Jefferson. But all Davis got from Jefferson was a sinister disquisition on the anatomy of the housefly. After blandly asserting that "wholesale removals" of Federalist officeholders would hurt Republicans' efforts to win them over later, Jefferson snatched a fly out of the air and dangled it before Davis by a leg. "Note," the president said, "the remarkable disproportion between one part of the insect [its large head] and its entire body." Davis was certain that Jefferson was making an analogy to Burr and his Little Band.

Burr himself furnished Jefferson and the Republicans with more reasons to undercut him. During the Senate debate in January 1802 over the repeal of the Judiciary Act, the vice president cast two tie-breaking votes. His first vote helped advance the repeal measure to final consideration, in conformance with Republican wishes. But his second tiebreaker, on the following day, aroused the Republicans' wrath. Believing it wrong to railroad the measure through the Senate without giving Federalists a chance to modify it, Burr voted with Federalists to send the bill to a committee— where it was duly amended by them. When the bill reached the Senate floor, the Republicans purged the amendments. Burr then compounded the sin of giving the Federalists a fair hearing by accepting an invitation to a Federalist banquet, where he offered the toast, "To the union of all honest men," words that Republicans took to be an insinuation that Burr regarded the Federalists as honest, but not Jefferson and his party.

The Jeffersonians, who were busy trying to prevent radical Old Republicans from fracturing the party, grew alarmed at the possibility that Burr might make an alliance with Federalists. Were he also to attract disaffected Republicans like John Randolph and William Branch Giles, Burr could mount a credible threat to Jeffersonians. As Republican newspapers assailed Burr for sending the Judiciary Act repeal to committee and for his banquet toast, Jefferson's officials wracked their brains for new avenues of attack. Treasury Secretary Albert Gallatin hit upon the idea of a Constitutional amendment: requiring presidential and vice-presidential candidates to run on a party ticket, for which electors then would cast one vote. Should all of his other countermeasures against Burr fail, Jefferson could always select another running mate and keep Burr off the ticket altogether.

Burr's final rupture with Republicans came over his well-intended effort to suppress John Wood's libelous *History of the Administration of John Adams esq. Late President of the United States.* Wood had written the book hastily, basing it on James Callender's slanderous works and articles that had been published in William Duane's virulently anti-Federalist Philadelphia *Aurora.* Upon reading an early copy of Wood's book in December 1801, Burr became convinced that its outrageous libels would backfire on Republicans. He instructed Wood to buy back from the publisher the 1,250 copies in print, but Wood did not have enough money. Burr and his friends raised $1,100, and an agreement was reached whereby Burr would purchase the entire first printing. Unfortunately, one of the publishers disclosed the arrangement to members of the Clinton family. Seizing the opportunity to embarrass Burr, the Clintons gave the information to their kinsman, James Cheetham, the thirty-year-old co-publisher of the New York *American Citizen,* but asked him not to print it until after the April 1802 New York state election.

The scathing attacks on Burr began in late May 1802, with Jefferson's evident approval. By newspaper, handbill, and pamphlet, Burr was assailed for his supposed recent secret political maneuverings; his alleged conniving during the 1800 election; his debts; and, not inaccurately, his mistresses scattered throughout the North and East. Cheetham's notorious pamphlet, *A Narrative of the Suppression by Col. Burr, of the Hist. of the Administration of John Adams,* asserted that Burr wished to win favor with the Federalists in order to form a coalition that would then try to defeat Jefferson. Several months before the campaign against Burr began in the *American Citizen,* Jefferson, at Cheetham's request, inspected his plan of attack, and read a draft of Wood's *History* pamphlet. The impending offensive against his vice president apparently met with Jefferson's approval: "I shall be glad hereafter to receive your daily paper by post as usual," the president wrote Cheetham, but asked that their collaboration be kept a secret.

"I shall not frank this to avoid post office curiosity, but pray you to add the postage to your bill."

Stubborn and proud, Burr refused to defend himself against his many detractors. "It is not worth while to write any thing by way of comment or explanation," he wrote to his son-in-law, Joseph Alston. "It will, in due time, be known what they are, and what is DeWitt Clinton, their colleague and instigator. These things will do no harm to me personally." Ironically, the very New York Federalist newspapers that had pummeled Burr during the 1800 elections now defended him. So did his friends, sometimes bodily. As a result of an exchange of heated words over Burr, John Swartwout dueled with DeWitt Clinton on July 31, 1802; each man fired five shots, and Swartwout was hit twice.

But the scurrilous attacks soon became too much even for the stoical Burr to abide, and he founded his own newspaper, the New York *Morning Chronicle*, naming Peter Irving editor. To Irving's credit, but not necessarily to Burr's benefit, Irving proved to be too gentlemanly to mudsling with Cheetham, although he staunchly defended his benefactor.

By the end of 1802, the attacks had taken such a toll on Burr's name that Federalist Robert Troup was moved to write, "Burr is a gone man." Troup had studied law with Burr and had once been his close friend. Writing to another prominent New York Federalist, Rufus King, Troup observed, "Jefferson hates him [Burr] as much as one demagogue can possibly hate another who is aiming to rival him, yet Burr does not come forward in an open and manly way against him . . . Burr is ruined in politics as well as in fortune."

In December 1803, with his reputation in ashes, Burr launched a full-scale counteroffensive against his enemies—a pamphlet titled *An Examination of the Various Charges Exhibited Against Aaron Burr*. It went a long way toward restoring Burr's credibility and setting his character assassins back on their heels, but, ultimately, not far enough. Burr's decision to at last defend himself arose from the realization that his last chances for reviving his political career were fast approaching: selection of a vice presidential candidate in

February 1804 for the fall election, and New York's gubernatorial election in April. Another reason was Burr's tardy recognition that he had been wrong not to battle his enemies from the start. "I fear I have committed a great error; the men who knew their falsity are dead, and the generation who now read them may take them for truths, being uncontradicted." Too late, Burr attempted to counteract his misjudgment, with the indispensable aid of his friend and Little Band member William P. Van Ness, who had written *An Examination* under the nom de plume "Aristedes."

An Examination sold more copies than any U.S. pamphlet except Thomas Paine's 1776 *Common Sense*, the fiery denunciation of Great Britain. Van Ness struck hard at all of Burr's Republican enemies: the Clinton family, but especially DeWitt Clinton, the "leader of a band of hired calumniators"; James Cheetham; the Livingston clan; and President Jefferson, who, Van Ness said, had "bid" for the presidency. Besides arousing indignation, the pamphlet spawned libel suits. Burr's supporters rallied around him, and the *Morning Chronicle* published a series of articles, *Who Shall be our next Vice-President?*, that made the case for Burr.

By the end of January, however, Burr knew that he would not be renominated as vice president. Irving's *Morning Chronicle* was reporting that the Virginians would deny Burr the nomination to ensure that Jefferson's successor in 1809 would be another Virginian. Using his position as New York mayor, DeWitt Clinton tried to advance himself as a vice presidential candidate, but discovered that Jefferson was not interested in replacing one potential rival with another. So Clinton endorsed his uncle, Governor George Clinton. The elder Clinton was more to the Jeffersonians' liking, seventy years old and a "safe" candidate.

—m—

On January 26, 1804, Burr met with Jefferson to discuss the future. He offered to withdraw from consideration as vice president "for the interest of the republican cause." But his offer made no impression on Jefferson, who had already dismissed him from consideration.

Jefferson's intense dislike for his vice president is abundantly evident in the memo that he wrote afterward: "I had never seen Colo. B. till he came as a member of Senate. His conduct very soon inspired me with distrust. I habitually cautioned Mr. Madison against trusting him too much . . . there never had been an intimacy between us, and but little association. When I destined him for a high appmt, it was out of respect for the favor he had obtained with the republican party by his extraordinary exertions and successes in the N.Y. election in 1800." In other words, Burr couldn't be counted on to always follow the Virginians' lead.

By offering to withdraw as vice president, Burr hoped to keep the president neutral during the April New York governor's race— which Burr intended to enter, provided that George Clinton did not run again. Perhaps sensing a decline in Clinton's vigor due to his age, Burr was counting on him not to pursue the governorship. Clinton, in fact, was considering accepting the vice presidential nomination *and* running for governor, just to keep it out of Burr's hands. He would then resign the governorship, after first naming a successor, Robert R. Livingston, who was stepping down as Minister to France. Known as "The Old Incumbent," Clinton had been governor of New York for twenty-one of the twenty-seven years dating to 1777. Clinton, his nephew DeWitt, and their supporters had built a powerful political apparatus by liberally dispensing patronage; appointees named by the Clinton-controlled Council of Appointments held more than fifteen thousand civil and military posts, from judges, district attorneys, and coroners to auctioneers, turnpike inspectors, and notaries public. It was no wonder that The Old Incumbent was reluctant to give it all up for the vice presidency.

But Clinton did; he announced in February 1804 that he would not seek a seventh term as governor. Days later, he was nominated by the Congressional Republican Caucus for the vice presidency.

Now seeing a clear path to the governorship, Burr began campaigning. One of his first actions was to sue James Cheetham for libel; Cheetham had accused him of conspiring to win the 1800 election. Burr hoped that his lawsuit would come to trial before the election, but it did not.

As Burr solicited support for his campaign for New York governor, his many enemies closed their ranks against him and his Little Band. Alexander Hamilton, the Livingstons, the Clintons, and, most significantly, President Jefferson and the Virginians were all determined to prevent Burr from reviving his political career. Of even greater concern to them was the possibility of an alliance between Burr and the New England Federalists. Fearing that the recent Louisiana Purchase would add more states to the Union—states that would look to Virginia for leadership, dooming the fading Federalist Party—the Federalists had begun secretly making plans to form a Northern Confederacy of New England states that would then secede from the Union.

At a dinner with Burr in Washington in early 1804, Federalist Senators Timothy Pickering of Massachusetts, James Hillhouse of Connecticut, and William Plumer of New Hampshire pledged to support him for New York governor if he would promise to bring New York into their confederation. While Burr listened attentively and even sympathetically, Plumer later concluded, after carefully parsing what Burr had said, that he had actually committed himself to nothing. Plumer could only marvel at Burr's deft evasiveness. "Perhaps no man's language was ever so apparently explicit, and at the same time, so covert and indefinite."

The mere threat of a Burr–Federalist alliance, however, galvanized the Jeffersonians, as well as Hamilton, who opposed secession as much as he loathed Burr. Hamilton began persuading New York Federalists to vote against Burr, knowing that without their votes, Burr would lose.

As usual, Jefferson's role was practically invisible. He knew from the 1800 election that rapidly growing New York was essential to Republican success. He could not permit Burr to swing it away from Virginia, because power would then flow back to New England and jeopardize his quest for a Virginia dynasty. Moreover, the president was fully informed about the New England secessionist talk, due to the confidential memos that arrived regularly from his diligent postmaster general, Gideon Granger, one of his most loyal and astute political informants. Granger had access not only to the mails, which he wasn't above snooping through, but to excellent sources inside the New England Federalist Party, sources which he mined on the president's behalf.

As the April gubernatorial election drew near, Clinton and Livingston Republicans nominated John Lansing, chancellor of the New York state court system. But Lansing withdrew when George and DeWitt Clinton demanded his unquestioning obedience. Lansing's replacement, State Supreme Court Chief Justice Morgan Lewis, had all the right credentials: He was a Clinton appointee, he would do as he was told, and he was married to Gertrude Livingston, Robert Livingston's sister.

Burr tried to distinguish himself from Lewis by declaring himself an "independent Republican," a patriotic man of the people, and an underdog facing a candidate who had been handpicked by New York's most powerful families.

With the Clintons, Livingstons, and Hamilton arrayed against him, Burr knew that Jefferson's neutrality was critical. On March 11, 1804, Burr met privately with the president to ask him not to intervene in the race. As Jefferson recounted their conversation to DeWitt Clinton, who was still directing Cheetham's savage attacks against Burr, the president had pledged to remain neutral, but had told Burr that "if either party [Burr or Lewis] aimed any blow against the Administration such party would meet my most hearty Opposition." Jefferson, however, was anything but neutral. When he first learned that Burr was going to run for governor, he had instructed Gideon Granger's brother, Erastus, to notify DeWitt Clinton. "It was thought advisable that the persons of influence in that State should be put on their guard. . . ."

By early April, all vestiges of Jefferson's professed impartiality had evaporated like morning fog. After the Federalist *Commercial Advertiser* reported that Jefferson had personally assured Oliver Phelps, a New York Republican, that he was indifferent to the outcome of the New

York election, Cheetham, Jefferson's editor friend, published a different account in the *American Citizen*. According to Cheetham, New
York Congressman Beriah Palmerot, after reading Phelps's report,
had met with the president to ascertain his true position. In the presence of Palmerot, New York Congressman Thomas Sammens, and
U.S. Attorney General Levi Lincoln, Jefferson confirmed that he had
told Phelps he would remain neutral in any contest "among real
Republicans." But the president said that he had then also told Phelps:
"But remember, Mr. Phelps, that I do not consider the *Little Band* as
making any part of the real Republican interest."

The Burr campaign never recovered from this body blow, or
from what William Coleman's New York *Evening Post* described as
"the very extraordinary attacks on his private character, which were
circulated with an industry and at an expence hitherto unexam-
pled." These accounts accused Burr of indulging in "abandoned
profligacy," despoiling women, and having invited "a considerable
number of *gentlemen of colour*—upwards of twenty" to a supper at
his home.

Morgan Lewis was so disgusted by the personal assaults on his
opponent that he said "that he would rather have seen the government in . . . than he would have been a candidate, had he known
how the election would have been conducted."

To no one's surprise, Lewis easily won the election, with 30,829
votes to Burr's 22,139.

—∽∾∿—

The Society of the Cincinnati celebrated Independence Day, July 4,
1804, with a banquet at Fraunces Tavern. Located at Broadway and
Pearl in Manhattan, Fraunces Tavern bore a special significance for
the former Revolutionary War officers; it was there that George
Washington had bid them farewell at the war's end in 1783, after
the withdrawal of the defeated British from New York.

Aaron Burr, seated at the same banquet table as Alexander
Hamilton, was out of sorts and unusually silent; Hamilton was
talkative and in high spirits. The bitter political enemies said little

to one another, if anything at all. Few knew it at the time, but Burr and Hamilton had agreed to duel in exactly one week.

During the dinner, Hamilton leaped atop a table and sang his favorite song, whose lyrics were supposedly written by British General James Wolfe the night before he died leading his troops in their successful assault on Quebec in 1759:

> *Why soldiers, why*
> *Should we be melancholy, boys?*
> *Why, soldiers, why*
> *Whose business 'tis to die!*
> *Damn fear, drink on, be jolly, boys!*
> *'Tis he, you, or I*
> *Cold, hot, wet, or dry*
> *We're always bound to follow, boys,*
> *And scorn to fly.*

A few weeks before the New York governor's election in April, Hamilton had denounced Burr at a dinner party in Albany. Dr. Charles D. Cooper related the comments in an approving letter to Hamilton's father-in-law, Philip Schuyler. The letter found its way into the April 24 edition of the *Albany Register,* and a copy of the newspaper made its way into Burr's hands on June 18, while he was recovering from the flu and brooding about his election loss. According to Cooper's account of Hamilton's rant, Burr was "a dangerous man" who should not be permitted to hold elective office. Cooper's letter also hinted darkly, "I could detail to you a still more despicable opinion which General Hamilton has expressed of Mr. Burr." (There has never been a verifiable explanation of Hamilton's "still more despicable opinion.")

Burr's cordial requests to Hamilton for an explanation of his remarks indicated that he was willing to resolve the matter peacefully; he gave Hamilton ample latitude to either retract his words, disavow them, or apologize. Three years earlier, in 1801, Hamilton's fevered disparagement of Burr, in order to prevent him from

winning the presidency, had nearly resulted in a duel; Hamilton
had averted it by disclaiming any malice. In 1797, Burr had dis-
suaded Hamilton from dueling James Monroe. (Hamilton had
accused Monroe of leaking to James Callender a confidential report
that had cleared Hamilton of federal corruption charges, but that
had also revealed that Hamilton, who was married with eight children, had been blackmailed by a pair of grifters over an adulterous
affair. Monroe had not leaked the report, and he denied having
done so, but Hamilton called Monroe a liar, forcing him to issue a
challenge. Monroe named Burr as his second, imploring him to
resolve the matter without bloodshed, and Burr did.)

This time, Hamilton would neither deny, modify, nor satisfactorily explain what he had reportedly said about Burr. Perhaps he
thought it impossible to retract the comments after everything that
he had said and done to thwart and malign Burr over fifteen years;
perhaps he saw a duel as his only option. Whatever the reason,
Hamilton adopted an unmistakably defiant tone in his letters to
Burr: "I deem it inadmissible, on principle, to consent to be interro-
gated as to the justice of the inferences, which may be drawn by
others from whatever I have said of a political opponent in the
course of fifteen years competition. . . . I trust, on more reflection,
you will see the matter in the same light with me. If not, I can only
regret the circumstances, and must abide by the consequences."

—◊◊◊—

At daybreak on July 11, Hamilton and Burr were in separate boats
on the Hudson, on their way to the dueling ground known as
Weehawken. Neither man had eaten breakfast, believing an empty
stomach would improve his chances of surviving a wound. No
more than a six-foot-wide ledge on the New Jersey shore,
Weehawken was named for the town on the Palisades above it. It
was popular among duelists—at least seventy duels were fought
there, and upwards of thirty-five men killed—because steep cliffs
above and below made it accessible only by water, and tall bushes
partly screened it from the Hudson. Duelists were not concerned

so much with privacy as with the authorities; dueling was illegal in most states.

Hamilton and Burr had both dueled before at Weehawken. In fact, Hamilton had been in twelve duels, without ever firing a shot or being fired on. This wasn't unusual; many duels ended with an apology and a handshake. Burr had dueled twice—once with Hamilton's brother-in-law, John Barker Church, who had shot a hole in Burr's coat.

Weehawken also bore a special, melancholic significance for Hamilton that he surely pondered during the river crossing. In 1801, his nineteen-year-old son, Philip, had been mortally wounded there during a duel with a Manhattan lawyer, George I. Eacker. Philip could easily have avoided the meeting by simply apologizing for his rowdy misbehavior—he and a friend had barged into Eacker's box at the Park Theater and mocked him. But he would not apologize. He died in agony at the Hamilton home, his family wild with grief. The trauma of watching Philip die had caused his devoted sister, Angelica, a talented musician, to lose her mind.

For his duel with Aaron Burr, Alexander Hamilton had borrowed John Barker Church's pistols, the same ones used by Philip Hamilton and Eacker, the ones with which Church had ventilated Burr's jacket. They were .544 caliber—large-bore even for dueling pistols—with handsome dark walnut stocks and solid brass barrels. (The pistols, today owned by Chase Manhattan Bank, are stored in a bank vault.) Burr's second, William P. Van Ness—"Aristedes" of the pamphlet war—and Hamilton's second, Nathaniel Pendleton, cast lots to determine position and who would give the order to fire. Winning both casts, Hamilton chose to have his back to the cliff so that Burr would be outlined by the glare off the river, even though this meant that Hamilton would face into the sun. The nearsighted Hamilton donned his spectacles, and he and Burr marked off ten paces, or about thirty feet. They turned, standing sideways to offer the smallest possible target. Pendleton asked if they were ready, then barked, "Present!"—meaning they could fire at will. The loud pistol reports occurred nearly simultaneously.

Hamilton's shot struck a cedar tree four feet away from Burr at twelve feet above the ground, but Burr was on target. His bullet hit Hamilton above the right hip, plowing through his liver and lodging in his spine. Hamilton fell on his face. Letting out a small, involuntary cry, possibly of regret, Burr took a step toward Hamilton, but Van Ness quickly led him to the boat, and they immediately departed for Manhattan. The Hamilton family doctor, Dr. David Hosack, who heard the shot while on the river, found Hamilton sprawled in Pendleton's arms. "This is a mortal wound, doctor," Hamilton said. Hosack was only able to numb the pain with laudanum (an opium–alcohol mixture) until Hamilton died the next day, July 12, at the home of merchant William Bayard, near the New York City docks. Hamilton's wife, Eliza, and their seven surviving children were by his side.

Stricken New York Federalists, inflamed by an "Apologia" that Hamilton had written for posterity suggesting that he planned to "throw away" his shot, demanded Burr's indictment for murder, even though the duel was fought in New Jersey. Of Hamilton's supposed intention to not hit Burr, Burr's only recorded comment was, "Contemptible, if true."

Pressured by New York Mayor DeWitt Clinton, a coroner's jury indicted Burr, and a New Jersey grand jury also returned a murder indictment. There was angry talk of burning down Burr's Richmond Hill home, where the vice president had taken refuge. In an attempt to quell the mounting public outcry, Van Ness and Pendleton released a joint written account of the duel, and included copies of Burr's and Hamilton's letters. But no one was interested in cool analysis.

Mayor Clinton closed down the city for Hamilton's funeral, held at public expense, on July 14. New York suspended its ordinance prohibiting the ringing of church bells at funerals. Citizens were asked to wear black crepe armbands for thirty days. The Sixth Regiment of the New York militia, and a band beating muffled drums, led the funeral procession, which included Hamilton's favorite horse, its master's boots and spurs facing backward in the stirrups, from John Barker Church's home to the Trinity Church burial ground. Cannon salutes were fired from the Battery and Governor's Island, and by men-of-war in the harbor.

Federalists exploited Hamilton's death to promote party unity, while Jeffersonian Republicans could not pass up the opportunity to once again abuse Burr. Treasury Secretary Albert Gallatin assayed the public feeling: "unquenchable hatred of Burr and federal policy have combined in producing an artificial sensation much beyond what might have been expected; and a majority of both parties seems disposed . . . to deify Hamilton and to treat Burr as a murderer. The duel, for a duel, was certainly fair."

Burr was not reviled everywhere; in the South and West, many thought he was justified in killing Hamilton. So did some Federalists. "A caitiff had come to a bad end," remarked former President John Adams, clearly remembering Hamilton's decisive role in Adams's defeat in 1800. Burr, Adams suggested, had repaid Hamilton for "fifteen years of slander." Richard Peters, a prominent Pennsylvania Federalist, said that he "never knew Colonel Burr [to] speak ill of any man, and he had a right to different treatment from what he experienced."

A blunt bit of doggerel made the rounds:

O Burr, O Burr, what hast thou done?
Thou hast shooted dead great Hamilton!
You hid behind a bunch of thistle,
And shooted him dead with a great hoss pistol.

Burr fled to Philadelphia. There, he slipped aboard a ship to St. Simon's Island, Georgia, and Senator Pierce Butler's rice and cotton plantation, "Hampton." Burr's normally steady nerves briefly unraveled in the face of the daunting public hostility toward him. In a note to Theodosia on August 2, he displayed uncharacteristic anxiety: "Don't let me have the idea that you are dissatisfied with me a moment. I can't just now endure it." But his old spirit had returned by the next day, as he drolly described to her the reported wild plots to assassinate him, and his new reputation as a deadly marksman. "Those who wish me dead prefer to keep at a very respectful distance." He even managed some gallows humor, remarking to Theodosia about "a contention of a very singular nature between the states of New-York and New-Jersey . . . The subject in dispute is which shall have the honor of hanging the vice president. . . . Whenever it may be, you may rely on a great concourse of company, much gayety, and many rare sights; such as the lion, the elephant, etc."

While Burr roamed the Southeast, the 1804 presidential campaign pushed the sensational duel into the background. Jefferson and George Clinton crushed Federalist Charles Cotesworth Pinckney in one of the most one-sided presidential elections in American history, receiving 162 electoral votes to Pinckney's 14. Jefferson's presidential authority now surpassed that of his predecessors, for federal power had sharply increased during his first administration. The Republican Party also was changing; its blazing advocacy of states' rights and curbs on federal power was ebbing.

Looking for business opportunities to pursue after he left office, Burr explored the Georgia coast and scouted northern Florida and its barrier islands, but abandoned the effort upon learning that Florida's Spanish governor despised Americans. While Burr was on the Georgia coast, a hurricane nearly destroyed the home of his host, Pierce Butler, and drowned nineteen of his slaves. What Burr wryly said of himself in later years appeared to be true: "It seems I must always move in a whirlwind."

Creditors now joined prosecutors, Federalists, and Jeffersonians in demanding their due from Burr. He was forced to sell Richmond Hill and its furnishings—practically everything except his books and wine—satisfying $25,000 in debts. A former fur trader, John Jacob Astor, bought the land and divided it into four hundred small residential lots, making a small fortune upon which he built a great one.

Still $8,000 in debt, publicly reviled, and facing murder charges in two states, Burr returned to Washington in late 1804 to complete his vice presidency.

—∿∿—

During his four years as the Senate's presiding officer, Burr had imposed decorum for the first time on the unruly body. Senators had previously brought their barking bird dogs, and had invited women friends to visit at their desks. They had snacked on apples, pies, and biscuits during debates, while messengers roamed the aisles, loudly calling out senators' names. There were so many distractions that one legislator took to calling the Senate "Babeltown." Burr demanded order and silence during debates, and barred all visitors from the floor, except House members.

On March 2, 1805, his final day on the Senate rostrum, Burr addressed his fellow senators for the last time. He had recently presided over the Chase impeachment trial with what everyone agreed was impeccable impartiality. Two weeks earlier, he had performed what must have been a painful ceremony, formally notifying Thomas Jefferson and George Clinton of their elections as president and vice president. Now it was time to say farewell, and every member of the Senate knew what this moment meant for Aaron Burr, who had come within a hair's breadth of the presidency, who had been denied a second term as vice president, who had lost his bid to become governor of New York, and who had then shot and killed Alexander Hamilton.

Speaking without notes, Burr began his final address by recalling how, four years earlier, he had promised to bring dignity to the Senate. He apologized for being curt at times, and thanked the senators for their support. The Senate, he said, was where "our Country must ultimately find the anchor of her safety; and if the Constitution is to perish, which may God avert, and which I do not believe, its dying agonies will be seen on this floor."

Burr's twenty-minute extemporaneous speech tapped the senators' most heartfelt feelings. "Every gentleman was silent, not a whisper was heard, and the deepest concern was manifested," Senator Samuel Latham Mitchill of New York reported to his wife. "When Mr. Burr had concluded he descended from the chair, and

in a dignified manner walked to the door, which resounded as he
with some force shut it after him. On this the firmness and resolution of many of the Senators gave way, and they burst into tears.
There was a solemn and silent weeping for perhaps five minutes."
The *Washington Federalist* called the speech "the most dignified, sub-
lime, and impressive that ever was uttered." Burr noted cryptically
in a letter to Theodosia: "I neither shed tears nor assumed tender-
ness; but tears did flow abundantly."

[6]

The Grand Jury Convenes

Would to God that I did stand on the same ground with every other man!
—AARON BURR

*In the hands of power, on the brink of danger, as composed, as immovable,
as one of Canova's living marbles.*
—WINFIELD SCOTT, DESCRIBING AARON BURR IN COURT

RICHMOND, MAY 1807

Not since Benedict Arnold's lightning campaign in 1781 had Richmond throbbed with such excitement, or seen so many strangers in the streets and public buildings. Almost overnight, the city's population had doubled to ten thousand or more. Every unoccupied home, every spare bedroom, and every bed in every tavern and boarding house was taken. Latecomers and the cash-strapped slept in tents, in their wagons, or under the stars along the banks of the James River. They had all journeyed to Richmond to see Aaron Burr, either the greatest villain since Judas or the most unjustly vilified man since Christ, fight for his life.

Richmond had fallen under Burr's spell two years earlier, when townspeople had lined up at the Washington Tavern to view the wax effigies of the dueling Aaron Burr and Alexander Hamilton, displayed by a man named Hallum, who charged fifty cents admission. Richmond residents might reasonably have been expected to loyally take the side of President Thomas Jefferson against Burr. Jefferson, after all, was a fellow Virginian, their former governor and congressman, and the man whose architectural vision had guided the construction of the state Capitol. In reality, the Burr trial had fanned Richmond's fierce political rivalries. The Federalist-leaning upper classes were sympathetic to Burr, while the Scots-ancestry merchants and working people voted Republican and supported Jefferson. During the XYZ Affair and the Quasi-War, Richmond Federalists and Republicans had brawled in public, stopped patronizing the same taverns, and crossed the street to avoid one another. Republicans had even gone so far as to stockpile arms and organize militia units such as the Richmond Light Infantry Blues.

In less turbulent times, Richmond citizens liked to proudly point out that their city, like Rome, was spread over seven green hills, and that the Virginia Armory in 1806 produced 1,265 muskets with bayonets; 205 without; 579 pistols; 84 rifles; 852 cavalry swords; 444 polished iron scabbards; 164 artillery swords; and 158 sword tips. In 1807, between one-third and one-half of the city's five to six thousand residents were slaves, and the chief industries were flour-milling, tobacco manufacture—mainly chewing tobacco, in flavored plugs—and iron, gunpowder, and ceramics. The James River, which in the springtime foamed with spawning shad, was Richmond's commercial turnpike, bringing the city seafood from the coast and finished goods from abroad. The shipments were landed at City Point and poled in flatboats upstream to City Market, where farmers from throughout the region sold meat, poultry, fruit, and vegetables. In their leisure time, the city's men jammed the Fairfield and Broad Rock horseracing tracks and watched the cockfights at Haymarket Gardens, betting up to fifty dollars a round. And everyone was wild for lotteries.

The city's leading newspapers—the zealously Republican Richmond *Enquirer* and the less rabidly Republican *Virginia Argus*—were committed to covering the Burr trial, gavel to gavel.

The *Enquirer's* habitual bias against Burr was on display in a March 27 report—inside, of course; page one was reserved for advertisements—about Burr's arrival in Richmond the day before. Without any pretense to impartiality, the article noted that Burr would probably be charged with treason, "the crime of a traitor. It is the crime of a parricide in arms against his country." Next came a free-verse description of Burr as:

> *A Prisoner.*
> *Covered with a crown of thorns.*
> *Degraded by plots of treason.*
> *Suspected by all.*
> *His own conscience, re-echoing the decisions of the world.*

The medley of front-page advertisements included Alexander Plainville's announcement that he had for sale "a fresh assortment of Claret Wines, Champaigne, Mousseux by the box, Bergundy, Sautern, VideGrave, Laffitte . . . and also, a fresh supply of Olives, Capers, Anchovies, Cayenne Pepper, Mustard, Pruines, Raisins by the box . . . All Kind of West-indian Sweetmeats . . . and different articles of Perfumery." Ten-dollar rewards were offered for a missing bay mare and a missing slave, Billy or Will, described as a good sawyer of about thirty who walked with his toes turned out. Dentist John Le Tellier, who conducted his business in a room at the Eagle Tavern, held out the prospect of restoring teeth "to their natural elegance, without injuring their enamel" by removing tartar, which he blamed as the cause of bad breath, tooth decay, tooth loss, and even scurvy.

—⁂—

On May 22, 1807, shortly after sunrise, hundreds of people on foot, on horseback, and in carriages began to fill Richmond's unpaved streets. They were headed toward the Capitol, where they hoped to claim a courtroom seat and witness the selection of a federal grand jury that would decide whether Aaron Burr should be charged with treason. The walkers and riders passed gracious oak-shaded homes that often adjoined meaner habitations where pigs and cattle grazed in the yards.

The pillared, porticoed Capitol, made of plain brick and not yet twenty years old, rested on a green hill overlooking the James River where it tripped out of the Piedmont hills. Thomas Jefferson, who admired classical architectural style, had instructed the Capitol's architect to use as his model a first-century Roman temple in Nismes, France, the Maison Caree. Streets led to the Capitol's north side; the south side, overlooking the James, was reached by climbing steep stone steps sunk into the weedy, gullied hillside, from where one then entered the Capitol by either the east or west door.

The House of Delegates was so full of people that when Chief Justice John Marshall arrived shortly before noon, he had trouble making his way to the bench. Every inch of the dingy, sparely furnished room was occupied—all of the curving benches, every seat in the balcony, every bit of floor space right up to the fluted pilasters, with the exception of the sand-filled boxes placed on the floor for the benefit of the large number of tobacco-chewers. Men even stood in the nine open windows. Had not statues occupied the wall recesses, spectators would have taken those places too.

The crowd spanned a broad demographic, as evidenced by its diverse attire. The outlanders, their hair hanging long and free, wore fringed deerskin jackets, coarsely spun red-woolen shirts, corduroy trousers with suspenders, leggings, and coonskin hats. Sometimes seated shoulder-to-shoulder with them were fashionable East Coast urbanites, elegantly dressed in ruffled shirts, cutaway coats, black silk, and knee breeches, their hair freshly powdered, their silver-buckled shoes gleaming.

Andrew Jackson of Tennessee, wearing a backwoodsman's rough clothing, stood near the back wall. He was tall, lean, and dangerous-looking. His hair hung in his face and was tied in a queue in back with a piece of eel-skin. A loyal friend of Burr's, Jackson had never forgotten his outspoken endorsement of Tennessee statehood. Jackson was staunchly Republican, but detested Jefferson.

A strapping young man stood on the enormous lock of the chamber's huge door, on the other side of which were scores of people awaiting their chance to go inside. The young man was twenty-year-old Winfield Scott, who, forty years hence, would lead a conquering army into Mexico City—realizing Burr's unfulfilled dream. The future general and presidential candidate had just finished riding his first courtroom circuit after passing the Virginia Bar.

David Robertson, a Richmond lawyer, took down everything that was said in shorthand, a facility for which he was as well known as he was for his fluency in several languages. His indefatigable recording of the proceedings over the next several months—there was no court stenographer—would yield two plump volumes of dense text running to nearly twelve hundred pages, and a modest income from their sale. Even Robertson's iron will occasionally wilted beneath the blizzard of words, and he would resort to paraphrasing. "A desultory conversation here ensued . . ." was a refrain he used often when the proceedings bogged down in tedious arguments before the bench.

Aaron Burr quietly conferred with his attorneys in the oval center aisle, where both the defense and prosecution tables had been placed. Flanking them were the rows of curving benches where House of Delegates members usually sat, but which spectators now occupied, facing one another across the aisle in the style of the British House of Commons. Opposite the balcony stood the House speaker's platform from which Marshall would look down upon the benches and attorneys' tables. Clad in black silk, his hair brushed back from his pale face and neatly tied in a powdered queue, Burr was, as Scott observed, "in the hands of power, on the brink of danger, as composed, as immovable, as one of Canova's living marbles." Confident and dignified in demeanor, he was where he was at his best, in the courtroom.

Burr's composure did not escape the sharp eyes of another admirer, twenty-four-year-old Washington Irving, who was sending publishable reports on the proceedings to his brother Peter Irving's New York *Morning Chronicle*, established by Burr four years earlier. Washington Irving, whose future literary masterpieces would include *The Legend of Sleepy Hollow, Rip Van Winkle,* and *Life of Washington,* indignantly observed to a friend, "I am very much mistaken if the most under hand and ungenerous measures have not been observed toward him [Burr]. He, however, retains his serenity and self-possession unshaken and wears the same aspect in all times and situations."

Privately, however, Burr seethed. "The most indefatigable industry is used by the agents of government, and they have money at command without stint," he wrote to his daughter, Theodosia. "If I were possessed of the same means, I could not only foil the prosecutors, but render them ridiculous and infamous."

President Jefferson had appropriated $11,000 from the government's "continuing fund" for U.S. Attorney George Hay to hire prosecutors. But much more than that was being spent to transport and lodge a hundred and forty government witnesses from nearly every region; in all, the Jefferson administration would spend nearly $100,000, without congressional authorization, the rough equivalent of $2 million today. Besides throwing open the executive purse, the president had sent Hay a sheaf of blank pardons. Use them, he instructed Hay, "at your discretion, if you should find a defect of evidence, and believe that this would supply it. . . ."

But Jefferson's most powerful weapon of all remained public opinion, which, due to the diligent efforts of the *Enquirer* and *Argus,* remained as fully inflamed against Burr in May as it had been after the president's Special Message to Congress in January. This fact did not escape Burr. "Nothing is left undone or unsaid which can tend to prejudice the public mind, and produce a conviction without evidence."

—⁓—

Less than a week after Chief Justice Marshall freed Burr on bond in early April, Burr and Marshall unwittingly handed the press a juicy scandal. The judge attended a dinner at the home of his good friend and Shockoe Hill neighbor, John Wickham, one of Burr's attorneys. Besides inviting Marshall to dinner, Wickham had also asked Burr. A long, awkward moment passed when the men noted one another's presence, which, in another era, would have furnished a perfectly reasonable ground for a mistrial. Instead of leaving when he saw Burr, Marshall stayed through the meal, an incredible lapse of his usual good judgment. The two sat at opposite ends of the table without speaking to one another, and Marshall left soon afterward.

The *Virginia Argus*, in its April 7 edition, carried the first report of the infamous dinner. According to the *Argus*, Marshall knew that Burr would be at Wickham's home—but attended the dinner anyway, because he believed that his private life was his own business. "We hope to God this part of the report is not true," clucked the *Argus* writer. (A Jefferson biographer, Professor George Tucker, who happened to also be a Wickham dinner guest on that day, wrote that Marshall knew Burr would be there, but attended because his absence would have implied criticism of his good friend Wickham.)

Three days later, the *Enquirer*, whose stories routinely appeared in other major East Coast newspapers, weighed in with its own account, signed by "A Stranger from the Country"—undoubtedly editor Thomas Ritchie. While the "Stranger" acknowledged that he had never trusted Marshall's political principles, he had nonetheless believed that Marshall possessed "excellent judgment," until learning of Wickham's dinner. Although it is doubtful that the Stranger ever held such a generous opinion of Marshall, he clearly did no longer. "We regard such conduct as a willful prostration of the dignity of his own character, and a wanton insult he might have spared his country." Marshall had dined with a man accused of "the abominable design . . . of assassinating the president, dissolving the Congress, disrobing the chief justice himself of his ermine, overturning all of our sacred institutions, state and federal, and erecting an execrable despotism on the ruins of freedom." The Stranger snidely suggested that Marshall would have been insulted if the lawyer for a common criminal whose case was before

Marshall had invited defendant and judge to dinner. "Is it only the grandeur and sublimity of the crime, which redeems the character of the criminal and exalts him to a level with a federal judge?"

Unreported by either newspaper was the fact that Congressman John Randolph, a leader of the radical "Old Republicans," was also a dinner guest of Wickham's.

The dinner inspired a young Richmond lawyer, Benjamin Watkins Leigh, to parody Marshall's imagined treatment of more ordinary defendants, when compared with his supposed regard for Burr:

> *Their lot forbade; nor circumscribed alone*
> *Their groveling vices, but their joys confined.*
> *To them luxurious banquets were unknown,*
> *With these poor rogues their judge had never dined.*

The much-abused dinner host, George Wickham, evidently didn't begrudge Leigh his verse; he later permitted Leigh to marry his daughter.

—◊◊◊—

At noon on May 22, Chief Justice John Marshall brought the court to order with a bang of his gavel. Seated beside Marshall, since this technically was a session of the 5th U.S. Circuit Court, was U.S. District Judge Cyrus Griffin, a federal judge for eighteen years. Like Marshall, Griffin was a Federalist. Educated in England and married to the daughter of a Scottish peer, Griffin had been president of the Continental Congress. During the weeks of testimony and arguments to come, Griffin would not utter a single word.

U.S. Attorney George Hay ostensibly led the prosecution team, although President Jefferson was really in charge. From Washington and, later, from Monticello, Jefferson kept a steady stream of suggestions, comments, and directives coming to Hay. As everyone knew, and as Winfield Scott noted, "It was President Jefferson who directed and animated the prosecution, and hence every Republican clamored for execution. Of course, the Federalists, forgetting [that Burr had killed] Hamilton . . . compacted themselves on the other side."

Hay, forty-one, was the son of Anthony Hay, proprietor of the Raleigh Tavern in Williamsburg, a favorite meeting place for Jefferson, Marshall, and other William and Mary students down through the years. Assisting him was William Wirt, already a respected courtroom orator, although only thirty-four years old. The third member of the prosecution team was Alexander McRae, Virginia's lieutenant governor—a middle-aged man known for being sarcastic and sour-tempered. Attorney General Caesar Rodney, who had argued for Burr's arraignment, would not appear again during the proceedings.

Months earlier, grand juries in Kentucky and Mississippi had refused to indict Burr on any charge, and Burr's defense team wanted to ensure that the grand jury picked in Richmond would not, either. Thus, two young Richmond attorneys who knew everyone of consequence in Virginia—Benjamin Botts and John Baker—had been added to the defense contingent of Edmund Randolph, John Wickham, and Charles Lee, who had represented Burr in March and April.

Sixteen grand jurors were initially selected—fourteen Republicans and two Federalists. Burr objected to two of them on the ground that, even for Jeffersonian Republicans, they were too strongly biased against him. Virginia Congressman William Branch Giles was Jefferson's floor manager in the U.S. House, and former Virginia senator Wilson Cary Nicholas was being groomed by Jefferson to run for the U.S. House and the Republican leadership position. Burr objected to Giles because he had advocated suspending habeas corpus during the proceedings against Dr. Justus Bollman and Samuel Swartwout. "It was therefore to be inferred," said Burr, "that Mr. Giles did suppose that there was a rebellion or insurrection, and a public danger of no uncommon kind." As for Nicholas, "The objection is that he has entertained a bitter personal animosity against me." Giles and Nicholas unhappily withdrew.

Congressman John Randolph, who was Jefferson's cousin and in 1805 was Judge Samuel Chase's prosecutor, was named the grand jury foreman. The appointment of this prominent Republican drew no defense objections, for good reason. Edmund Randolph was John Randolph's uncle, and had guided his nephew's legal studies. John Randolph was also a leader of the "Old Republicans" who were now giving the Jeffersonians fits. Randolph was known as a champion of personal liberty and a tireless worker. He was also thin-skinned, headstrong, and a bona fide eccentric who unfailingly dressed in boots and spurs and carried a whip, and lived in a Virginia town named Bizarre.

On the distinguished grand jury were three future Virginia governors and U.S. senators: Littleton W. Tazewell, James Pleasants, and James Barbour. Another panelist was Virginia Governor William H. Cabell's brother, Joseph C. Cabell, who would help Jefferson found the University of Virginia. Robert Barraud Taylor, another juror, carried a bullet in his body from a duel with John Randolph when they were William and Mary students, but there were no apparent hard feelings. Also seated was John Ambler, a first cousin of John Marshall's wife and a Marshall neighbor on Shockoe Hill.

Upon learning of Burr's objections to Giles and Nicholas and of their withdrawal, Jefferson began to plan for the unpleasant possibility that Burr might escape indictment altogether. "If there be no bill, & consequently no examination before court, then I must beseech you to have every man privately examined by way of affidavit, and to furnish me with the whole testimony," the president instructed Hay. "Go into any expense necessary for this purpose, & meet it from the funds provided by the Attorney General for the other expenses."

MAY 25, 1807

The government's main hope of indicting Aaron Burr for treason was General of the Army James Wilkinson; if his testimony did not persuade the grand jury to issue an indictment, then it had no case. But Wilkinson, busy subjecting New Orleans to his iron-fisted military regime, had not yet arrived in Richmond. No one was sure whether he had even left New Orleans. As Wilkinson's absence stretched from days into weeks, the patience of the attorneys, the grand jury, the spectators, and Chief Justice Marshall began to wear thin.

The attorneys' irritation occasionally erupted in blazing fireworks over seemingly innocent matters, as when Burr asked Marshall to instruct the grand jurors about the admissibility of certain evidence.

Hay sprang to his feet to object to Burr's temerity in suggesting any action by the judge regarding the jurors. Burr, he snapped, "stood on the same footing with every other man charged with crime."

In a rare display of emotion, Burr, his voice trembling, declared, "Would to God that I did stand on the same ground with every other man! This is the first time [since his arrest in Alabama] that I have been permitted to enjoy the rights of a citizen!"

Burr deeply resented his unceremonious arrest, his brusque treatment by Lieutenant Gaines, and especially the government's peremptory seizure of his expedition's boats and provisions—property that by rights belonged to him. "It is not easy for one who has been robbed & plundered till he had not a second Shirt, and all under Colour of Authority if not of law, to contend with a Govt. having Millions at Command & active & Vindictive agents in every quarter," he complained to his friend, Charles Biddle of Philadelphia. But his fighting spirit remained intact: "Yet in Justice to my reputation & to the feelings of my friends, nothing within my power will be left undone—."

Fearing that Burr, free on $10,000 bond, would flee when General Wilkinson reached Richmond, Hay made a motion to commit him to jail for treason, even though he had not even been charged with that crime. "The evidence is different now," Hay said.

Marshall agreed to hear Hay's evidence, over the strenuous objections of Burr, who was certain the government had no proof that he had committed treason. "Six months ago, [President Jefferson] proclaimed that there was a civil war," Burr said sarcastically. "And yet, for six months [government officials] have been hunting for it, and still can not find one spot where it existed. There was, to be sure, a most terrible war in the newspapers; but nowhere else."

Prosecutor William Wirt shot back that the defense was attempting to frame the case as "a political question; they would make it a question between Thomas Jefferson and Aaron Burr . . . this is not our business; at present we have an account to settle, not between Aaron Burr and Thomas Jefferson, but between Aaron Burr and the laws of his country."

But prosecutors soon ran up against the immutable fact that in order to send Burr to jail on suspicion of treason, they would need to first prove that there had been an "overt act" of treason. This was the key that would unlock the entire Burr case, a key now buried in the immense dragnet loosed by Jefferson and Attorney General Caesar Rodney. If Hay and his government lawyers hoped to win their case, they would first have to sift the statements of 140 witnesses to find two who could testify that Burr had committed an overt act of treason.

Marshall made Hay's task more difficult by refusing to allow the government to submit two depositions that supposedly proved that just such an act had occurred. Wilkinson's and William Eaton's depositions, which might have illuminated Burr's intentions, described no overt acts, Marshall said. So Hay tried a different tack, summoning two witnesses to the stand—Peter Taylor, who was a gardener on the Ohio River island where the alleged overt act had occurred, Blennerhassett Island, owned by Burr's Irish émigré friend, Harman Blennerhassett; and Jacob Allbright, a laborer who had built a corn-drying kiln on Blennerhassett Island while expeditioners were assembling there. Burr immediately objected that the government could not suddenly begin presenting evidence unless the defense was given an opportunity to rebut it. Marshall agreed with Burr, permitting Taylor and Allbright only to say whether or not they had firsthand knowledge of possible treasonous acts, without giving specifics. They possessed such knowledge, said Taylor and Allbright.

Aware that ending arguments on the motion might make him appear biased toward Burr, Marshall let the debate ramble for four days. However, it soon became obvious that the motion was going nowhere. Hay's first report to Jefferson reflected his frustration: "I do not believe that the C. Justice does wrong with his eyes open, but that his eyes are mostly closed, is a position of which no man can doubt who has observed his conduct. . . ."

Burr unexpectedly provided a way out of the quandary over how to ensure that he would not take flight. While still asserting that the court could not hold him on bail for a charge that had not been filed against him, he volunteered to increase his own bond if the court would stop arguments on the motion without issuing an opinion. Happy to be given a way out of his predicament, Marshall readily consented. Burr then voluntarily doubled his own bail from $10,000 to $20,000. Four men promptly put up $2,500 each. For a second time, the government had failed to show probable cause that Burr had committed treason, and he remained free.

[7]

"The Most Finished Scoundrel"

A mammoth of iniquity . . . the only man I ever saw who was from the bark to the very core a villain.
—JOHN RANDOLPH ON GENERAL JAMES WILKINSON

June brought mounting impatience over the exceptionally tardy chief government witness, General of the Army James Wilkinson. U.S. Attorney George Hay tried to stem the complaints of Aaron Burr's attorneys by asking that they make allowances for a man "of General Wilkinson's age and bulk to travel to this city." Edmund Randolph shot back: "Surely there is enough time to travel from New Orleans to this city in seventeen days, even with the gigantic bulk of General Wilkinson himself."

Pompous and brash, conniving and boastful, self-important and sly, fifty-year-old James Wilkinson, although endowed with talents better suited to a politician than an Army officer, had still managed to reach the highest rank, without ever having led a major combat operation. He looked every inch the martial hero, in uniforms tailored to fit his bloated figure, and sumptuously decked out in a kingly array of epaulets, medals, and gold braid and trim designed to satisfy even his outsized ego. The Spanish governor of Louisiana,

Baron Francisco Luis Hector de Carondelet, who paid Wilkinson thousands of dollars to spy for Spain, had been so dazzled by the general that he took to calling him "the Washington of the Western states." Others were decidedly less impressed. John Randolph, the congressman and grand jury foreman, would one day describe Wilkinson as "the most finished scoundrel that ever lived," and "a mammoth of iniquity . . . the only man I ever saw who was from the bark to the very core a villain."

Had not James Wilkinson come along with his intrigues, Aaron Burr would probably have found tamer projects than he did for his boundless creative energies between 1804 and 1807. At every stage of Burr's amorphous schemes, from their inception through his arrest and trial, Wilkinson was indispensable to what became known as "the Burr conspiracy." Yet Thomas Jefferson, in his eagerness to prosecute Aaron Burr, had placed all his faith in the same General Wilkinson, even though, as Senator William Plumer of New Hampshire had observed in January 1807, "All parties & all classes of people who are informed, appear to distrust Genl. Wilk. the commander of our armies."

Wilkinson had pledged allegiance to Spain in 1787, when he was a civilian businessman in Lexington, Kentucky. He became a Spanish spy. During the next twenty years, he received $34,563 for his services. When he reached the pinnacle of the U.S. Army, Spanish officials were careful to conceal his identity in their official correspondence, referring to him as Spy No. 13. In all of American history, there was never a higher-ranking U.S. military officer than General of the Army James Wilkinson in the secret employ of a foreign power.

In return for his fealty to Spain, businessman Wilkinson was permitted to buy and sell goods in New Orleans and freely use the Mississippi River for transit—a huge commercial advantage because, in 1784, the Spanish had closed the Mississippi to nearly all other American tradesmen. The U.S. government tried to circumvent the Mississippi River restrictions by building a road through the wilderness to New Orleans, but Creek Indians attacked the reconnaissance party. The attack was at the instigation of the Spanish, to whom the tactic had been suggested by none other than James Wilkinson. The road project was abandoned.

The son of a well-to-do Maryland merchant–planter, Wilkinson initially studied medicine and practiced briefly in Maryland. But when the Revolutionary War began, he joined the Continental Army and never returned to the medical profession. He was an aide to Generals Nathaniel Greene and Charles Lee, and to General Horatio Gates during Gates's triumph at Saratoga. He was at Quebec with Burr. Wilkinson shot through the officer ranks and became a brigadier general at just twenty. But political intrigue, Wilkinson's making and unmaking throughout his career, undid him. After repeating the contents of a confidential letter addressed to Gates that denounced George Washington, he was forced to resign. He returned to the Continental Army in 1779 as Clothier-General, in charge of furnishing the army with uniforms, but was so inept that he was pressured into leaving a second time, in 1781.

When the war ended, Wilkinson, his wife Ann, and their young children moved to Kentucky and opened the first store in what became Lexington. Wilkinson speculated in land development, laid out the city of Frankfort, naming its streets for Revolutionary War generals and for his wife, and led the movement to separate Kentucky from Virginia, writing the petition to the Virginia General Assembly. In 1787, Wilkinson asked John Marshall, then Virginia's political agent overseeing Kentucky, to get him a passport to the Spanish Southwest. No passport was ever sent.

Undeterred, Wilkinson loaded tobacco, hams, and butter onto a barge and floated down the Ohio and Mississippi rivers to New Orleans, in defiance of the Spanish ban on American river trade. In New Orleans, he presented a letter to the Spanish governor, Esteban Rodriguez Miro, that proposed Kentucky's secession from Virginia and its union with Spain—the infamous "Spanish Conspiracy." Impressed by Wilkinson's brashness and intelligence, Miro obtained his pledge of loyalty, and together they invented a cipher in which to cloak future communications. Wilkinson's

Spanish Conspiracy attracted followers, but never graduated from words to action. Its one quantifiable result was the $2,000 annual pension that Wilkinson began receiving from Spain.

Over the next years, Wilkinson served his Spanish patrons well: He betrayed a plan to colonize land at the Yazoo River's confluence with the Mississippi, and spoiled another American colonization scheme intended for Spanish territory in present-day Missouri, opposite the Ohio River's mouth. George Morgan, the Missouri colony organizer and a former Revolutionary War colonel, committed the egregious error of arousing Wilkinson's jealousy, with the consequence that Wilkinson told Spanish officials that Morgan was scheming against them. That was enough for the Spanish, who snatched back their land grant from Morgan before he was able to do much more than launch the town of New Madrid. Wilkinson's Spanish patrons also had reason to smile on Spy No. 13 when he broke up George Rogers Clark's embryonic expedition against St. Louis, Natchez, and New Orleans. But when Miro was recalled to Spain in 1791, Wilkinson's ties to the New Orleans government languished.

—m—

After Wilkinson led a punitive militia campaign against the Wabash Indians in southern Indiana, President George Washington rewarded him with a commission as lieutenant colonel in the regular U.S. Army. In August 1794, Wilkinson commanded the right wing of General Anthony Wayne's army against fifteen hundred Miami and Canadian militia during the victory at Fallen Timbers (in present-day northern Ohio). Afterward, Wilkinson criticized Wayne's battle tactics in letters to Army Secretary Henry Knox, who turned the letters over to Wayne. When a tree fell on Wayne's tent—he suffered only a knee injury—it was rumored that Wilkinson was behind the "accident."

While campaigning with Wayne, Wilkinson revived his relationship with the Spanish in letters to the new New Orleans governor, Baron Hector de Carondelet. Carondelet eagerly reciprocated—

after all, Wilkinson was now general and deputy commander of U.S. ground forces—by sending him $6,000 for stopping George Rogers Clark years earlier. When the courier was murdered and robbed, Carondelet sent Wilkinson $9,000 in Spanish silver, packed in barrels of coffee and sugar.

Upon General Wayne's death in 1796, Wilkinson was promoted to General of the U.S. Army. Carondelet, envisioning Wilkinson at the head of a Western insurrection, was initially ecstatic: "At the slightest movement the people will name him General of the new republic; his reputation will raise an army for him, and Spain, as well as France, will furnish him the means of paying for it." But there was little support for secession in the West, Wilkinson said, and his correspondence with the Spanish—along with his $2,000-a-year pension—once again went into hiatus.

—∿—

During the republic's first twenty years, the states and territories west of the Alleghenies were a cauldron of plots and intrigues. The frontiersmen and tradesmen in the thinly settled regions felt disconnected from the Union. The U.S. capital was not only geographically distant, but, to the Westerners' thinking, politically detached from the West as well. While they were taxed like Easterners, the Western settlers believed that they received little in return from the government. Proof lay no farther than John Jay's suggestion to Congress in August 1786 that America acquiesce to Spain's closure of the lower Mississippi River for twenty-five to thirty years in exchange for Spain's agreement to a commercial treaty with the United States. To Westerners of that era, neither secession, nor any action, for that matter, that would further their parochial interests—such as campaigns against the Spanish, English, or French—was objectionable.

The universal belief in a single, indissoluble Union lay many decades and one terrible war in the future. To many Western leaders, there was nothing sacred about the Union, and nothing prevented the formation of a *second* republic west of the Alleghenies.

During the 1780s, even Thomas Jefferson looked favorably upon the notion of separate American republics. "If they [Western settlers] see their interests in separation, why should we take sides with our Atlantic rather than our Mississippi descendants? God bless them both, and keep them in union, if it be for their good, but separate them, if it be better."

Thus, in the late eighteenth and early nineteenth centuries, it was unsurprising that the restive West tempted patriots, adventurers, grand schemers, and scoundrels. Spain, England, and France also recognized opportunities there for curbing America's growth. Tantalizing before discontented Western leaders with promises of money and support, as well as dreams of a sovereign empire, they hoped to lure the region away from the young New World power.

Troubled by this very possibility, George Washington wrote: "The Western settlers (I speak now from my own observations) stand as it were, upon a pivot. The touch of a feather would turn them any way. . . . It is by the cement of interest alone we can be held together."

However much secession may have tempted some Westerners during the republic's first decade, its attraction diminished as the years passed, and as, one by one, the Ohio, Tennessee, and Kentucky territories became states. Now, Spain's Gulf Coast and Southwest possessions appeared more alluring to the restless adventurers known as "filibusters."

—∞—

"Vrijbuiter," the Dutch word for pirate, became the English "freebooter" and then the Spanish "filibustero." In early American parlance, a "filibuster" was an overland expedition by a private army to steal another nation's territory. It had not yet acquired its later meaning—talking nonstop to steal an opponent's time in order to block legislative action.

Spain's crumbling North American empire tempted several ambitious men to go so far as to organize filibusters. Although unsanctioned by the U.S. government, the filibuster leaders nonetheless were encouraged by popular anti-Spanish sentiment and by the widespread belief that the United States was entitled to Spanish-controlled southern Alabama, southern Mississippi, and Florida.

When James Wilkinson unmasked George Rogers Clark's 1780s filibuster, thereby pocketing a tidy Spanish reward, he had only fired Clark's determination to try again. Thomas Jefferson, to whom Clark had often sent large, unusual bones from his excursions into the West, may have suggested to Clark that he sound out Citizen Edmond Charles Genet, the flamboyant new French minister whom Secretary of State Jefferson had so warmly welcomed to the United States in April 1793. Whatever Jefferson's role may have been, Genet sent an envoy to Clark in Indiana, where he was busy organizing a volunteer army to capture Spanish Louisiana and Florida. Clark was encouraged in the belief that France might give him cash to maintain an army of eight hundred and send two or three frigates to support it.

But before Clark's latest filibuster got off the ground, President George Washington ordered Jefferson to rebuke Genet for having outfitted privateers in Charleston harbor to send against the British, and then to brazenly bring a captured British ship into Philadelphia harbor. Jefferson quickly dropped Genet. "I saw the necessity of quitting a wreck, which could not but sink all who would cling to it," Jefferson informed James Madison. Genet was recalled, and General Anthony Wayne swooped down on Clark's tiny invasion fleet and destroyed it.

The failed plot led directly to Congress's adoption of the Neutrality Act, in 1794. The act made it a high misdemeanor, punishable by three years in prison and a $3,000 fine, to organize a military expedition against any nation at peace with the United States.

Four years later, after Clark's thwarted filibuster, Senator William Blount of Tennessee, a signer of the Constitution and Tennessee's first territorial governor, tried to interest the British in underwriting a similar scheme. In an interesting coincidence, but perhaps something more, Blount, during the winter of 1796–1797 when he was planning his filibuster, dined with Vice President-elect Jefferson and

General of the Army James Wilkinson. But if Blount had revealed his intention to involve Britain, Jefferson, the passionate Francophile, would certainly have turned a cold shoulder to the scheme.

Blount, however, never had a chance to launch his expedition. To his intense embarrassment, a letter that he had written to a confederate was intercepted and given to President John Adams. Adams made sure that it was read before the Senate, which then voted 25–1 to impeach Blount. He fled to Tennessee and adamantly refused to stand trial in Philadelphia, where Jefferson—whose involvement in Blount's scheme was rumored, as was Wilkinson's—was busy helping prepare his defense. Blount was never tried.

The filibusters' dangerous potential to introduce a foreign threat aimed at the United States' jugular moved President George Washington to warn in his Farewell Address: "Will they [Westerners] not henceforth be deaf to those advisers, if such they are, who would sever them from their Brethren, and connect them with Aliens?"

—ᨸᨸ—

As a Spanish infantry captain, Francisco de Miranda had led the successful assault on British-held Pensacola during the American Revolution. As a lieutenant general in the Revolutionary French army, he had participated in the capture of Antwerp, Belgium, from the British. During the late 1790s, Miranda tried to enlist the British and American governments in helping him to liberate his native Venezuela from Spanish rule. At war again with France, Britain was uninterested. Alexander Hamilton volunteered to lead an American unit, but President Adams wanted nothing to do with Miranda. Then, in 1805, President Jefferson and Secretary of State Madison indicated to Miranda that he could recruit volunteers and raise money on U.S. soil without their interference. Miranda, aided by his American friends—they included New York U.S. Marshal John Swartwout; William S. Smith, who was John Adams's son-in-law and surveyor of the Port of New York; and former Senator Jonathan Dayton, Aaron Burr's old Revolutionary War friend—obtained ships, money, and volunteers in New York.

But Venezuelan troops and sailors, forewarned by newspaper stories of Miranda's departure from New York, were ready when he reached the coast of his native land in early 1806. They captured the would-be liberators, executing many of them. The debacle cost Swartwout and Smith their government jobs.

—⁓—

On May 23, 1804, three weeks after Aaron Burr had lost the New York governor's race, a mysterious visitor arrived at his Richmond Hill home at nightfall. The visitor spent the night, departing at daybreak. Burr's only notice of the guest's impending arrival had come that day in a note: "I propose to take a bed with you this Night, if it may be done without observation or intrusion—answer me & if in the affirmative, I will be with [you] at 30 of the 8th hour." Although he was ill with the flu and in low spirits after his defeat, Burr could not very well refuse to see General James Wilkinson, a friend of thirty years, for whom Burr had recently used his considerable influence with the College of New Jersey to obtain the admission of Wilkinson's sons, James and Joseph. Wilkinson was married to Ann Biddle of Philadelphia, a first cousin of Burr's confidant, Charles Biddle.

All that Wilkinson and Burr discussed that night will never be known, but Louisiana was one of the subjects that came up. The next day, after Wilkinson had returned to his own quarters in New York City, the general sent the vice president a note that included the line: "You are deceived, my friend, with respect to the size of the Rum Barrel of Louisiana the answer being 450 lbs." Wilkinson then invited Burr to his quarters to meet some of his friends "and see my Maps." Burr left that meeting in higher spirits than he had enjoyed in weeks, going so far as to suggest in a letter to Theodosia that they both read Shakespeare's collected works and mark passages "beautiful, absurd or obscure" and compare notes. "Gods!—how much you might accomplish this year." He might have been speaking of himself.

From the events that followed, it is likely that Wilkinson broached the subject of an expedition against Spanish-ruled

Mexico, preposterous as that might seem, given his secret allegiance to Spain. But as General of the Army, Wilkinson saw that relations between Spain and the United States had been steadily deteriorating since the Louisiana Purchase, a transaction that France had assured Spain would never occur.

France had possessed this territory from the 1680s until 1763, when, as part of the treaty ending the French and Indian War, it had transferred Louisiana to Spain. In late 1802, owing France either money or troops under the terms of their military alliance, Spain had reluctantly given its vast Louisiana holdings—territory lying within the massive Missouri River and Mississippi River watersheds—back to France, with one caveat: that France *not* hand over the territory to the United States. Having to give up Louisiana was painful for Spain, but at least the Spanish could take consolation from France's buffering the Spanish Southwest from the muscular young republic in the East. France immediately broke her promise. Napoleon, in need of money for his grandiose plan to invade Great Britain, agreed to sell Louisiana to the United States for $15 million, one of history's great real estate bargains.

Wilkinson was one of the commissioners who formally took possession of Louisiana on behalf of the United States, on December 20, 1803, at a ceremony in New Orleans. The Louisiana Territory's vagaries caused an immediate spike in the simmering tensions between the United States and Spain; especially contentious was the matter of the border between the future states of Louisiana and Texas.

At Richmond Hill and later at Wilkinson's quarters, the Vice President and the General of the Army very likely discussed how a war with Spain could redound to their advantage and profit. With Wilkinson's army and Burr's volunteers, they would march to Mexico City, where Wilkinson and Burr would rule a vast kingdom stretching to Louisiana. But their plan depended on war with Spain. Without a war, Wilkinson could not deploy the U.S. Army. Without a war, Burr would be just another filibuster leader, like Clark and Blount, risking prosecution under the Neutrality Act.

—∞—

As if matters weren't complicated enough for Wilkinson, who was never able to pass up an opportunity to make money through intrigue, he renewed his secret ties to Spain. With war threatening, the general knew the Spanish would pay him well for information.

At a meeting in the spring of 1804 with Florida Governor Don Vicente Folch, Spy No. 13 named his price: $20,000, for past and future services. As Wilkinson put it, the sum would "indemnify me for the eventual loss of the office which I hold, and which probably it will seem necessary for me to abandon in case of hostilities." To sweeten his offer, Wilkinson translated into Spanish a recent analysis of the Western territories that he had written for the War Department, and shared his supposed insights into what lay "concealed in the heart of the President." For his "Reflections" Wilkinson was paid $12,000 by Folch, who promised to ask his superiors in Madrid for the other $8,000, and to renew Wilkinson's pension—at $4,000 a year, double what he had been paid previously.

Perhaps in gratitude for the consideration shown him and for being granted the right to export 16,000 barrels of flour each year to Havana, Wilkinson gave the Spanish some advice: Arrest Meriwether Lewis and William Clark, who were then exploring the reaches of the Missouri River at Jefferson's behest; and fortify the Texas and Florida frontiers against the very army Wilkinson commanded.

Wilkinson and Burr met often in Washington during the winter of 1804–1805 to refine their invasion plan for the Spanish territories. In his spare time, the general amused himself—and, undoubtedly, Washington's citizens—by going for horseback rides around the capital while outfitted in gold stirrups and spurs, and bestriding a leopard-skin saddlecloth.

When Burr returned to Washington in November 1804 from his exile following the Hamilton duel, he, no doubt to his wry amusement, found himself the object of friendly overtures from Jefferson and his officials, who wanted him on their side during the Samuel Chase impeachment trial, scheduled for January. During this brief cease-fire in the Jeffersonians' hostilities toward Burr, the vice president persuaded Jefferson to name Wilkinson Governor of Upper Louisiana, whose provincial capital was St. Louis. The appointment placed Wilkinson close to the flashpoint of any war with Spain, and in an excellent position from which to launch an invasion of the Southwest and Mexico.

—∽—

Wilkinson began to play a deep game with his Spanish paymasters, to screen his and Burr's true motives while attempting to raise money for the Mexican expedition. To Folch and other Spanish colonial officials, Wilkinson presented Burr as a confederate—in a scheme to detach the U.S. western territories and create a republic friendly to Spain. Burr, he said, would soon come asking for money, and it would be to Spain's benefit to give him what he needed. The vice president and the general had evidently discussed this bold ploy at Richmond Hill in May, for Burr, through an intermediary, ex-British Army Colonel Charles Williamson, laid out a similar secession scheme to the British minister, Anthony Merry, in the summer of 1804, but with the added feature of an invasion of Mexico. Williamson told Merry that Burr needed British cash to levy troops, and British ships to transport his invaders to Mexico.

Just as the full extent of Wilkinson's traitorous arrangement with Spain would not be known for nearly a century, so, too, would his and Burr's unscrupulous attempts to solicit money from Spain and England remain secret until late–nineteenth-century historians discovered documentation of them in archives in London, Madrid, Texas, and Mexico. Had these overtures become known during Burr's prosecution for treason in 1807, government lawyers could have confidently erected the scaffold on which to hang the former vice president.

—∽—

Anthony Merry was unhappy with Thomas Jefferson and his administration during the summer of 1804, when Burr's emissary,

Colonel Williamson, first approached him about the Burr scheme. Merry had undergone a harrowing baptism by fire during his first week as minister in November and December 1803. First there had very nearly been a rupture in U.S.–British relations over neutrality rights and British impressments of American seamen. Then the Senate had refused to ratify a proposed Canadian boundary agreement with England. On top of these troubles had come the contretemps over President Jefferson's attempt to introduce Republican equality to his President's House dinners—his so-called "rule of pele mele."

Instead of the usual custom of guests taking assigned dinner seats, Jefferson's "Rules of Etiquette" called for everyone to enter en masse without regard to rank, on the arm of whoever happened to be close by, and to sit in any empty chair. At two dinners hosted by Jefferson and the James Madisons, the Merrys—as well as the Spanish minister, Don Carlos Martinez de Yrujo, and his wife— had found themselves far down the table. Mrs. Merry took particular offense when Jefferson escorted a cabinet member's wife, and not Mrs. Merry, into the dining room. With Washington society at the same time courting Napoleon Bonaparte's brother, Jerome, and his new wife, Elizabeth Patterson of Baltimore, the Merrys and Yrujos believed their shabby treatment to be deliberate, and refused further dinner invitations until they received instructions from their governments. Jefferson made an effort to explain pele mele to Merry, but evidently failed, for neither Mrs. Merry nor Mrs. Yrujo accompanied her husband on his customary New Year's Day call on the president. Jefferson blamed Mrs. Merry and not the minister, sardonically observing to James Monroe: "If his wife perseveres she must eat her soup at home, and we shall endeavor to draw him into society as if she did not exist."

The Merrys, who disliked Washington's isolation and climate, were spending the warm months in Philadelphia, where, in early August 1804, Col. Williamson met with Anthony Merry. Having no friendly feelings for Jefferson, Merry listened with interest as Williamson described Burr's brazen scheme. Williamson, a trusted

Burr friend, was well-connected in Great Britain; one of Williamson's good friends was Henry Dundas—Lord Melville—a powerful figure in Scotland and England. Burr and Williamson had become acquainted in the 1790s when Burr, as a New York state assemblyman, aided Williamson's development of the region around Rochester and Syracuse, New York. As agent for English speculators who had purchased 1.2 million acres, Williamson was responsible for the establishment of townships, roads, and taverns, as well as a hotel on Seneca Lake.

After Merry had heard Williamson out, he wrote to Lord Harrowby, England's Secretary of State for Foreign Affairs, "I have just received an offer from Mr. Burr, the actual Vice President of the Un. States (which situation he is about to resign), to lend assistance to his Majesty's Government . . . particularly in an endeavouring to effect a Separation of the Western Part of the Un. States from that which lies between the Atlantick and the Mountains, in its whole Extent."

When Burr's term as vice president ended in 1805, he met again with Merry, before leaving for the West. To carry out his scheme to separate the Louisiana Territory and the western states from the union and invade Mexico, Burr said he would need a $500,000 loan and a British squadron at the mouth of the Mississippi River. Merry wrote to Lord Harrowby that Burr had told him that Westerners longed for independence, "and that the execution of their design is only delayed by the difficulty of obtaining previously an assurance of protection and assistance from some foreign Power. . . ." Merry said he was confident that Burr "certainly possesses, perhaps in a much greater degree than any other individual in this country, all the talents, energy, intrepidity, and firmness which are required for such an enterprise."

Burr applied to Spanish Minister Don Carlos Martinez de Yrujo for a passport to Mexico, but the suspicious Yrujo rejected the request and instructed Spanish officials to arrest Burr if he entered Spanish territory. Perhaps Yrujo had heard the rumors then beginning to circulate that Burr intended to lead a filibuster against Mexico, or he may have seen Wilkinson's secret reports on Burr's activities.

Even if there were not an expedition against Mexico, Burr believed that something would turn up for him in the West, the only place left to him. A pariah in the East, his political career there over because of the Hamilton duel, he could not even resume his former law practice in New York, because he could be arrested and extradited to New Jersey to face a murder charge. "In New-York I am to be disenfranchised, and in New-Jersey hanged," he wrote to his son-in-law, Joseph Alston, but spiritedly added, "You will not . . . conclude that I have become disposed to submit tamely to the machinations of a banditti."

The West, however, afforded many opportunities, the Mexican expedition only one of them. The Louisiana Territory was ripe for development. There were plans for a canal to bypass the treacherous Falls of the Ohio at Louisville, long an obstacle to Ohio River navigation. And Burr had already received overtures to re-enter public life as a Western senator. The West, where Hamilton had never been popular and where dueling bore no stigma, promised to be friendlier than the East to Burr.

With all of these possibilities in mind, Burr bought "a floating house" for $133 in Pittsburgh and set off down the Ohio River and to a promising future. Sixty feet long and fourteen feet wide, his new home had a dining room, a kitchen with a fireplace, two bedrooms, and glass windows. Steps led to the flat roof, where passengers could walk and sightsee. It was a pleasant way to travel down the Ohio River to the Mississippi River, and then all the way to New Orleans.

Below Pittsburgh, Burr by chance met Congressman Matthew Lyons of Vermont, and they lashed their boats together. As they floated leisurely down the Ohio, they discussed the possibility of Burr moving to the West and running for Congress. At Marietta, Ohio, Burr learned that twelve miles away, on a lush island in the middle of the Ohio River, lived a wealthy Irish émigré and his family. Burr's host in Marietta, Dr. Robert Wallace, a fellow Revolutionary War veteran, asked Burr to deliver a microscope his son had purchased in Philadelphia for the island's gentleman-scholar owner, Harman Blennerhassett. With the microscope in hand, Burr landed at Blennerhassett Island in early May 1805 and introduced himself.

—-w—-

Harman and Margaret Blennerhassett, who had emigrated from Ireland to America in 1796, had purchased 169 acres on the upper end of the five-hundred-acre, hourglass-shaped island in 1797, with part of Harman's $160,000 inheritance. Over the next three years, they built a seven-thousand-square-foot, fourteen-room Palladian-style home with porticos linking the main house to a large kitchen on one side and Harman's study on the other. Despite their attempts to raise cattle and produce, the Blennerhassetts' "Eden" steadily lost money, although Harman enjoyed the life of a scholarly country squire. He played the violin, studied medicine, electricity, and chemistry—his laboratory was just the second one in the Ohio valley—and indulged his love of literature by filling the floor-to-ceiling shelves of his large library with thousands of books. Margaret, twenty-eight years old and the mother of four sons— John, Dominic, Harman Jr., and Joseph—was tall, graceful, and slender from horseback riding and walking up to ten miles a day. Fluent in French and Italian and fond of Shakespeare's plays and Rousseau, she undoubtedly found the well-read Burr, who was fond of pretty young women, an engaging conversationalist.

The Blennerhassetts' neighbors must have wondered why an educated, cultivated couple with meager survival skills would retreat to the American wilderness, then invite their neighbors to lavish parties to dispel their isolation. There were two reasons: First, Margaret, thirteen years younger than Harman, was her husband's niece; she was the daughter of Harman's sister, Catherine Agnew. Their scandalous marriage had violated church, but not civil, law. The more compelling reason for their emigration was Harman's membership in the Society of United Irishmen, a secret patriotic club committed to Irish independence at a time when the

British were arresting and executing dissidents. Exiles from the society that had nurtured them, the Blennerhassetts were soul-mates of Aaron Burr.

Burr reached Blennerhassett Island on May 6, 1805, and was warmly welcomed by Harman and Margaret. It was nearly midnight when they broke off their animated conversation and Burr retired to his houseboat. After breakfast the next morning, he resumed his journey downriver.

Later, Burr sent Harman a letter inviting him to participate in an unspecified future enterprise that he said Harman would find stimulating and profitable. Flattered by Burr's interest, Harman replied in December that he was ready for anything that Burr might suggest—words he would come to regret. "I hope, sir, you will not regard it indelicate in me to observe to you how highly I should be honored in being associated with you, in any contemplated enterprise you should permit me to participate in."

—∾—

Burr toured a proposed canal site that would give river travelers a safe passage around the Falls of the Ohio, and met with three friends who wanted him to become a partner in the venture (the canal was never dug): Senators John Smith of Ohio and John Brown of Kentucky, and his friend from college, former New Jersey Senator Jonathan Dayton, now an Ohioan. But before long, the men were discussing the Spanish, and Burr's proposed expedition against Mexico. This subject absorbed them—especially the prospects of glory and riches for everyone involved.

In Nashville, Senator Andrew Jackson, whose loyal friendship dated to Burr's efforts in the 1790s on behalf of Tennessee statehood, honored Burr at a banquet. Jackson, also major general of the Tennessee militia, despised "the hated Spanish dons and their allies, the savage hostiles." Jackson, said Burr, was "a man of intelligence, and one of those prompt, frank, ardent souls whom I love to meet."

Then Burr went to Fort Massac, near the mouth of the Ohio River, huddling with General James Wilkinson, and probably also with Senator John Adair of Kentucky, to whom Wilkinson had written in May: "He [Burr] understands your merits, and *reckons* on you. Prepare to visit me, and I will tell you all. We must have a peep at the unknown world beyond me."

In late June 1805, bearing letters of introduction from Wilkinson, Burr found steamy New Orleans a congenial stopping place. The city's leaders were full of grievances about the federal government's administration of the Louisiana Territory, and took the former vice president's side against Jefferson and his officials. Wilkinson's letters connected Burr to New Orleans society and men such as Daniel Clark, the city's most prominent merchant, who would one day dedicate himself to exposing Wilkinson as a traitor. Wilkinson's letter to Clark asked him to place himself at Burr's service, adding cryptically, "To him I refer you for many things improper to letter, and which he will not say to any other." A Wilkinson letter introducing Burr to the Spanish commissioner, the Marques de Casa Calvo, revealed that the general was in top double-dealing form: "Your great family interests will promote the view of Colonel Burr and the great interest of your country will be served by following his advice."

—∽∾∽—

New Orleans, Western America's major port, was an amalgam of French, Spanish, Creoles, and Americans—a lingual polyglot. The city simmered with discontent. During the previous three years, it had been governed successively by the Spanish, the French, and, for the preceding six months, the Americans. The French were currently the unhappiest inhabitants, over having become subjects of the barely civilized Americans. But other dissidents and secret organizations thrived in New Orleans's tropical climate—many of them American, and some advocating the liberation of Mexico from Spain. Of these, the Mexican Association, with three hundred members, was the most influential, and the most single-minded: It wished for nothing less than the conquest of Mexico.

The Mexican Association's leaders and collaborators included some of New Orleans's most prominent men, Daniel Clark foremost among them. Others were Edward Livingston, one of Burr's few patronage appointments, forced to resign as New York City U.S. attorney when shortages were discovered in his office accounts; and Judge James Workman. The association's free-wheeling schemes revolved around a cherished core plan: capturing Baton Rouge from Spain, rifling New Orleans's banks, seizing the city's shipping, and sailing to Mexico with the support of British warships.

Burr met with the Catholic bishop of New Orleans, a man who would be essential to his expedition's success in Mexico. The bishop had been quietly sending Jesuit priests to Mexico to gather intelligence and to organize local insurgencies for a future uprising. After Burr and the bishop finished discussing business, the prelate escorted Burr to the Ursuline convent, from which he had received a welcoming letter. Burr and the nuns conversed through the convent grates before he was admitted inside and served wine, fruit, and cakes. "None of that calm monotony which I expected. All was gayety, *wit* and sprightliness," he noted. "All is neatness, simplicity and order. At parting, I asked them to remember me in their prayers. . . ."

—⁂—

In oppressive Deep South summer heat, Burr struck out east from New Orleans on a long ramble through the Mississippi Territory, following the Yazoo River through Mississippi and into Alabama, then turning north into Tennessee. The 450-mile trek enabled him to assay the sympathies of the region's scattered settlers and to reconnoiter the Spanish Florida–U.S. border. It was "vile country, destitute of springs and of running water—think of drinking the nasty puddle-water, covered with green scum, and full of animalculae—bah!" At the Tennessee River, the terrain improved, "all fine, transparent, lively streams, and [the Tennessee] a clear, beautiful, magnificent river."

By September, Burr was back in St. Louis and poring over maps of the Southwest with General Wilkinson. They "settled the plan for an attack on Mexico," Burr wrote Andrew Jackson. Wilkinson began laying the groundwork by asking War Secretary Henry

Dearborn to authorize him to send an expedition into the Southwest if the United States went to war with Spain. As Wilkinson and Burr bent over their sketchy maps, it must have occurred to them that Wilkinson should send out an exploratory party to make better maps and find a serviceable route to Santa Fe, the Spanish colonial capital and the logical staging area for any overland invasion of Mexico.

—m—

In November 1805, Burr returned to Washington to find the city buzzing with rumors about his journey. Much of the talk was the handiwork of Spanish Minister Don Carlos Martinez de Yrujo. Possibly at Yrujo's instigation, Stephen Minor, a wealthy Spanish sympathizer in Natchez, had whispered it about that Burr intended to cause the western states to secede by promising them Mexican treasure. General James Wilkinson was implicated in some accounts. Daniel Clark, the New Orleans merchant, informed the general, "Even I am now supposed to be of consequence enough to combine with Generals and Vice-Presidents." Yrujo added fuel to the speculation by publishing anonymous articles that appeared under the heading, "Queries," in the Philadelphia *United States Gazette*. Yrujo predicted that Burr would call a convention of the Mississippi River and Ohio River states, and urge them to secede from the Union and conquer Mexico with the British navy's help.

The stories were reprinted in all the major newspapers, and, as Yrujo intended, aroused conjecture in the East, where the loyalty of the western settlements had always been considered suspect, and where Burr's reputation was blackest. Louis Marie Turreno, the French minister to the United States, reported to France's foreign minister, Charles Maurice de Talleyrand, that "Louisiana thus is going to be the seat of Mr. Burr's new intrigues; he is going there under the aegis of General Wilkinson." Not everyone was taken in by Yrujo's mischief; to Thomas Ritchie of the Richmond *Enquirer*, the "Queries" sounded like nothing more than a ghostly reprise of the Blount conspiracy of 1797.

In a report to his superiors in Madrid, Yrujo, with what must have been great satisfaction, sniffed at the rumors that he had concocted. "The supposed expedition against Mexico is ridiculous and chimerical in the present state of things."

—⁓—

Over dinner at the President's House on November 30, 1805, Burr described his Western trip to Jefferson; he also met with administration officials. "My views have been fully explained to several principal officers of the government," Burr wrote to Henry Clay, a young Kentucky lawyer and politician who was one of his new western friends. Burr told Clay that his ideas "are well considered by the administration and seen by it with complacency."

Exactly which views Burr propounded is unclear, because before he met with Jefferson, he had learned from one of his many government contacts that Jefferson's cabinet two weeks earlier had decided to buy the Floridas from Spain. France, which was arbitrating the secret negotiations, had set a $10 million price. Burr now knew there would be no war with Spain, even though Jefferson, in his Fifth Annual Message to Congress on December 3, had continued to wax hawkish: "Our citizens have been seized and their property plundered [by the Spanish] in the very parts of the former [Orleans] which had been actually delivered up by Spain."

After his dinner with Burr, Jefferson received an anonymous letter warning him that Burr's trip west had a dark purpose: a coup, possibly aided by British Minister Anthony Merry.

"You admit him at your table, and you held a long a private conference with him a few days ago *after dinner* at the very moment he is meditating the overthrow of your Administration. . . . Yes, Sir, his abberations [sic] through the Western States had *no other object*."

[8]

The Burr Expedition, and Ruin

Our project my dear friend is brought to the point so long desired. I guaran-
tee the result with my life and honor, with the lives, the honor and the for-
tune of hundreds, the best blood of our country. . . . The gods invite us to
glory and fortune. It remains to be seen whether we deserve the boons.
—EXCERPT FROM FAMOUS "CIPHER LETTER" TO
GENERAL JAMES WILKINSON

Burr, now aware of the administration's secret negotiations to buy the Floridas, knew that he would not be able to raise a volunteer army to invade the Southwest and Mexico if America and Spain kept the peace. But if a border war suddenly flared in Louisiana, he wanted to have a force ready to mount a lightning expedition into Texas and Mexico. Burr hit upon a simple solution to this dilemma: Establish a Louisiana colony of able-bodied volunteers who could invade the Southwest on hours' notice if war did break out. Plentiful land was for sale on the Ouachita River in northeast Louisiana (near present-day Monroe), the former Spanish land grant known as the Bastrop Tract.

The fine, black river-bottom soil was ideal for growing cotton, and thus well suited to slave-owning plantation owners from the South. But Burr would not be inviting slaveholders to join his colony; he was a longtime abolitionist. He envisioned 336-acre plots—too small for growing cotton, sugar, or indigo, but large enough for wheat cultivation—with settlers living in habitations designed by Burr's friend, the master architect Benjamin Latrobe.

Burr's chimerical plans for Bastrop were in step with the tract's checkered history. Felip Neri, the Baron de Bastrop, had received the 1.2-million-acre land grant in 1797 from Spanish Governor Francisco Luis Hector de Carondelet. Bastrop planned to establish a colony of five hundred families. But when Carondelet was recalled, Bastrop's title was called into question, and rather than defend his claim, the baron sold the land in 1799, sowing the seeds of a bitter dispute over ownership among several claimants. Into this imbroglio stepped Burr. With $5,000 cash, he made a down payment on 400,000 acres and promised to pay the $30,000 balance at a later date. Title questions made Burr's ownership shaky at best, but it supplied him with an alternative plan if there was no Spanish–American war. By the fall of 1806, when war with Spain once again appeared probable, Burr described to Ohio Senator John Smith how the Bastrop tract figured in his plans: "If peace should be preferred, which I do not expect, I shall settle my Washita [sic] lands, and make society as pleasant as possible."

Falsely claiming that he intended to launch a separatist movement, Burr unscrupulously lobbied Britain and Spain for money that he intended to use for either an expedition against Mexico or to complete his Louisiana land purchase. It was not Burr's finest moment; he evidently had no compunction about lying when it advanced his schemes. Yet, as the government would learn a year later, Burr took no actual steps to separate the West, but only suggested the idea to men who might be persuaded by such talk to aid him. Acting in concert with Burr, ex-Senator Jonathan Dayton intimated to Spanish Minister Yrujo that for $40,000, he would divulge Burr's secret plans, suggesting that they included the dismemberment of the Western states and territories. Yrujo played along, already aware of what Burr was really up to. At their second meeting in late December 1805, Dayton changed his approach, admitting to Yrujo that he was serving as Burr's agent and had invented the story of revealing Burr's plan in order to persuade the Spanish to advance him money. Hoping that by admitting a small lie he would persuade Yrujo to swallow a whopper, Dayton said Burr planned to overthrow the U.S. government, rob the banks, and plunder the federal arsenal. If he met no resistance, Burr would remain in Washington and negotiate with individual states on how they would be governed. Otherwise, if there was fighting, he intended to commandeer ships from the Washington Navy Yard, burn what he didn't take, and sail with his loot to New Orleans, where he would proclaim the independence of Louisiana and the West.

Amazingly, Yrujo believed it, and recommended to his superiors in Madrid that Spain give Burr up to $1 million. Dayton and Burr "counted on her [Spain's] friendship because of her obvious interest in the success of the enterprise; that the matter of the Louisiana boundary would be arranged to our entire satisfaction . . . that the Floridas would be undisturbed. . . ." But Yrujo's superiors were more skeptical than he; they counseled caution and consented to advance Burr just $2,500.

Once again approaching British Minister Anthony Merry, Burr reiterated the daring proposal that he had outlined to him earlier: With a volunteer army financed by a $500,000 English loan and backed up by British warships, Burr would detach the Louisiana Territory and the West from the Union. But it was an untimely solicitation. Immersed in preparing Britannica's defenses for a seemingly imminent invasion by Napoleon Bonaparte, Prime Minister William Pitt had no time for American affairs. Moreover, Lord Melville, the powerful patron of Burr's friend, Colonel Charles Williamson, was leaving the government under a cloud of corruption accusations. Nonetheless, in his report to the home office, Merry was as ebullient as ever about Burr's chances of carrying off his fantastic scheme:

> He [Burr] observed, what I readily conceive may happen, that when once Louisiana and the Western country became independent, the Eastern States will separate themselves immediately from the Southern; and that thus the immense power which is now risen

up with so much rapidity in the western hemisphere will, by such a division, be rendered at once informidable; and that no moment could be so proper for the undertaking in question and particularly for Great Britain to take part in it as the present. . . .

—◊◊◊—

In early 1806, the administration's negotiations for the Floridas collapsed, and tensions began rising again between America and Spain. Neither the United States nor Spain had been as enthusiastic about the discussions as France, which had hoped to pocket all of the sale proceeds to square Spain's debts to her. Jefferson's apathy toward the negotiations arose from his belief—an article of faith held by many in Congress as well—that the Louisiana Purchase gave the United States title to not just the Louisiana Territory, but also to West Florida. Jefferson, in fact, favored breaking off relations with Spain and taking the Floridas and Texas, which goes a long way toward explaining his ambivalence toward Burr throughout 1806. "I do not view peace as within our choice," he wrote to Secretary of State Madison.

His cabinet, however, was not in unanimous agreement. Treasury Secretary Albert Gallatin and others believed that by buying the Floridas, the United States would avoid a war, while resolving spoliation claims by American merchants against Spain for ships captured during the Quasi-War. But West Florida's disputed ownership ultimately undid the negotiations.

Unaware that the negotiations for Florida were unraveling, Burr explored peaceful options besides his Louisiana colony. He bid for a Pennsylvania judgeship, and even swallowed his pride and asked President Jefferson for a position. After their meeting, on March 22, 1806, the president wrote in his diary that Burr was "willing to engage in something . . . if I should have anything to propose to him." Jefferson, of course, offered Burr nothing. While acknowledging that Burr surely "would use his talents for the public good, . . . the public had withdrawn their confidence from him," Jefferson said he told Burr. Burr reminded Jefferson of his indispensable role in Jefferson's election and also darkly hinted, as Jefferson retold it in his *Anas* entry, "He could do me much harm . . . [but] wished, however, to be on different ground." But Burr could do no harm to Jefferson, the president strenuously explained in his journal entry, whose date happened to coincide with the taking of depositions in the "wager suit" filed in 1806 by former Little Band members; the testimony revealed Jefferson's collaboration with Federalists in his election in 1801.

—∽—

Burr attempted to enlist two former U.S. military officers who were unhappy with the Jefferson administration in his expedition–colonization plan. Captain Thomas Truxtun, the hero of the Quasi-War with France, had been forced to resign from the Navy when, during the Tripolitan War, he had refused to assume command of a squadron and his own flagship, too, arguing that the squadron commander should not be required to do both. Burr invited Truxtun to command a fleet whenever Burr invaded Mexico. Truxtun listened with interest, until Burr admitted that the expedition wasn't government-sanctioned; Truxtun then politely declined the offer.

Burr's other prospect was William Eaton, who had led a motley, four hundred-man army of dissident Tripolitans, mercenaries, Arab cavalry, and eight U.S. Marines across 520 miles of desert and captured Derna, Tripoli's second-largest city during the Barbary War. Unfortunately for Eaton, his victory had pushed Tripoli into a negotiated peace, spoiling his plan to march at the head of an army into the city of Tripoli, overthrow the ruler, and dictate peace. Eaton was now in Washington, trying to recoup his expenses for the expedition and from his days as U.S. consul to Tunis, and complaining loudly about the Jefferson administration's foot-dragging to anyone who would listen. Burr contacted him. According to Eaton's dubious later testimony—dubious because Burr normally was close-mouthed, unless he had abandoned his usual sobriety to carouse with the hard-drinking Eaton—Burr had offered him a generalship in his volunteer army. He had then outlined a wild plot to overthrow the government, assassinate the president, and seize the Navy and the national treasury. Eaton's response was to go to Jefferson to warn him about Burr, suggesting that the president remove him from the country by appointing him to a remote European ministry. Jefferson took no action.

Other rumors and reports about Burr's activities, besides those appearing in the newspapers, began to reach Jefferson. Kentucky U.S. Attorney Joseph Daviess, a Federalist and John Marshall's brother-in-law, penned several letters to the president during 1806, warning him that Burr—and Jefferson's top army commander, James Wilkinson—were plotting the separation of the West, and that Wilkinson had received thousands of dollars from Spain. Daviess reminded Jefferson that in 1788 at a convention in Danville, Kentucky, Wilkinson had proposed that Kentucky secede from the United States and unite with Spain. Daviess added: "I am convinced Wilkinson has been for years and now is a pensioner of Spain." Jefferson initially asked Daviess for more names and details, but then, perhaps because he thought that Daviess, a Federalist, was only trying to embarrass the Republicans—or, possibly, that Burr might serve a useful purpose by invading the Southwest and Mexico—he wrote nothing further to Daviess. Jefferson's last note to him, a response to Daviess's request that he confirm receipt of his letters, was a curt acknowledgment that they had reached him. Frustrated, Daviess and his brother-in-law, Humphrey Marshall, founded *The Western World* to expose the alleged conspiracy.

—∿—

By the spring of 1806, U.S.–Spanish relations had broken down again, and Spanish troops were massing along the Sabine River (the boundary between present-day Louisiana and Texas). When this news reached Washington in early May, orders immediately went out directing Wilkinson to leave St. Louis "with as little delay as practicable," and to take command of the six hundred troops in Louisiana to repel any attack.

The sudden developments also caused Burr to lobby Spanish Minister Yrujo and British Minister Merry one last time for money. But neither of them would promise financial support for his secession scheme, even though Burr warned both ministers that if they did not help him, he would seek the aid of their respective enemies.

Burr prepared to return to the West, only this time "never to return." Lacking a clear plan, financial backing, or knowledge of General James Wilkinson's whereabouts, Burr was making it all up as he went. He intended to retrace the journey that he had made the previous year, down the Ohio and Mississippi rivers to Louisiana, with a thousand to fifteen hundred volunteers raised in the Northeast and the West. They would join forces with General Wilkinson against the Spanish. But if the fluid border situation suddenly turned peaceful again, Burr and his recruits would colonize the 400,000 acres that he had purchased along the Ouachita River.

In Philadelphia, Burr conferred with Jonathan Dayton and the expedition quartermaster, Comfort Tyler, who was a friend from Burr's New York Assembly days. They studied Burr's maps—of the Spanish empire from Louisiana to California and south to Panama; admiralty charts of the Mexican Gulf Coast with information on inlets, islands, and water depth; and a topographical map of Mexico's interior, between Vera Cruz and Mexico City. Tyler arranged for the shipment of pork, flour, beef, and whiskey from Pittsburgh to Natchez.

Wilkinson had fallen virtually silent in his correspondence with Burr, except for a May 13 letter that Burr and Dayton had both found disturbingly evasive. Hoping to inspire Wilkinson to renew his commitment to the expedition and also to inform him of their plans, they wrote him two letters. The encrypted July 22 letter, ostensibly written by Burr, would become known as the "cipher letter" and have enormous ramifications for Burr, Wilkinson, and Jefferson, while igniting a controversy over its authorship lasting a hundred and seventy years. A single copy of a second letter, written by Dayton to Wilkinson two days later, along with two copies of the July 22 cipher letter, were handed to messengers to deliver to Wilkinson in Louisiana by land and sea, to reach him, so Burr and

Dayton hoped, before Burr and his men boarded their boats on the Ohio River to sail to Louisiana.

But Wilkinson, although ordered to Louisiana May 6, lingered in St. Louis through July, and he did not reach Natchez until September 7, four months after his orders were signed. What delayed him? Besides the fact that the general was by nature a comfort-loving procrastinator, he had been busy organizing an exploratory expedition into the West, to be led by twenty-seven-year-old Lt. Zebulon Pike, who had explored the upper Mississippi River Basin in 1805. Pike and his twenty-two men, who left Fort Belle Fontaine above St. Louis on July 15, 1806, carried written orders instructing them to escort some former Osage captives of the Pottawatomie to their homes on the Grand Osage River in present-day Missouri; to arbitrate a peace between the Kansas and Osage tribes; to make a truce with the Comanches, who lived near the Arkansas River headwaters; and to take detailed notes on the region's natural history, population, and geography, collecting mineral and plant specimens.

But the true, secret purpose of the Pike expedition was to find a route of march to Santa Fe suitable for supply wagons and artillery. Any lingering doubts as to Pike's motives were dispelled by his October 2, 1806, letter to Wilkinson, written while camped on the Republican River:

> Any number of men who may reasonably be calculated on would find no difficulty in marching by the route we came, with baggage, wagons, field artillery, and all the usual appendages of a small army; and if all the route to Santa Fe should be of the same description, in case of war I would pledge my life, and what is infinitely dearer, my honor, for the successful march of a reasonable body of troops into the province of New Mexico.

Against the backdrop of the Rocky Mountains and the towering Colorado peak that would one day bear Pike's name, Pike and his men built breastworks at present-day Pueblo, Colorado, and, moving west, marveled at the sight of the Royal Gorge, a heart-stopping 1,100 feet deep. Detained by Spanish army scouts, they were escorted to Santa Fe, probably Pike's intention all along, and from there to Chihuaha, Mexico. The publication of Pike's journal in 1810 caused a sensation in America and Europe.

Pike didn't have long to enjoy his fame; in 1813, Brigadier General Zebulon Pike was fatally wounded while leading the American attack on Toronto.

—◊—

In Pittsburgh, Burr and Colonel Julien De Pestre, a French Revolution refugee, canvassed for volunteers. For agreeing to a six-month commitment, recruits were promised $10 a month in wages and 150 acres in the Ouachita colony. On August 25, Burr visited Colonel George Morgan, an old friend and fellow Princeton alumnus, whose plan for a Spanish-grant colony at New Madrid, Missouri, had been ruined by Wilkinson. While at Morganza, as Morgan called his home outside Pittsburgh, Burr tried to enlist in his expedition Morgan's two sons, John and Thomas, who later claimed, as did their father, that Burr discussed separating the West from the Union. Perhaps the Morgans embellished—George Morgan may have recognized an opportunity to speed up government validation of his Indian land grants in the Indiana Territory—or Burr may simply have gotten carried away. Whatever was said, Burr hastily left early the next morning, before his hosts arose. Morgan sent a letter to President Jefferson informing him of Burr's assertions, and hinting at a possible quid pro quo as a reward for his information: "A knowledge of the persons who may reject, as well as those who may accept parricide propositions will be peculiarly useful."

In late August, Burr reached Blennerhassett Island. His daughter, Theodosia, and her husband, Joseph Alston, were already there. Burr plunged into preparations for the expedition, which he hoped to set in motion in December. He signed contracts for a hundred barrels of provisions, and for the construction of fifteen boats, to be built by Joseph Barker on the Muskingum River above Marietta,

Ohio. Five of the shallow-draft galleys would be fifty feet long; the other ten, forty feet.

In Nashville, Burr asked Andrew Jackson to build him five large boats. Jackson and two partners operated a racetrack, tavern, and boatyard on a branch of the Cumberland River. Jackson was recuperating from a nearly fatal dueling wound that he had received May 30. Charles Dickinson, a lawyer, speculator, and one of the best shots in Tennessee, had made insulting remarks in a tavern about Jackson's wife, Rachel. The fiery Jackson challenged him to a duel. Aware that Dickinson was the better and quicker marksman, Jackson decided to let him fire first, so that he would not rush his own shot and possibly miss his mark. Dickinson's round smashed into Jackson's chest, shattering ribs. Jackson swayed but kept his feet. Gritting his teeth against the pain as blood began to fill his shoe, Jackson took careful aim at Dickinson, who gazed at Jackson in horror, clutching his empty pistol. Jackson fired, and Dickinson fell, hit below the ribs. Dickinson bled to death. "I should have hit him if he had shot me through the brain," Jackson said afterward. His wound took years to heal completely and caused him chronic pain.

Jackson, happy to see Burr, "a true and trusty friend of Tennessee," readily agreed to build the boats. He despised the dons, and had applauded the collapse of the negotiations to buy the Floridas, because it meant that America was free to "conquer not only the Floridas, but all Spanish America." With a few thousand volunteers under "firm officers and men of enterprise [we] . . . will look into Santa Fe and Mexico, give freedom and commerce to those provinces and establish peace. . . ."

—∽∼—

But the fates were turning against Burr. *The Western World* was trumpeting every rumor about Burr and Wilkinson, and the stories were being reprinted in all the major Eastern newspapers. Harman Blennerhassett added to the growing uproar, writing essays that advocated Western secession. They appeared under the nom de plume, "Querist," in the *Ohio Gazette* in Marietta, but any air of authorial mystery evaporated after Blennerhassett went around boasting in Wood County, Virginia, just across the river, that he had written them.

Morgan's letter reached Jefferson about the same time as a warning from Thomas Truxtun. A letter from James Taylor, a Kentuckian to whom Blennerhassett had expressed secessionist views, landed on the desk of Secretary of State James Madison. Then, more letters came to Madison—a second-hand account of Burr's meeting with the Morgans, another about Comfort Tyler's activities in New York, and one forwarded by William Eaton, describing how an Ohio mob had serenaded Burr with the "Rogue's March." But it was U.S. Postmaster Gideon Granger's letter to the president, recounting Eaton's meeting with Burr the previous winter, that prompted Jefferson to convene his cabinet to discuss Burr and Wilkinson.

—∾—

Burr made Lexington the expedition headquarters. Supplies arrived at the Louisville docks, a staging area supervised by Davis Floyd, later a Burr co-defendant. On Blennerhassett Island, a kiln was built for making cornmeal. Burr seemed to be everywhere at once, making sure preparations were advancing. Theodosia and Joseph Alston departed for South Carolina in October as the Blennerhassetts packed their belongings, intending to join the flotilla that would embark in December for either the Ouachita River Valley or Mexico.

Meanwhile, leaders throughout the West were growing alarmed at Burr's mysterious preparations on Blennerhassett Island and at Marietta, Lexington, and Louisville—to what purpose, they need only have read *The Western World*'s shrill warnings of uprisings, secession, foreign intrigue, and plunder. At a public meeting in Wood County, Virginia, residents decided to raise a militia and discussed invading the island. When Margaret Blennerhassett learned of the meeting, she sent the family gardener, Peter Taylor, to warn her husband and Burr. Taylor looked for them first in Cincinnati, but in vain. Ohio Senator John Smith directed him to Lexington, Kentucky, after writing a letter warning Burr that the "mystery and rapidity" of his movements had aroused suspicions throughout Ohio, and admitting that the rumors of a Western uprising worried him too.

"I have no political views," Burr replied to Smith. He assured the senator that he only wished to begin a settlement on the Ouachita River in Louisiana. "I never harbored or expressed any such intention to anyone, nor did any person ever intimate such a design to me," Burr wrote, conveniently overlooking the glaring fact that he had just sent his chief of staff, Colonel de Pestre, to Philadelphia to try once again to wring money from Spanish Minister Yrujo with suggestions of just such a plot, and with reassurances that Burr had no designs on Mexico.

—◊—

On October 22, 1806, Jefferson convened the cabinet to address the Burr–Wilkinson situation. Joseph Daviess's letters, William Eaton's warning, *The Western World*'s sensational stories, and Colonel George Morgan's account of Burr's strange behavior had failed to rouse the president to action, but Gideon Granger's letter about Eaton's meeting with Burr, Jefferson later acknowledged, "gave a specific view of the objects of this new conspiracy." Jefferson and his advisers reviewed all the reports about Burr's statements and movements, "which had excited suspicions, as every motion does of such a Catalinarian nature." They wrote confidential letters to the Western governors and district attorneys, instructing them to arrest Burr for treason or high misdemeanors if he committed any "overt act." The cabinet decided to dispatch gunboats to Fort Adams on the Mississippi, with orders to stop any suspicious-looking groups of men traveling downriver.

And what to do about James Wilkinson, the General of the Army? Burr supposedly had told William Eaton that Wilkinson was in league with him. And Wilkinson had moved with incredible slowness when ordered by the War Department to take charge of troops in Louisiana. What was one to make of that? Jefferson tersely noted, "Suspicion of infidelity in Wilkinson being now become very general, a question is proposed what is proper to be done as to him on this account." But no action was taken on the explosive question.

Gravely watching the disturbing reports about Burr and Wilkinson gather like storm clouds, the cabinet judged it prudent to send Captains Edward Preble and Stephen Decatur, the Tripolitan War's naval heroes, to New Orleans to command the ships and gunboats going to Fort Adams.

Then the reports about Burr abruptly dried up. Thinking there was no crisis after all, Jefferson rescinded the orders to Preble and Decatur, and instead sent John Graham, the new secretary of the Louisiana Territory, to follow Burr's trail. Graham, named to succeed Dr. Joseph Browne, the Burr brother-in-law appointed before the Chase impeachment trial, as territorial secretary, also was instructed to gather intelligence on Burr, to consult with the Western governors, and to have Burr arrested if he broke the law. Granger sent an agent to New Orleans, a Mr. Pease, with orders to dismiss any western postal agent whose fidelity to the government was doubtful. The cabinet did nothing about Wilkinson.

—⁓—

In August, seven hundred Spanish troops under Lieutenant Colonel Simon de Herrera y Leyva, governor of Nuevo Leon, crossed the Sabine River. Herrera was acting on Spain's presumption that the proper border was thirty miles east, at Arroyo Hondo. Louisiana officials, who, astonishingly, believed that the true border was really the Rio Grande, hundreds of miles west, could not abide Spain's incursion. Governor William C. C. Claiborne called out the Louisiana militia, while sourly expressing regret over General of the Army Wilkinson's continued absence. The Spanish marched to within twelve miles of Natchitoches, the American military headquarters. War Secretary Henry Dearborn ordered Wilkinson to drive the Spanish back across the Sabine. But Wilkinson, who had only reached Natchez, countermanded Dearborn's orders, instructing Colonel Thomas Cushing, the commander at Natchitoches, not to act until Wilkinson reached the scene.

Wilkinson was in a quandary. As commander of U.S. forces, he was duty-bound to drive the Spanish back across the Sabine. As a Spanish pensioner, he could not very well make war on Spain. And what was he to do about Aaron Burr? He had also recently received Dayton's disturbing July 24 letter exhorting him to joint action with Burr while slyly warning him that he was going to be replaced as army chief during the next congressional session. "Jefferson will affect to yield reluctantly to the public sentiment, but yield he will; prepare yourself, therefore, for it; you know the rest." By "the rest," Dayton evidently meant the Burr expedition. "You are not a man to despair, or even despond, especially when such prospects offer in another quarter. Are you ready?" Dayton asked. "Are your numerous associates ready? Wealth and glory, Louisiana and Mexico." But instead of inspiring Wilkinson to join Burr, Dayton's letter only made him more cautious.

At the Natchez plantation of the rumor-monger Stephen Minor, Wilkinson made up his mind not to attack the Spaniards. "I shall drain the cup of conciliation," he wrote to War Secretary Dearborn. The general then leisurely made his way toward Natchitoches, taking two weeks to travel 250 miles. Not wanting to put his army in the field, Wilkinson sent the Spanish commander, Colonel Herrera, a letter cordially requesting that he withdraw to the Sabine River. For reasons unknown, Herrera amazingly did just that on September 27. Wilkinson ordered his army to prepare to march to the eastern bank of the Sabine, but the ponderous general did not budge from Natchitoches until October.

While performing this delicate balancing act between his two paymasters, Spain and the United States, General Wilkinson, on October 8, received a most unwelcome visitor—Burr's messenger, young Samuel Swartwout, bearing one of the two copies of the coded July 22 letter. In the presence of Colonel Cushing, Swartwout told Wilkinson that he had come to volunteer. But when Cushing left the general's tent, Swartwout handed him the letter. Working steadily until nearly dawn, Wilkinson laboriously deciphered it, using the key that he and Burr had devised: the 1800 edition of

Entick's New Spelling Dictionary; the letter's seemingly random jumbles of numbers and letters referred to page numbers in the dictionary and the locations on those pages of the decoded words.

The bombastic letter, so stylistically alien to Burr's usual cool, measured phrasing, was, in fact, written by Dayton. Dayton's nephew, Peter Ogden, had overtaken Swartwout on the way to Louisiana and substituted his uncle's letter for Burr's, possibly because Dayton believed Wilkinson needed bracing up. Besides being outdated, the letter gave Wilkinson one more good reason to disassociate himself from Burr.

"Your letter postmarked 13th May is received," the letter began—critical words, future developments show. The letter described plans to recruit volunteers, build boats, and rendezvous on the Ohio River, and from there to descend to the Mississippi and the Deep South. The expeditioners would join Wilkinson in Natchez, and decide whether to seize Baton Rouge, or to proceed directly to their unnamed destination, presumably New Orleans—the embarkation point for Mexico. "The people of the country to which we are going," the letter said cryptically, "are prepared to receive us."

"Naval protection of England is secured. Truxton [*sic*] is going to Jamaica to arrange with the [British] admiral there and will meet us at Mississippi," the letter said untruthfully, adding:

> Our project my dear friend is brought to the point so long desired.
> I guarantee the result with my life and honor, with the lives, the
> honor and the fortune of hundreds, the best blood of our country.
> . . . The gods invite us to glory and fortune. It remains to be seen
> whether we deserve the boons.

Wilkinson spent an anxious, sleepless night brooding about what he should do. A misstep could mean his utter ruin. By morning, he was settled on a breathtaking plan—one that was the polar opposite of what he and Burr had decided upon. Now, rather than collaborating with Burr in an expedition against Mexico, Wilkinson would save the republic from a treasonous plot, while simultaneously reaffirming his fealty to Spain.

Summoning Colonel Cushing, Wilkinson announced to his startled field commander that he intended to settle the Spanish crisis peacefully and then march his troops from Natchitoches to defend New Orleans against a new threat. Without consulting anyone, Wilkinson sent Colonel Herrera a communiqué proposing that the Spanish withdraw from the Sabine west to Nacogdoches, and that Wilkinson pull back to Natchitoches. Neither army would venture into the 120 miles of disputed territory between. Herrera, without *his* government's authorization, readily accepted. The informal agreement, known henceforth as the Neutral Ground Treaty, stood until 1821, even though it was never submitted to the U.S. Senate for approval.

At his field desk, Wilkinson began to compose an all-important letter to the president that he knew must sound just the right note of shock and urgency. The general devoted several days to writing and revising it, completing the final version on October 20. Then, evidently concerned about the *Western World* stories implicating him in Burr's plans, Wilkinson wrote the president a second letter, dated October 21. The general handed the letters to Colonel Thomas Smith, who slipped them into the sole of one of his shoes for safekeeping during the thousand-mile journey to Washington. When Smith delivered the letters on November 25, it was like a bomb going off.

Deliberately matter-of-fact, Wilkinson's first letter announced that he had uncovered a powerful conspiracy, stretching from New York to New Orleans, and aimed at the conquest of Mexico. It is unlikely that this letter alone would have inspired the tumult that followed, for Jefferson had heard all of this before, although not from the General of the Army. The incendiary second letter, however, touched off the cascading events that followed.

Unnamed conspirators intended to separate the West from the Union and attack Mexico, according to this letter, a strange fusion of false piety and Wilkinson's usual grandiloquence:

The desperation of the plan, and the stupendous consequences with which it seems pregnant, stagger my belief and excite doubts of the reality, against the conviction of my senses; and it is for this reason I shall forbear to commit names, because it is my desire to avert a great public calamity.

In order to confound the deadly plot, Wilkinson would "make the best compromise" with the Spanish—in fact, he already had—"and throw myself with my little band into New Orleans to be ready to defend the capital against usurpation and violence." Here, the general indulged his weakness for theatrical self-aggrandizement: "It is the highest ambition of my soul on a proper occasion, to spend my last breath in the cause of my country." He showed that he was not above resorting to abject flattery, either, if it furthered his purposes. "To you [Jefferson] I owe more than I will express, lest I should be suspected of adulation, which I detest." Then, he reached the true purpose of the second letter, expressing the sincere hope that the *Western World* stories, which had left him "bespattered with obloquy and slandered with a degree of virulence and indecency surpassing all example," had not damaged Jefferson's confidence in him. Should this fail to convince Jefferson of his loyalty, he reminded the president that his two predecessors, George Washington and John Adams, had never doubted him.

Handcuffed until now by the many reports from informants and newspapers of Wilkinson's involvement with Burr, Jefferson saw his way clear to act against Burr. Wilkinson's quicksilver loyalty was not the only reason; other factors were the rising public anxiety about Burr, and the unsettled international climate. War with Spain might bring Spain's ally, Napoleon Bonaparte, and the French army to America. There was Gideon Granger's report of Burr's supposed insurrectionist declarations to William Eaton. Moreover, Southern Republicans disliked the idea of an avowed abolitionist, Burr, on the loose in the West and possibly closing off Louisiana and the Southwest to the expansion of slavery. Having exhausted the soil in their home states with relentless cotton cultivation, plantation owners did not want to find their westward migration barred by free territories or their congressional power threatened by new free-soil states. Finally, Burr's conspiracy had revived Jefferson's ancient antipathy toward his former rival.

Convening his cabinet the very day that Wilkinson's letters reached him, Jefferson said he intended to warn the nation of the dangerous threat to its peace. Scarcely a page long, the president's carefully worded proclamation of November 27 announced the discovery of a

> military expedition or enterprise against the dominions of Spain, against which nation war had not been declared by the constitutional authority of the U.S.; that for this purpose they are fitting out & arming vessels in the western waters of the U.S., collecting provisions, arms, military stores & other means. . . .

The unnamed conspirators were ordered to desist, and were warned that they persisted "at their peril, and will incur prosecution with all the rigors of the law." All state and judicial officials, militiamen, and members of the armed services were directed to find and stop anyone involved in the expedition.

Unmentioned in the proclamation was perhaps the most serious threat of all to the peace: the potential Western insurrection of which Wilkinson had warned. Nor did Jefferson's Sixth Annual Message to Congress on December 2 allude to an insurrection, but only to "military expeditions against the territories of Spain."

Why? The reason was Jefferson knew that because the Constitution's framers had not foreseen such a development, he could not use troops to stop an insurrection, but he could order the Army to stop a violation of the Neutrality Act. Jefferson immediately drafted legislation remedying this oversight, and Congress passed it on March 3, 1807.

—◊—

Burr's plans now began unraveling under the pressure of powerful government forces animated by Jefferson's proclamation. U.S.

Attorney Joseph Daviess convened a grand jury in Frankfort, and asked it to indict Burr and his friend, Kentucky Senator John Adair, for allegedly plotting to violate Spain's neutrality. Burr hired his young lawyer friend, Henry Clay, to defend him, but neither Clay nor the grand jury had anything to do because Burr's quartermaster, Davis Floyd, the only witness Daviess planned to present, could not be located in Kentucky. The jury was dismissed. When Floyd turned up in Kentucky two weeks later, the grand jury reconvened. But even after hearing Floyd's testimony, it still could find no ground for indicting Burr or Adair. "There has been no testimony before us which does in the Smallest degree criminate the conduct of either of those persons. . . ." Jefferson was so disgusted with Daviess's misbegotten prosecution that he fired him. Later, Daviess avenged himself by circulating a pamphlet documenting how Jefferson had disregarded his warnings about Burr and Wilkinson. Five years later, Daviess was killed at the Battle of Tippecanoe, and he posthumously became the namesake of a Kentucky county.

In early December 1806, Jefferson's agent, John Graham, was on Burr's trail, listening to the rumors that saturated the Ohio River Valley: that twelve hundred stands of arms were being assembled, that twenty thousand armed men were poised to storm down the river, that Andrew Jackson was raising troops in concert with Burr. Graham informed Ohio Governor Edward Tiffin that Burr planned to seize New Orleans, establish a new government, and force the West to join him, and Tiffin convened an emergency session of the legislature. On December 9, Ohio militia seized the fifteen shallow-draft galleys that Joseph Barker was building for Burr on the Muskingum River near Marietta.

These alarming reports reached the expeditioners assembling on Blennerhassett Island like a thunderclap, greatly accelerating their preparations. On the night of December 10, a bonfire burned on the island waterfront as work parties led by Comfort Tyler and including Harman Blennerhassett hastily loaded their half-dozen boats and pushed off into the Ohio River. At daybreak the next morning, Virginia militiamen from Wood County swarmed onto the island, only to discover that their quarry was gone. They drank up the wine in the Blennerhassetts' wine cellar and rampaged through the mansion as Margaret Blennerhassett and her sons cowered upstairs. Militiamen dragged down the fence rails to make fires, and cattle foraged in the cornfields. A week later, Margaret was permitted to collect some of her silver, books, and furniture, and her husband's musical instruments and papers, and follow Harman downriver. She never saw her island home again.

—⁓—

Aware that wild rumors were flying, but not of the events on Blennerhassett Island, Burr and Adair rode to Nashville to claim the five boats being built for them by Andrew Jackson. Jackson, to their surprise, was cold and distant. A recent visitor, Captain John Fort, had told him disturbing things: that Burr was allied with Wilkinson, whom Jackson despised, and that they intended to capture New Orleans, detach the West, and invade Mexico. While Jackson would not have hesitated to lead a filibuster against the Spanish (he later did), he was steadfastly loyal to the Union. After Fort's visit, Jackson sent warning letters to President Jefferson, Senator Daniel Smith of Tennessee, and New Orleans Governor William C. C. Claiborne, to whom he declared, "I will die in the last ditch before I would yield a foot to the Dons or see the Union disunited."

Only by disavowing any intention to sever the West and by falsely claiming that the government had sanctioned his Mexican expedition was Burr able to win back Jackson's friendship. Jackson recounted Burr's declarations to Tennessee Congressman George W. Campbell:

> He always held out the idea of settling Washita [sic] unless a war with Spain, in that event he held out the idea, that from his intimacy with the S. of War, he would obtain an appointment and if he did he would revolutionize Mexico.

Later, when War Secretary Dearborn, citing a Richmond *Enquirer* story, insinuated that Jackson was a Burr confederate, the future president wrathfully turned on Jefferson and Dearborn for standing by Wilkinson, whom Jackson believed to be the actual villain.

In Nashville, Burr learned that Wilkinson had reached a truce with Spain and had occupied New Orleans. Not yet knowing of Wilkinson's betrayal, Burr still hoped that he would join him at Fort Adams to attack Baton Rouge, the capital of Spanish West Florida, and then sail to Mexico with him.

Only two of the boats that Burr had commissioned from Jackson were completed, and Jackson scrupulously refunded Burr the money he had paid for the other three. With a small party that included Stokely Hays, Mrs. Jackson's nephew, Burr set out on the Cumberland River, rendezvousing at the confluence of the Cumberland and Ohio with his expeditioners, now numbering about sixty people, and including Harman Blennerhassett, Comfort Tyler, and the party that had fled Blennerhassett Island early December 11. Kentucky's legislature called out the state militia to stop Burr, but his flotilla had reached the Mississippi by then and had begun its descent into the South.

Stopping at an Army fort on Chickasaw Bluffs, the site of present-day Memphis, Tennessee, Burr bought lead and tomahawks, and his men repaired their arms and made five hundred musket balls. Burr tried to persuade the fort's commander, Lieutenant Jacob Jackson, and his men to join him, but they did not.

The expeditioners reached Bayou Pierre in the Mississippi Territory in the middle of the coldest January in memory. Four inches of snow lay on the ground. Against this aptly forbidding backdrop, Burr learned from the January 6 Natchez *Mississippi Messenger* about Jefferson's proclamation and Wilkinson's treachery. Not only did this mean the death of Burr's dreams of a colony on the Ouachita and his expedition against Mexico: It meant that he was a wanted man.

At the home of Thomas Calvit, at the mouth of Cole's Creek, Burr arranged to surrender to Mississippi authorities. He did not want to fall into Wilkinson's hands in Louisiana; having disavowed Burr, the general might decide to eliminate him altogether. Burr was escorted to Washington, Mississippi's territorial capital, seven miles inland from Natchez. Judge Thomas Rodney, the father of Caesar Rodney, the U.S. Attorney General, set Burr's bond at $5,000, which Burr's new planter friends posted.

While waiting for the grand jury to meet on February 2, Burr divided his time between his demoralized expeditioners, shivering in their riverside camp, and the Mississippi planters, who were sympathetic to him and hostile to Wilkinson. He even found time to romance a local beauty, Madeline Price, and to propose marriage. Nothing came of the casual courtship.

After two days' deliberation, the grand jury refused to indict Burr for treason. Instead, it condemned his ill-treatment and Wilkinson's flagrant civil rights violations in New Orleans. Judge Rodney, however, would not release Burr from his $5,000 bond, and required him to report to court daily so that he would be at hand whenever Wilkinson decided to seize him.

That day wasn't long in coming. After placing a $5,000 bounty on Burr, Wilkinson sent six picked men armed with pistols and dirks, but with no warrants, to apprehend him and bring him back to New Orleans for a drumhead court-martial—or, perhaps, to kill him.

Burr, wanting nothing to do with Wilkinson's bounty hunters or his idea of justice, fled into the Mississippi wilderness with Robert Ashley, a local man who guided him. As he explained in a note to Territorial Governor Robert Williams, "The vindicative [sic] temper and unprincipled conduct of Judge Rodney [in refusing to release him from bond] have induced me to withdraw for the present from public view. . . ."

Wilkinson's men arrived too late to capture Burr. After detaining and questioning the expeditioners still camped along the Mississippi River, they sank their boats and let them go. Few of them returned to the North; instead, they made Mississippi their new home. Governor Claiborne later wrote, "They dispersed themselves throughout the territory and supplied it with schoolmasters, singing masters, dancing masters, clerks, tavern keepers, and doctors."

[9]

A Landmark Subpoena
and Indictments

*Any person, charged with a crime, in the courts of the United States, has a
right . . . to compel the attendance of his witnesses.*
—CHIEF JUSTICE MARSHALL,
IN GRANTING A SUBPOENA AGAINST PRESIDENT JEFFERSON

*Wilkinson strutted into court . . . swelling like a turkey-cock. . . . Burr
turned his head, looked him full in the face with one of his piercing regards,
swept his eye over his whole person from head to foot, as if to scan its dimensions, and then coolly resumed his former position. . . .*
—WASHINGTON IRVING, DESCRIBING GENERAL OF THE ARMY
JAMES WILKINSON'S ENCOUNTER WITH AARON BURR

RICHMOND, JUNE 8, 1807

The House of Delegates' tall windows were thrown open to catch
the faint breeze off the James River, but it provided scant relief
from the unseasonably sultry heat that oppressed Richmond. While
the sun-dazed city remained packed with visitors, there were empty
seats in the sweltering courtroom, where Aaron Burr's commitment
hearing was in limbo pending the arrival of General of the Army
James Wilkinson, who reportedly had left New Orleans weeks earlier. The heat becalmed the attorneys, the courtroom audience, and
even Chief Justice Marshall, who generously permitted frequent
breaks in the listless proceedings. "We are now enjoying a kind of suspension of hostilities," Washington Irving wrote to a friend, a Mrs.
Hoffman, "the grand jury having been dismissed the day before yes-
terday for five or six days, that they might go home, see their wives,
get their clothes washed, and flog their negroes."

Amid the general lethargy, Burr rose from his chair and in a measured voice began to speak. In his January Message to Congress, said Burr, President Jefferson had alluded to a letter from General Wilkinson and to orders that had been issued to the Army and Navy. Burr had requested those documents from Navy Secretary Robert Smith, but he had refused to hand them over. The Wilkinson letter of October 21—which had spurred Jefferson to issue his proclamation against Burr—and the military orders were essential to his defense, said Burr. In the same calm voice, he said that since the Jefferson administration had refused to share the documents with the defense, he was forced to ask Chief Justice Marshall to issue a subpoena duces tecum (literally, "bring with you") to the president, compelling him to appear in court with the documents.

Burr's motion landed like a thunderbolt. Stammering and red-faced, U.S. Attorney George Hay jumped to his feet. No subpoena was necessary, he said; he would supply the documents the court needed. But Burr and Marshall were not so easily appeased. How could Hay promise to produce the documents when he did not know which ones the defense needed? the chief justice asked. Marshall said the motion merited a full hearing. Seeing that he was in for a fight, Hay defiantly declared that the court could not require the President of the United States to appear in court. Moreover, "no individual charged with a crime has any right to legal process until the grand jury have found a true bill," he said, and the grand jury had not yet begun its work.

Once before, in 1806, two members of Burr's Little Band had attempted to subpoena some of Jefferson's cabinet officers to their trial in connection with the disastrous Francisco de Miranda expedition to liberate Venezuela. The defendants, Samuel G. Ogden and William S. Smith, asked the court to subpoena Secretary of State James Madison, War Secretary Henry Dearborn, Navy Secretary Robert Smith, and three State Department clerks. The government officials had all refused to appear on the ground that President Jefferson needed them in Washington. The court, unwilling to force a showdown with the president, would not order the men's appearance. Smith and Ogden were acquitted anyway.

—∽—

The news that Burr wished to subpoena President Jefferson was soon all over Richmond. When Marshall banged his gavel the next morning, the courtroom once again overflowed with spectators. With high anticipation, the crowd watched portly, red-faced Luther Martin rise to argue the motion on Burr's behalf.

For the many who had traveled to Richmond to see the famous defense attorney in action, their moment had arrived. Arguably the best courtroom lawyer in the country—better even than Burr—Martin had won the acquittal of Samuel Chase at his impeachment trial in 1805, the trial over which Burr had presided as vice president.

Middle-aged and bibulous, with a hoarse bullfrog voice and small, bloodshot eyes, the former Maryland attorney general was known far and wide as "the Bulldog of Federalism," and, less flatteringly, by his Baltimore colleagues as "Lawyer Brandy Bottle." Like Jefferson and Marshall, Martin was a former student of the legendary William and Mary law professor George Wythe. Martin was Jefferson's contemporary—their acquaintance dated to 1771 Williamsburg, where Martin had taken an instant dislike to young Jefferson. His antipathy deepened with the publication of Jefferson's *Notes on Virginia*, which described the murder of an Indian chief's family by Europeans. The man held accountable for the killings—but unnamed in Jefferson's book—was Colonel Michael Cresap, the father of Luther Martin's wife, Maria Cresap.

Martin mocked Hay's many objections to the defense attorneys' occasional long-winded statements to the court:

> Mr. Hay makes, I think, about a dozen times as many speeches as any other gentleman, and each speech longer than those of other persons, and yet we cannot open our mouths without his sounding loudly his complaints to this hall. On this case of unequaled magnitude, shall we not be suffered to declare our opinions, without

this unnecessary complaint about the consumption of the court's
time?

The defense, said Martin, believed that the Jefferson administration's orders to the Army and Navy would reveal that Burr's "property and his person were to be destroyed—yes, by these tyrannical
orders, the life and property of an innocent man were to be exposed
to destruction." The government might argue that it had more
pressing business, as it had in the Smith–Ogden case, in order to
deny the defense the requested documents. But Martin let the
court know what he thought of that, addressing his remarks to his
friend, Chief Justice Marshall:

> This is a peculiar case, sir. The president has undertaken to prejudge
> my client by declaring that "Of his guilt there can be no doubt." He
> had assumed to himself the knowledge of the Supreme Being him-
> self, and pretended to search the heart of my respected friend.

Martin's voice rose in indignation.

> He has proclaimed him [Burr] a traitor in the face of that country
> which has rewarded him. He has let slip the dogs of war, the hell-
> hounds of persecution, to hunt down my friend.
>   And would this president of the United States, who has raised
> all this absurd clamor, pretend to keep back the papers which are
> wanted for this trial, where life itself is at stake?

After a pause, he added, "Can it be presumed that the president
would be sorry to have Colonel Burr's innocence proved?"

A gasp went up in the courtroom, and Alexander McRae leaped
to his feet at the prosecution table. As a private individual, McRae
said, the president might be subpoenaed, but to order him to produce "confidential communications" was an entirely different matter.

The lawyers began talking over one another. The debate raged
for two days.

—◊—

On the third day, June 13, Hay announced that President Jefferson had responded to his request for the Army and Navy orders and the Wilkinson letter. The lawyers and spectators ceased their whispering and fidgeting as Hay read the president's response: He would send the Wilkinson letter, he wrote, but with instructions to Hay to exercise Jefferson's right to discretion, "by withholding the communication of any parts of the letter, which are not directly material for the purposes of justice." As for the requested military orders, Jefferson would instruct the Army and Navy to comply, but the defense must specify which orders it wished to see. Short of opening all the records, the president said disingenuously—and exhibiting no willingness to do so—it would be extremely difficult to comply, even "with a perfect willingness to do what is right."

When Hay finished reading Jefferson's response to the court, Marshall announced that he had reached a decision on the landmark question of whether the president and his documents could be subpoenaed. The president could be subpoenaed, Marshall declared. While the people had elected him, he remained a citizen and, thus, subject to the same laws as other citizens. Only if his presidential duties occupied his every waking moment could the chief executive reasonably claim an exemption:

> But it is apparent, that this demand is not unremitting; and if it should exist at the time when his attendance on the court is required, it would be sworn on the return of the subpoena, and would rather constitute a reason for not obeying the process of the court, than a reason against its being issued.

Furthermore, the president could not withhold any documents on the ground that they might contain state secrets; that was for the court to decide, after they were handed over. And Burr needn't prove the documents' importance to his defense, but must only believe them to be important. "Any person, charged with a crime, in the courts of the United States, has a right, before, as well as after indictment to the process of the court to compel the attendance of his witnesses."

Marshall's next words on the prosecution's expectations caused a commotion:

> It is not for the court to anticipate the event of the present prosecution. Should it terminate *as is expected on the part of the United States* [author's italics], all those, who are concerned in it, should certainly regret, that a paper, which the accused believed to be essential to his defense, which may, for aught that now appears, be essential, had been withheld from him.

The chief justice's implication that prosecutors *expected* Burr's conviction impelled Alexander McRae to ask whether Marshall was insinuating that the government "wished" for a guilty verdict. The government, McRae said, wanted only "a fair and competent investigation."

Marshall wasn't having any of that. Prosecutors, he said, "had so often repeated it [Burr's guilt] before the testimony was perceived . . . that it appeared . . . probable that they were not indifferent on the subject." The chief justice later offered the excuse that "he had been so pressed for time, that he had never read the opinion, after he had written it," George Hay reported to Jefferson.

Before Hay's dismal day ended, he invited more misfortune by calling on Dr. Justus Erich Bollman to testify about his supposedly confidential statement to the president and Secretary of State Madison about Burr's intentions. Outraged that the president had reneged on his pledge to not release the statement, Bollman refused to answer Hay's questions.

Hay then produced one of Jefferson's blank pardons—which Bollman contemptuously spurned. "I say no," Bollman said, because accepting the pardon would imply guilt, and he had done nothing wrong—although he had been arrested without a warrant, marched against his will onto a ship bound for Washington, and held in jail at Marine Corps headquarters without any charges filed against him.

Hay then announced that the doctor was pardoned anyway, whether he accepted the pardon or refused it. Bollman rejected this absurdity, as did Luther Martin: "Doctor Bollman is *not* pardoned, and no man is bound to criminate himself." Bollman was released from the witness stand without having testified.

—✕—

The subpoenas were delivered to Thomas Jefferson, Navy Secretary Robert Smith, and War Secretary Henry Dearborn. Up to a point, Jefferson complied. He asked Dearborn "to furnish copies of the orders which had been given respecting Aaron Burr and his property," and directed Attorney General Caesar Rodney to send him Wilkinson's October 21 letter and other documents that Rodney had taken with him to Richmond in March. The president wrote to George Hay:

> To these communications of papers, I will add that if the defendant supposes there are any facts within the knolege [*sic*] of the Heads of departments, or of myself, which can be useful for his defence . . . we shall be ready to give him the benefit of it, by way of deposition, through any persons whom the Court shall authorize to take our testimony at this place.

But regarding his personal appearance, Jefferson made his stand, thereby laying the groundwork for the principle of executive privilege:

> As to our personal attendance at Richmond, I am persuaded the Court is sensible, that paramount duties to the nation at large control the obligation of compliance with their summons in this case; as they would, should we receive a similar one, to attend the trials of Blannerhassett [*sic*] & others, in the Mississippi territory, those instituted at St. Louis and other places on the western water. . . . To comply with such calls would leave the nation without an executive

branch, whose agency, nevertheless, is understood to be so constantly necessary, that it is the sole branch which the constitution requires to be always in function.

Rational and restrained as he was in these public statements, privately Jefferson fumed over the subpoena. The president's anger crept into his private correspondence with Hay. Luther Martin, he suggested, might be committed for treason particeps criminis with Burr, for hadn't Martin known for at least a year of Burr's traitorous plans? The president pointed Hay to a Baltimore flour merchant, Philip Graybell, who Jefferson said could attest to Martin's complicity. He ordered Rodney to interview Graybell, and Hay to subpoena him.

Graybell will fix upon him [Martin] misprision [concealing his knowledge] of treason at least. And at any rate, his evidence will put down this unprincipled & impudent federal bull-dog, and add another proof that the most clamorous defenders of Burr are all his accomplices. It will explain why L M flew so hastily to the aid of his "honorable friend." . . .

After brooding some more over Marshall's ruling, Jefferson shot off another aggrieved letter to Hay the next day. How would Marshall like it, Jefferson wondered, if he were required to appear before judges in New Orleans, Virginia, and Maine? The president also carped over Marshall's swipe at his presidential duties:

The Judge says, "*it is apparent* that the President's duties as chief magistrate do not demand his whole time, & are not unremitting." If he alludes to our annual retirement from the seat of government, during the sickly season, he should be told that such arrangements are made for carrying on the public business, at and between the several stations we take, that it goes on as unremittingly there, as if we were at the seat of government. I pass more hours in public business at Monticello than I do here, every day; and it is much more laborious, because all must be done in writing.

Returning to the higher ground of political philosophy, Jefferson gloomily mused on the opinion's negative effect on the Constitutionally prescribed autonomy of the Legislative, Executive, and Judicial branches:

> But would the executive be independent of the judiciary, if he were subject to the commands of the latter, & to imprisonment for disobedience; if the several courts could bandy him from pillar to post, keep him constantly trudging from north to south & east to west, and withdraw him entirely from his constitutional duties?

Chief Justice John Marshall, Jefferson believed, had extended the Judiciary's penumbra over the Executive Branch, much as *Marbury v. Madison* had thrown the Judiciary's shadow over the Legislative Branch.

—〰—

General James Wilkinson's tardy arrival on Saturday, June 13, diverted attention from the subpoena ruling and the disastrous Bollman appearance, and temporarily restored George Hay's optimism. The prosecutor's relief was evident in his letter to Jefferson describing Wilkinson:

> His erect attitude, the serenity of his countenance, the composure of his manners, the mild but determined expression of his eye, all conspired to make me think that he has been most grossly calumniated.

On Monday, anticipation of the General of the Army's arrival in the courtroom and his face-to-face meeting with Burr brought as many spectators to the House of Delegates as had the grand jury's opening day. Impeccably turned out in a dress uniform, his medals and epaulets gleaming, Wilkinson arrived with an impressive entourage that included Lt. Edmund P. Gaines, the Army officer who had arrested Burr. "Wilkinson strutted into court . . . swelling like a turkey-cock," wrote Washington Irving. Burr

did not take notice of him until the judge directed the clerk to swear General Wilkinson; at the mention of the name Burr turned his head, looked him full in the face with one of his piercing regards, swept his eye over his whole person from head to foot, as if to scan its dimensions, and then coolly resumed his former position, and went on conversing with his counsel as tranquilly as ever. The whole look was over in an instant; but it was an admirable one. There was no appearance of study or constraint in it; no affectation of disdain or defiance; a slight expression of contempt played over his countenance.

A far different description of the encounter appeared in Wilkinson's letter to Jefferson:

In spite of myself my eyes darted a flash of indignation at the little traitor, on whom they continued fixed until I was called to the Book;—here, sir, I found my expectations verified—this lion-hearted, eagle-eyed Hero, jerking under the weight of conscious guilt, with haggard eyes in an effort to meet the indignant salutation of outraged honor; but it was in vain, his audacity failed him. He averted his face, grew pale, and affected passion to conceal his perturbation.

As David Robertson took down everything in shorthand, he noted only: "On appearance of the general in court, it was said that his countenance was calm, dignified, and commanding, while that of Colonel Burr was marked by a haughty contempt."

Now the grand jury would hear the General of the Army describe his relationship with Burr, and explain the significance of the mysterious cipher letter, now just a meaningless jumble of numbers and letters. In a closed hearing room, the grand jury began interviewing Wilkinson, as well as Thomas Truxtun, William Eaton, George Morgan and his two sons, Andrew Jackson, and dozens of other witnesses—forty-eight in all.

Truxtun related how Burr had offered him command of the naval force that was to have transported his army to Mexico. Eaton, the hero of Derna, cut a swashbuckling figure, decked out in an enormous brimmed hat and a fiery-red sash. No sooner had Wilkinson entered the jury room than a federal marshal escorted him outside, with instructions from foreman John Randolph to remove the general's sword. "I will allow no attempt to intimidate the jury," Randolph said.

Day after day, Wilkinson disappeared into the hearing room, inspiring Washington Irving to drolly observe, "Wilkinson is now before the grand jury, and has such a mighty mass of *words* to deliver himself of, that he claims at least two days more to discharge the wondrous cargo."

—◊◊◊—

Wilkinson's absence from New Orleans undoubtedly was a relief to its seventeen thousand inhabitants, who, for six long months, had labored under Wilkinson's heavy-handed military regime. In December 1806, he had marched into the city at the head of six hundred troops, ostensibly to defend it against Burr and the thousands of volunteers that Wilkinson claimed Burr commanded. The general's true purpose, however, appeared to be more sinister: muzzling anyone who could connect him to Burr. Lacking the authority to impose martial law, Wilkinson urged Governor William C. C. Claiborne to do so: "Under circumstances so imperious, extraordinary measures must be resorted to, and the ordinary form of civil institutions must for a short period yield to the strong arm of military law." When Claiborne balked at handing the city over to Wilkinson, the general warned the governor that without martial law, "dangers of which you dream not" would flourish, fungus-like, in the damp climate:

Many, very many enemies in this city, who in concert with Mr. Burr, aim to subvert the Constitution and the laws under which we live, to pillage this city, to seize your shipping and to carry an expedition against a country in peace with the United States.

But Claiborne stubbornly refused to declare martial law, and, in fact, suggested that Wilkinson, instead of occupying New Orleans, should occupy the Army forts upriver near Natchez, where he could intercept Burr's force before it reached the city. Wilkinson ignored the advice; it would have meant allowing men who could implicate him to go free, and he continued to pressure Claiborne to declare martial law. Claiborne feared that martial law would touch off a slave rebellion—New Orleans's free and enslaved blacks outnumbered whites, two to one. The governor informed Wilkinson that only the territorial legislature could declare martial law and suspend habeas corpus. The legislature refused.

So Wilkinson proceeded as though Claiborne and the legislature did not exist. He jailed men without arrest warrants and denied them access to the courts; he clamped down on the newspapers and arrested the editor of the *Orleans Gazette*; he forced the City Council to pass an ordinance requiring every person entering the city to be detained for twenty-four hours; and, under his authority, letters were opened in the post office.

All the while, Wilkinson singlemindedly pursued Burr's co-conspirators. He jailed Dr. Justus Bollman; Peter Ogden, Jonathan Dayton's nephew; and Samuel Swartwout. A hundred soldiers burst in on Kentucky Senator John Adair while he was eating dinner. Adair's crime was having received a letter from Wilkinson, in which the general expressed enthusiasm for invading Mexico. "Unless you fear to join a Spanish intriguer [Wilkinson alluding to himself] come immediately—without your aid I can do nothing." The senator was in New Orleans on business, with two boatloads of provisions and three thousand gallons of whiskey to sell. Denied medicine and extra clothing, Adair was held for six days at a primitive camp twenty-five miles downriver from the city before being marched aboard the schooner

Thatcher and shipped off to Baltimore, where a judge promptly ordered his release. (Adair sued Wilkinson for false imprisonment and was awarded $2,500, ten years later.) James Alexander, a New Orleans lawyer, was imprisoned merely for attempting to provide legal representation for Bollman, Ogden, Swartwout, and Adair. Judge James Workman, a Burr sympathizer and member of the Mexican Association, adjourned Orleans County Court in disgust and resigned; then he, too, was seized by Wilkinson's soldiers.

In a petition to Congress, the indignant Louisiana territorial legislature denounced Wilkinson's "acts of high-handed military power." His actions—"too notorious to be denied, too illegal to be justified, too wanton to be excused"—had caused "the temple of justice" to be "sacrilegiously rifled." In Washington, Federalists complained to the Jefferson administration about Wilkinson's conduct, and there was even grumbling among Republicans. Senator William Plumer of New Hampshire deplored Wilkinson's violation of rights guaranteed even to "common *convicted* malefactors."

So loud was the outcry over Wilkinson's seizure of the city that, in self-defense, the general wrote to Jefferson that he had acted only "to destroy the concert and co-operation of the conspirators, to stem the torrent of disaffection, and to save the city from the horrors of civil commotion."

Describing the deadly peril in which he had placed himself by defending New Orleans, he waxed melodramatic: "Although I may be able to smile at danger in open conflict, I will confess I dread the stroke of the assassin, because it cannot confer an honorable death." Wilkinson needn't have worried about losing Jefferson's support; the president evidently was willing to tolerate any conduct by his general so long as he remained loyal to him and opposed to Burr. In his reply, the president informed Wilkinson that Burr's force on the Mississippi had consisted of only eighty to one hundred men and not the seven thousand or so estimated by Wilkinson, but Jefferson ascribed the gross disparity to the dampening effect on recruitment of his own November 27 proclamation. Jefferson also attempted to soothe his general's frazzled nerves:

You have indeed had a fiery trial at New Orleans, but it was soon apparent that the clamours were only the criminal, endeavoring to turn the public attention from themselves & their leader upon any other objection.

Immersed in New Orleans's affairs to the neglect of his duties as governor of the Louisiana Territory, Wilkinson was quietly replaced in St. Louis by Jefferson's former secretary, Captain Meriwether Lewis, the famed expedition leader. Jefferson never ceased to defend Wilkinson's actions in New Orleans, where "a law of necessity and self-preservation . . . rendered the *salus populi* supreme over the written law."

—∽∽—

While occupied in jailing anyone who could link him to Burr and mollifying President Jefferson, Wilkinson managed to keep his Spanish patrons fully informed of developments. Even as Burr was descending the Mississippi River, the general was assuring West Florida Governor Don Vicente Folch that he was making "every arrangement . . . to protect the dominions of Spain as to support the Government of the United States against all our lawless citizens." He went so far as to suggest a "common defence of the posts we respectively command."

Wilkinson normally used a trusted intermediary to deliver his letters to Folch; but once, at the height of the New Orleans turmoil, they managed to actually meet. "He has laid before me not only the information which he acquired, but also his intentions for the various exigencies in which he might find himself," Folch informed a superior. Wilkinson, he said, "acted conformably as suited the true interests of Spain." In gratitude, Folch used his influence in the Louisiana legislature to defeat a petition condemning Wilkinson, although another was approved and sent to Congress.

Wilkinson's actions may have perplexed or angered the American public and evoked the admiration of President Jefferson, but the Spanish ambassador, Carlos Martinez de Yrujo, understood perfectly what Wilkinson was up to. In a remarkable analysis written in January 1807 to his superiors in Madrid, Yrujo said Wilkinson had to betray Burr when Burr's plans jeopardized Wilkinson's

> honorable employment [as U.S. Army commander] . . . and the generous pension he enjoys from the King. These considerations, secret in their nature, he could not explain to Burr; and when the latter persisted in an idea so fatal to Wilkinson's interests, nothing remained but to take the course adopted.

Wilkinson's subsequent conduct, Yrujo said, safeguarded his high standing in the U.S. Army and with Spain, too. The ambassador predicted that Wilkinson

> will allege his conduct on this occasion as an extraordinary service, either for getting it increased, or for some generous compensation. . . . In such an alternative he has acted as was to be expected; that is, he has sacrificed Burr in order to obtain, on the ruins of Burr's reputation, the advantages I have pointed out.

Even as Yrujo wrote those words, a Wilkinson emissary, Walter Burling, a well-to-do Natchez farmer, was on just such an errand to Mexico City. In early February 1807, as Burr fled from Wilkinson's bounty hunters in the Mississippi woods, Burling delivered a letter written by Wilkinson the previous November to the Spanish viceroy of Mexico, Jose de Iturrigaray. For his valiant service to Spain in thwarting Burr's planned invasion of Mexico, Wilkinson requested payment of $121,000.

Iturrigaray contemptuously rejected the outrageous request. Wilkinson had only stopped a filibuster that had caused no alarm in Mexico, said the viceroy, and Spanish forces could easily have repelled the attempted invasion anyway. Burling was hustled off to Vera Cruz, put aboard the American schooner *Liberty*, and sent home empty-handed. In March, as Iturrigaray was describing the Burling visit in a letter to Don Pedro Cevallos, the Spanish foreign minister in Madrid, Wilkinson was forwarding to Washington a report, purportedly by Burling, about conditions in Mexico— along with a request for $1,500 to reimburse Burling for expenses incurred during his "fact-finding" trip. Jefferson paid the $1,500.

—⁓—

For four days, the Richmond grand jury interviewed Wilkinson, the government's star witness. As Washington Irving had sarcastically noted, the general had a "wondrous cargo" of testimony to deliver. But this occupied only a day or two. Then something wholly unexpected and dismaying to Wilkinson developed behind the grand jury's closed door. Some grand jurors, led by John Randolph, decided that *Wilkinson* should be indicted. With minimal instructions from Wilkinson, the brilliant, erratic Randolph had quickly mastered the cipher used by Burr and Wilkinson, and even its shorthand: the letter "O" standing for the president; "O" with a dot in the middle, the vice president; and ÷ signifying the secretary of state.

Randolph and his fellow jurors soon saw that the letter's parts didn't quite add up to the whole. It isn't clear what put the jurors on this track—no record was kept of their deliberations—but under intensive questioning, Wilkinson admitted that he had deliberately mistranslated the letter, evidently to conceal his true relationship with Burr. "Such a countenance never did I behold," Randolph told his friend, Judge Joseph H. Nicholson.

Wilkinson had omitted the incriminating opening line, "Your letter postmarked 13th May is received." (When asked about this letter, Burr refused, as a point of honor, to produce it, saying that he would do so only if forced by "the extremity of circumstances." Wilkinson reportedly gave friends at least four other cipher letters from Burr besides the one laid before the grand jury.) Another alteration, designed to hide Wilkinson's true relationship with Burr, was the line, written either by Burr or Jonathan Dayton, "Our object, my dear friend, is brought to a point so long desired." It had been changed to, "The project is brought to the point so long desired."

At the urging of Randolph, who was convinced that Wilkinson was at least as culpable as Burr, the panel voted on whether to indict the general for misprision of treason—concealing his knowledge of a treasonous plot. To Randolph's disappointment, only seven of the sixteen jurors voted for indictment. "The mammoth of iniquity escaped," Randolph wrote Nicholson:

> Not that any man pretended to think him innocent, but upon certain wire-drawn distinctions that I will not pester you with. [Wilkinson] is the only man that I ever saw who was from the bark to the very core a villain. . . . W. is the most finished scoundrel that ever lived. . . . Yet this miscreant is hugged to the bosom of government. . . .

Burr took pleasure in describing to Theodosia Wilkinson's discomposure as he left the grand jury room—"in such a rage and agitation that he shed tears, and complained bitterly that he had been questioned as if he were a villain." Wilkinson sputtered and fumed to Jefferson: "Merciful God what a Spectacle did I behold—Integrity & Truth perverted & trampled under foot by turpitude & Guilt, Patriotism appaled [sic] & Usurpations *triumphant*." Jefferson replied with words calculated to calm the ruffled general: "No one is more sensible than myself of the injustice which has been aimed at you."

The grand jury was far more impressed with Samuel Swartwout than with Wilkinson. While in Wilkinson's custody in Louisiana, the young man had attempted to escape; in recapturing him, guards opened fire—fortunately for Swartwout, their powder was damp—and an officer tried to stab him. Swartwout emphatically denied Wilkinson's assertions that he had told the general, while delivering the coded letter, that Burr had seven thousand men; that another force was poised to descend the Allegheny Mountains and incite the West to rebellion; that Burr intended to loot the New Orleans banks; and that Great Britain intended to supply naval protection. "The very frank and candid manner in which he gave his testimony,

I must confess, raised him very high in my estimation," wrote grand juror Littleton W. Tazewell, a future Virginia governor and U.S. senator. "The manner of Mr. Swartwout was certainly that of conscious innocence," observed another juror, Joseph C. Cabell, brother of Virginia Governor William H. Cabell.

Witnesses came and went from the grand jury room: Eaton, Truxtun, Andrew Jackson, and a host of others. Having recovered from his near-fatal dueling wound, Jackson was now under indictment for assault with intent to kill for brawling with a relative and business partner, Samuel Jackson, on a downtown Nashville street. Jackson had tried to run Samuel through with a sword concealed in his cane. He was later acquitted.

—◊◊◊—

While Wilkinson was being grilled by the grand jury about his alterations to the cipher letter, things were going just as badly for him in the courtroom. Burr asked Chief Justice Marshall to cite the general for contempt, for flouting the law in New Orleans by opening mail, jailing potential witnesses without charges being filed, and "extorting testimony by torture," for which Burr offered the deposition of James Knox, who claimed to have been brutalized during an interrogation. But Burr's motion was all but forgotten—Marshall later ruled against it—in the great stir caused by the grand jury's announcement on June 24 that it was ready to issue indictments.

—◊◊◊—

At 2 P.M., the grand jurors filed into the courtroom with their first pronouncement in the case: Aaron Burr and Harman Blennerhassett were both charged with treason, punishable by death, and with the high misdemeanor crime of violating Spain's neutrality. Later, when George Hay was grumbling to Jefferson about Chief Justice Marshall's supposed bias toward Burr, he would claim that when the grand jury announced its indictments, Marshall had gazed upon Burr "with an expression of sympathy & sorrow as strong, as the human countenance can exhibit without palpable emotion."

Burr, however, was stone-faced, although the pro-Republican Richmond *Enquirer* would gleefully claim that he reacted with "indescribable consternation and dismay."

Blennerhassett wasn't present. Left behind in Mississippi when Burr turned fugitive, he was traveling to his island home and, for the moment, was unaware that he was under indictment.

Five Burr associates were indicted on the same charges two days later: former Senator Jonathan Dayton of New Jersey; Senator John Smith of Ohio; Comfort Tyler and Israel Smith, both of New York; and Davis Floyd, of the Indiana Territory. No charges were filed against three men whom Wilkinson had arrested in New Orleans without warrants and had sent under guard to Baltimore and Washington—Samuel Swartwout, Dr. Justus Bollman, and Kentucky Senator John Adair.

Washington Irving dejectedly watched as Burr, after pleading not guilty, was led away to the Richmond City Jail, where he was held without bond due to the gravity of the crimes he was charged with. "Fallen, proscribed, prejudged, the cup of bitterness has been administered to him with an unsparing hand," noted Irving, adding that many of Burr's former friends "skulked from his side, and even mingled among the most clamorous of his enemies."

—⟪⟫—

The grand jury indictment mingled legal pedantry with flashes of fire and brimstone worthy of Burr's grandfather, Jonathan Edwards:

> Aaron Burr . . . being . . . under the protection of the laws of the United States, and owing allegiance . . . [thereto], not having the fear of God before his eyes . . . but being moved and seduced by the instigation of the devil, wickedly desiring and intending the peace and tranquility for the said United States to disturb and foster, move and excite insurrection, rebellion and war against the said United States, on the tenth day of December [1806] . . . at a certain place called and known by the name of Blennerhassett's Island in

the county of Wood, district of Virginia . . . with force and arms
unlawfully, falsely, maliciously and traitorously did compass, imagine and intend to raise and levy war, insurrection and rebellion
against the said United States. . . .

The indictment said the "overt act" of December 10 on Blennerhassett Island involved "thirty persons and upwards, armed and
arrayed in a warlike manner . . . with guns, swords, and dirks . . .
being then and there traitorously assembled. . . ." On December 11,
this armed force proceeded down the Ohio River, intending to capture New Orleans and then invade Mexico. The indictments were
based on the testimony of twenty-nine of the forty-eight witnesses
who testified, according to the Richmond *Enquirer*, which listed all
twenty-nine. Conspicuously absent from the list—evidently due to
their unhelpfulness—were Jackson, Truxtun, and Swartwout.

From his jail cell, Burr coolly analyzed the grand jury's findings
in a letter to Theodosia, pointing out what he believed to be the
flawed reasoning underlying them. While Colonel Comfort Tyler
and his men had stopped at Blennerhassett Island on their way
down the Ohio River, "these men were not armed, and had no military array or organization, and . . . they did not use force nor
threaten it." Yet, because their alleged purpose was to seize New
Orleans and Mexico, their assembly on the island constituted treason—"and therefore a war was levied on Blennerhassett's Island by
construction." By the same "construction of law," Burr said, he, too,
was present on the island—even though he really was in Frankfort,
Kentucky—and had also levied war on the island. "In fact, the
indictment charges that Aaron Burr was on that day present on the
island, though not a man of the jury supposed this to be true."

—m—

With Burr's treason trial scheduled to begin August 3, Marshall
knew that he too was about to be placed under a microscope. The
chief justice was troubled by the fact that the treason indictments

rested upon Burr's connection with an assembly from which he was absent. Clearly, the grand jury had looked to Marshall's words in *Ex Parte Bollman and Ex Parte Swartwout*, that

> if war be actually levied, that is, if a body of men be actually assembled for the purpose of effecting by force, a treasonable purpose, all those who perform any part, *however minute or however remote from the scene of the action* [author's italics], and who are actually leagued in the general conspiracy, are to be considered as traitors.

Even while the grand jury was deliberating, Marshall had begun to doubt this interpretation of "constructive treason." Did it meet the Constitutional requirement of an "overt act"? Could he have been wrong? He nervously solicited the opinions of his fellow Supreme Court justices, acknowledging that the Burr case "presents many real intrinsic difficulties," particularly the "doctrine of constructive treason":

> How far is this doctrine to be carried in the United States? If a body of men assemble for a treasonable purpose, does this implicate all those who are concerned in the conspiracy whether acquainted with the assemblage or not? Does it implicate those who advised, directed, or approved of it? Or does it implicate those only who were present or within the district?

English case law, he said, addresses this particular issue, "but in England, treason may be committed by imagining the death of the King. . . ."

Marshall's struggle with these perplexing questions would dominate the Burr proceedings.

[10]

Eye of the Storm

The scenes which have passed and those about to be transacted will exceed all reasonable credibility, and will hereafter be deemed fables, unless attested by very high authority.

—AARON BURR

This persecution was hatched in Kentucky. The chicken died, and they are trying to bring it to life here. . . . Mr. Jefferson can torture Aaron Burr while England tortures our sailors [referring to impressment].

—ANDREW JACKSON, DENOUNCING THE BURR PROSECUTION

"Treason" is a medieval English word for an ancient crime—the betrayal of one's tribe, nation, or God. Treason was considered to be so reprehensible that the bitter punishment visited on Satan in *Paradise Lost* for his revolt against God—he was cast into hell—was scarcely worse than the gruesome price paid by real traitors during John Milton's time: The victim was hanged, then cut down while still alive; his abdomen was slashed open, and his entrails were removed and burned before him. He then was beheaded, and his body torn into quarters.

Treason was codified as a crime under the so-called Statute of 25 during Edward III's reign; the Statute of 25 is the model for American Constitutional treason law, with one significant differ-ence: "constructive treason," making a capital crime of a remote asso-ciation with a treasonous conspiracy that might never have even been carried out, did not become part of United States treason law. Ruthless kings had found constructive treason to be extremely useful in eliminating enemies who might only have "wished" their king's death. Constructive treason was a tyrant's bludgeon.

The Constitution's framers, particularly Benjamin Franklin, attempted to prevent constructive treason from ever taking root in the United States, as it had in England, where it had "stained the English records with blood and filled the English valleys with innocent graves." The founders' shield was the Constitution's Article III, Section 3:

> Treason against the United States, shall consist only in levying War against them, or, in adhering to their Enemies, giving them Aid and Comfort. No Person shall be convicted of Treason unless on the Testimony of two Witnesses to the same overt Act, or on Confession in open Court.

In England, a secret meeting and seditious talk might get one hanged for treason, but in America, treason required an "overt act" of war witnessed by two people.

Article III's first test came during the trial of John Fries, charged in the so-called "Hot Water War"—"hot air war" might have been a better description—in northeastern Pennsylvania in 1799. Unhappy with a new federal tax to raise money for the Quasi-War against France, a housewife dumped a bucket of hot water on the head of a government revenue officer; after that, events snowballed. The tax collector tried to arrest the woman's husband, residents made the officer their prisoner, and the U.S. marshal arrested twenty-three men. They were freed by more than eighty armed men led by Fries, who was a former Continental Army captain and a leader of the Whiskey Rebellion several years earlier. President Adams ordered the group to disband, and when it did not, he sent federal troops, Pennsylvania activated the militia, and the troublemakers were rounded up. Fries was found hiding in the woods when his barking dog, Whiskey, gave him away.

At the outset of Fries's treason trial in Pennsylvania federal circuit court, before any evidence was introduced, the presiding judge,

Supreme Court Justice Samuel Chase, pronounced his interpretation of treason. He began by saying that English precedents were inapplicable to American treason law, but then efficiently destroyed the defense's hopes by stating that any actual insurrection, effectual or not, met the Constitutional definition of levying war, one of the key elements of treason. Believing the case lost, Fries's attorneys withdrew, leaving the defendant to continue without legal representation. Fries was convicted and sentenced to hang, but President Adams, who disagreed with the sentence, pardoned him and two other rebels.

Chief Justice John Marshall's Bollman ruling had muddied Chase's clear statement about English precedents. Reaching back to England's "constructive treason" doctrine, Marshall had declared that a conspiracy leader could be implicated in an "overt act" of war even if he was not present when the act was committed. While Marshall, fearing that he might have erred in the Bollman ruling, anxiously solicited the opinions of his Supreme Court colleagues, Burr and his attorneys recognized that this interpretation could send Burr to the gallows if prosecutors proved that there had been an overt act of war. In that event Burr's physical presence would not matter.

—◊◊◊—

The former vice president had been held in the hot, verminous Richmond City Jail only two days when his lawyers began badgering prosecutors and Chief Justice Marshall to transfer him. The jail was not just unhealthful, his lawyers said, but there was no place for Burr to work on his case, or to confer privately with his attorneys. U.S. Attorney George Hay reluctantly agreed to allow Burr to move in with Luther Martin, who was renting a home near the Capitol. The door was padlocked and the windows of Burr's room were barred. From the house next door, seven guards kept a watch. Benjamin Latrobe, the government's architect and a Burr friend, personally vouchsafed the security measures, although none of the arrangements was to the liking of government attorneys, who thought them too costly and Burr too mollycoddled.

With impeccable timing, the State of Virginia stepped in with a plan that suited nearly everyone: Burr could occupy three spacious "apartments" on the third floor of the federal penitentiary outside of Richmond. The new prison, on a hill overlooking the James River, had been designed by Latrobe according to President Jefferson's specifications. It resembled a medieval castle in nearly every particular, except for a moat and flowing banners over the battlements. Burr alone opposed the proposed arrangement; the prison was too far from the city, he complained. Overruled, he was escorted to his new quarters on July 3.

Burr did not want for company in his prison "penthouse," as he took to calling his quarters. Distinguished visitors came to see him at practically all hours, for the former vice president was admired by Richmond society as much as he was despised by its merchant and laboring classes. Catherine Gratton Gamble—the mother-in-law of Governor William Cabell, and future mother-in-law of prosecutor William Wirt—sent food and refreshments to Burr from her kitchen at Gray House, another Latrobe-designed structure that stood on the hill adjacent to the prison. Oranges, lemons, pineapples, raspberries, apricots, cream, butter, ice, and other gifts from "adoring females" arrived daily at Burr's door, he reported to Theodosia, to allay her concerns that he was suffering from deprivation. Indeed, Richmond society's women were especially devoted to Burr, Washington Irving noted after paying him a visit. While the accommodations might have been damp and dreary, with high, grated windows, Burr had so many visitors that Irving, during his brief visit, only "was permitted to enter for a few moments, as a special favor, contrary to orders."

Even Burr's jailer indulged his famous guest. When he informed Burr that the doors were customarily locked at nightfall and the lights extinguished at 9 P.M., Burr protested. "That, sir, I am sorry to say, is impossible," Burr said politely, "for I never go to bed till twelve, and always burn two candles."

"Very well, sir," replied the jailer, "just as you please. I should have been glad if it had been otherwise; but as you please, sir."

Burr rewarded the jailer for his cooperation by liberally sharing the delicacies and gifts that he received.

—◊◊◊—

On June 22, the 50-gun British frigate *Leopard* attacked the 36-gun frigate USS *Chesapeake* ten miles off Cape Henry, Virginia, arousing national indignation. The *Leopard's* captain had demanded that the *Chesapeake's* commander, Captain James Barron, hand over three crewmen who were supposedly deserters from the Royal Navy. When Barron refused, the *Leopard* fired five unanswered broadsides, killing three Americans and wounding eighteen others, including Barron, before he struck his colors without firing a shot.

At mass meetings throughout the country, speakers urged war against Britain. Judge Spencer Roane of the Virginia Court of Appeals presided over a Richmond rally at which a letter to the president was drafted, stating, "While we are sensible of the evils which must result from war, we are prepared to encounter them in defense of our dearest rights." Patriotic pledges were taken by the Light Infantry Blues at Bell Tavern, the Manchester Cavalry at Brooks Tavern, and the Richmond Troop of Cavalry at the Eagle Tavern. Caught in the riptide of patriotism, Winfield Scott, the strapping young attorney who had stood on the door lock of the House of Delegates, abandoned his fledging legal career and joined the cavalry, embarking on an illustrious 45-year military career.

Coming in the wake of the *Chesapeake* debacle, Richmond's Fourth of July celebration was unusually noisy and patriotic. Dawn was marked by the firing of a single gun; sunrise, by a seventeen-gun salute. At 9 A.M., there was a military parade to Capitol Square by a troop of light horse and several companies of infantry, with bands playing and flags flying. Throughout the day, the House of Delegates chamber rang with orations. At 2 P.M., Mayor William Foushee, as was his custom, read the Declaration of Independence to a large crowd, which, with the militia and volunteers drawn up in ranks, gave three cheers and sang "Yankee Doodle" and "Hail, Columbia." There was a funeral oration for the *Chesapeake* crewmen who had been killed, followed by muffled drums and the firing of minute guns. There was drinking at the Capitol, with Governor William Cabell making the first of the seventeen toasts. At Buchanan's Spring, the Barbecue Club held a dinner attended by all the regulars, including Chief Justice Marshall.

During an Independence Day celebration in Cecil County, Maryland, a mock toast was made to Aaron Burr that very quickly became a favorite among the habitués of Richmond's taverns: "Aaron Burr—may his treachery to his country exalt him to the scaffold, and hemp be his escort to the republic of dust and ashes." The celebrants also toasted Luther Martin: "May his exertions to preserve the Catiline of America procure him an honorable coat of tar, and a plumage of feathers that will rival in finery all the mummeries of Egypt."

As war fever spread at brush-fire speed, Jefferson and his cabinet prepared to call up a hundred thousand militiamen to defend the East Coast, and made plans for a possible winter campaign in Canada. Virginia officials were instructed to rush troops to protect Norfolk. But, after General of the Army Wilkinson said the Army was unready to fight England and Secretary of State Madison argued against war, Jefferson decided to retaliate with a trade embargo rather than armed force.

—m—

During the summer of 1807, Richmond, its population swollen by the Burr proceedings, was a magnet for renowned artisans, entrepreneurs of all stripes, and entertainers, such as Thomas Abthorpe Cooper, one of the era's best actors. The *Enquirer* was moved to express the sincere hope that the manager of a new Shockoe Hill theater would arrange an entertainment featuring "the celebrated Cowper" [sic]. Another conspicuous visitor was Charles Balthazar Julien Ferret de Sain-Memin, famed for his life-size portraits, drawn on pink paper with black and white crayons and hung in black-and-gold frames. The portraits, which cost $25 to $35—

about the price of a four-poster bed—in later years became price-less badges of social exclusiveness.

Young, single, well-to-do men and women played at courtship, with the women wearing racy "Empire fashion" dresses that bared shoulders and cleavage, provoking the censure of the city's ministers and the applause of the young men. "I am absolutely enchanted with Richmond, and like it more and more every day," wrote Washington Irving. "The society is polished, sociable, and extreme-ly hospitable." Irving himself was so much in demand that he was moved to complain unconvincingly to his friend and correspon-dent, Miss Mary Fairlie:

> By some unlucky means or other, I got the character, among three or four novel-reading damsels, of being an interesting young man; now of all characters in the world, believe me, this is the most intol-erable for any young man, who has a will of his own to support; particularly in warm weather. The tender-hearted fair ones think you absolutely at their command; they conclude that you must, of course, be fond of moonlight walks, and rides at daybreak, and red-hot strolls in the middle of the day, (Fahrenheight's [sic] Thermom. 98 1/2 in the shade,) and melting-hot-hissing-hot tea parties. . . .

Others, restless and idle during the weeks stretching until the August 3 trial, indulged in less refined pastimes—drinking, gam-bling, and going to the racetrack. Supposedly at the instigation of Andrew Jackson, Samuel Swartwout tried to provoke General James Wilkinson into dueling him. When they happened to meet one day on a sidewalk, Swartwout shouldered Wilkinson into the muddy street, then invited Wilkinson to challenge him to a duel. The general refused to issue a challenge, and bystanders jeered him. (After the trial, Swartwout challenged Wilkinson to a duel; the general replied that he did not traffic with "traitors or conspirators," to which Swartwout responded with an open letter in a newspaper accusing Wilkinson of perjury, treachery, forgery, and cowardice.

The men never dueled.) William Eaton caroused in the taverns in his red sash and "tremendous hat," betting heavily on Burr's conviction, and abandonedly spending the $10,000 in expense money that he had belatedly received from the government for his North African service.

Besides prodding Swartwout to goad the hated Wilkinson into a duel, Andrew Jackson loudly denounced the Jefferson administration from street corners around Capitol Square and from the Capitol steps. In one of his harangues, he said: "This persecution was hatched in Kentucky. The chicken died, and they are trying to bring it to life here. . . . Mr. Jefferson can torture Aaron Burr while England tortures our sailors [referring to impressments]." Jackson recalled the toast, "Millions for defense; not a cent for tribute," that he had once made at a dinner held for Aaron Burr. "Here it seems to be, 'Millions to persecute an American; not a cent to resist the English!' Shame on such a leader! Contempt for a public opinion rotten enough to follow him!"

Chief Justice Marshall passed the hot July days at his home in the "Court End" district of Shockoe Hill. Wherever Marshall went, it seemed that he encountered attorneys from the Burr case; Alexander McRae and Benjamin Botts inhabited the same square as the Marshalls, and nearby lived John Wickham, George Hay, and Edmund Randolph. William Wirt, who resided in another part of Richmond, was seen so often at Court End that he might as well have lived there.

—✦—

While the president should have been pleased with the treason indictments, he was pessimistic about winning a conviction. "Altho' there is not a man in the U.S. who is not satisfied of the depth of his guilt, such are the jealous provisions of our laws in favor of the accused, & against the accuser, that I question if he can be convicted," he complained to Victor Marie Dupont de Nemours, the naturalized French industrialist, in mid-July. Yet Jefferson could not help showing his pride, as he had to Wilkinson, in the effect wrought by his November 27 proclamation. "A proclamation alone, by undeceiving them, so compleatly [sic] disarmed him, that he had not above 30 men left," and they, he said untruthfully, were all "fugitives from justice, or from their debts, who had flocked there from other parts of the U.S. . . . and of adventurers & speculators of all descriptions."

Meanwhile, Jefferson was still trying to locate Wilkinson's October 21 letter; Caesar Rodney didn't have it. The president promised George Hay it would be found. "No researches shall be spared to recover this letter, & if recovered, it shall immediately be sent on to you."

His statement to Dupont de Nemours notwithstanding, Jefferson was aware that not everyone believed Burr to be guilty. He pressured Hay and his prosecution team to bring every witness they could find to Richmond, and to utilize every resource to convict Burr. Just as Burr had become the locus of all of Jefferson's fears and frustrations, so, too, had he become the lodestar for everyone unhappy with the government—Federalists, dissident Republicans, and men with personal grievances. Just as Burr, like a powerful magnet, had once before attracted Jefferson's enemies, he was again beginning to do so. This unhappy fact whetted Jefferson's desire to convict him at whatever cost—and to take measures against Chief Justice Marshall too, if he dared to thwart Jefferson's purposes.

—◊◊◊—

Might Jefferson, in fact, have been obsessed with Burr's prosecution in 1807? His letters often revealed a deep, abiding anger, and at times deteriorated into rants. In July 1807, Jefferson knew that Burr had traveled down the Ohio and Mississippi rivers not to commit treason, but possibly to invade Mexico, an objective that Jefferson did not necessarily deplore. Much earlier, Jefferson believed, Burr might have contemplated separating the Western states, but as the president himself noted, he very early saw that the fidelity of the Western country was not to be shaken and turned himself wholly towards Mexico and so popular is an enterprise for that country in this, that we had only to be still, & he could have had followers enough to have been in the city of Mexico in 6 weeks.

In December 1806, Jefferson had written to Louisiana Governor William C. C. Claiborne that the Spanish minister, Carlos Martinez de Yrujo, "has been duped by Burr to believe he means only the capture of New Orleans & the separation of the western country," when an expedition against the Spanish territories was his real aim.

Knowing this, why was Jefferson prosecuting Burr for treason? And why, if Burr's activities had truly alarmed him and if he had no ulterior motives, could not Jefferson have simply asked his former vice president to explain his actions? The former political allies had dined together at the President's House as recently as November 1805. Jefferson's quiet intervention might have persuaded Burr to launch his Louisiana colony, and there would have been no national manhunt, no dragnet for evidence, and no treason trial. But instead, Jefferson had flouted administrative procedures that he had himself helped establish, and had violated the very civil liberties that he had championed—for example, pronouncing Burr guilty before his arrest. His relentless pursuit of Burr and his associates for treason might have been motivated by corrosive hatred, or to make good on his public declaration that Burr's guilt was "beyond question." But these possible explanations do not seem altogether adequate, given the time that Jefferson devoted to the trial when he had more pressing matters before him: Great Britain, for example, whose impressments of American seamen and attacks on shipping Jefferson planned to punish with the ineffectual Embargo, the worst mistake of his presidency.

Undoubtedly, the year 1807 was the nadir of Jefferson's otherwise impressive tenure. Future historians and biographers who would otherwise hold Jefferson in high esteem would puzzle over

Revolutionary War hero, superb trial lawyer, and political operator, AARON BURR nearly became president in 1801 instead of Thomas Jefferson. But by 1805, all of Vice President Burr's political dreams had died, and he headed West, seeking fortune and glory. (*Yale University Art Gallery*)

This 1805 Gilbert Stuart portrait of PRESIDENT THOMAS JEFFERSON depicts the Revolution's inspired wordsmith as a wise, benevolent patriarch. While this was largely true, Jefferson could also be ruthless, vindictive, and irrational. (*Smithsonian National Portrait Gallery*)

THEODOSIA BURR was reared according to her father's then-radical belief that women should receive the same education as men. During her short life as a daughter, wife, and mother, Theodosia remained utterly devoted to her father. In 1813, the ship transporting Theodosia to New York to visit her father mysteriously vanished off North Carolina's coast. (*Smithsonian National Portrait Gallery*)

JAMES WILKINSON became General of the Army while serving as a paid spy for Spain. In Spain's official correspondence, Wilkinson was known as Spy No. 13. (*Smithsonian National Portrait Gallery*)

HARMAN BLENNERHASSETT was happily pursuing his studies of science, electricity, literature, and music, and raising cattle and corn when Aaron Burr arrived on Blennerhassett Island in the Ohio River near Parkersburg, W. Va. The Irish expatriate's participation in Burr's expedition cost him his wealth, reputation, and home. (*Blennerhassett Island Historical State Park*)

MARGARET BLENNERHASSETT, Harman's wife and niece, was bright, educated, well-read, and active. The loss of her beloved island home was a blow from which she never fully recovered. Her remains were interred on the island in 1998. (*Blennerhassett Island Historical State Park*)

BLENNERHASSETT MANSION as it probably appeared in 1806. It burned to the ground in 1811. This illustration is based on an 1840s oil painting by Sala Bosworth of Marietta, Ohio. (*Blennerhassett Island Historical State Park*)

BLENNERHASSETT MANSION WAS RECONSTRUCTED following the excavation of the original structure's foundation in 1973. Historians and archeologists worked together to build this replica. Flanking the main house is Harman's study (right) and the kitchen (left). *(Photo by Pat Wheelan)*

Titled "AARON BURR ADDRESSING HIS FOLLOWERS," this well-known illustration first appeared in *Popular History of the United States*. It shows Burr speaking to his expeditioners after they had embarked from Blennerhassett Island. *(Blennerhassett Island Historical State Park)*

The Barbary War hero
WILLIAM EATON declined
Aaron Burr's invitation to
become a leader of the
Burr expedition. Instead,
he warned President Thomas
Jefferson of Burr's plans. His
deposition and testimony were
central to the government's
treason case against Burr.
(*Naval Historical Center*)

AARON BURR was arrested by federal troops in present-day Alabama in March 1807.
(*The New York Public Library*)

JOHN MARSHALL, the "Great Chief Justice," walked a tightrope during Aaron Burr's treason trial, knowing that if he appeared to favor Burr, Congress and the president might emasculate the Federal Judiciary and impeach him. (*Smithsonian National Portrait Gallery*)

Virginia Congressman JOHN RANDOLPH, a distant cousin of both Thomas Jefferson and John Marshall, was foreman of the grand jury that indicted Aaron Burr and nearly indicted General of the Army James Wilkinson. (*Smithsonian National Portrait Gallery*)

ANDREW JACKSON stood by his friend Aaron Burr throughout his 1807 treason trial, denouncing the Jefferson administration in street-corner harangues near the Virginia State Capitol. (*Smithsonian National Portrait Gallery*)

LUTHER MARTIN, Aaron Burr's lifelong friend, was the lead defense attorney at Burr's treason trial. Martin, reputedly the best trial lawyer in America, was nicknamed "Lawyer Brandy Bottle" because of his affinity for liquor, which he freely imbibed during his courtroom orations. (*Smithsonian National Portrait Gallery*)

PROSECUTOR WILLIAM WIRT'S "Who Is Blennerhassett?" oration during Aaron Burr's treason trial became an instant classic of American rhetoric; he is shown delivering it here. On the left, arms folded, is Burr. Chief Justice John Marshall can be seen on the bench. (*The New York Public Library*)

Hundreds of people converged on the stately VIRGINIA STATE CAPITOL in 1807 to witness Aaron Burr's treason trial. The Capitol's design was largely the work of Thomas Jefferson, who admired classical architecture, as evidenced by the triangular gable, Ionic columns, and cornice detailing. Jefferson instructed the architect to use as his model a first-century Roman temple in Nismes, France, the Maison Caree. (*Photo by Pat Wheelan*)

In his roomy home in Richmond, Chief Justice John Marshall wrote what became the foundation of treason law for nearly the next century and a half. THE JOHN MARSHALL HOUSE today is a national historical site. (*Photo by Joseph Wheelan*)

Chief Justice John Marshall presided over the Burr trial from the imposing HOUSE OF DELEGATES SPEAKER'S CHAIR, of which this is an exact replica. The original, made in 1730, was retired in 1933 to the DeWitt Wallace Decorative Arts Museum in Williamsburg, Va. (*Photo by Joseph Wheelan*)

CHIEF JUSTICE JOHN MARSHALL'S BUST in the Old House of Delegates in the Virginia state Capitol. (*Photo by Joseph Wheelan*)

AARON BURR was buried with honors in the President's Plot of Princeton Cemetery beside his father, Aaron Burr Sr., and grandfather, Jonathan Edwards, the second and third presidents, respectively, of the College of New Jersey, now Princeton University. (*Photo by Pat Wheelan*)

his almost reptilian vindictiveness toward Burr and Marshall, without ever satisfactorily explaining the reason for it.

—◊◊◊—

On the eve of Burr's trial, Theodosia and Joseph Alston arrived in Richmond from South Carolina and rented a home near Burr's new lodgings. Burr had been permitted to move back into Luther Martin's leased house. He had argued that it would be too time-consuming to have to ride or walk a mile and a half to court and then return to the prison each day.

When Jefferson learned of the new living arrangement, he sarcastically noted that Blennerhassett, Dayton, and the other co-conspirators, too, might well demand

> private & comfortable lodgings. . . . In a country where an equal application of law to every condition of man is fundamental, how could it be denied to them? How can it ever be denied to the most degraded malefactor?

Burr found his new quarters doubly satisfactory with the Alstons now just a few houses away; they could enjoy one another's company every day. The situation agreed with Martin, too, for he had developed a mild infatuation with the charming Theodosia. "Our little family circle has been a scene of uninterrupted gayety," Theodosia wrote to the wife of one of her stepbrothers. "Thus you see, my lovely sister, this visit has been a real party of pleasure." Her flashing wit, charm, and dark good looks quickly won her many new friends in Richmond society. "From many of the first inhabitants I have received the most unremitting and delicate attentions, sympathy, indeed, of any I ever experienced."

Family amity might not have been as complete as Theodosia made it out to be, at least during the Alstons' initial reunion with Burr. In February, after publication of a translation of the famous "cipher letter," which named Joseph Alston, Alston had strenuously disavowed any connection with Burr's schemes in a letter to South

Carolina Governor Charles Pinckney. "I solemnly avow that, when that letter was written, I had never heard, directly or indirectly, from Colo. Burr, or any other person, of the meditated attack on New Orleans. . . ." Alston had obsequiously asked Pinckney to believe in his innocence and flagellated himself, "Conspirator! the blood now burns my cheek, as I write the word."

All was not well, either, with Theodosia, burdened with physical and emotional problems largely concealed by her beauty and intelligence. Since her son Aaron Burr Alston's birth in 1801, she had suffered from chronic weakness, fevers and lethargy, and bouts of depression. Joseph Alston did what he could to relieve her symptoms, shuttling her among their several Waccamaw Peninsula rice plantations and, in the summertime, moving the family out of the sticky heat to Debordieu Island and its refreshing sea breezes.

Familiar with his daughter's tendency to brood, Burr tried to inoculate her with some of his own stoicism: "I beg and expect it of you that you will conduct yourself as becomes my daughter, and that you manifest no signs of weakness or alarm." He invented a task to distract her from the mortal peril that he faced:

> I want an independent and discerning witness to my conduct and that of the government. The scenes which have passed and those about to be transacted will exceed all reasonable credibility, and will hereafter be deemed fables, unless attested by very high authority.

She should not worry about the possibility of having to witness her father's public disgrace: "I cannot be humiliated or disgraced," he wrote, then broached the real reason for wanting her with him in Richmond. "If absent you will suffer great solicitude. In my presence you will feel none, whatever may be the malice or the power of my enemies, and in both they abound."

In the first days of August, Harman Blennerhassett arrived in Richmond under guard. The scholarly landowner and his captors had traveled 564 miles on horseback from the place of his arrest, Lexington, Kentucky, "under a broiling sun, over a road, in which I was almost suffocated by the dust." He was placed in Burr's former Virginia penitentiary quarters. "My apartments are large and convenient, but very warm from the height of the windows preventing a free admission of air," he wrote in the epistolary journal that he kept for his wife Margaret throughout his confinement and court hearings.

Blennerhassett rued his decision to leave the island home in which he had invested his fortune, hopes, and dreams, in order to join Burr's quixotic scheme. He resentfully noted in his journal: "Burr lives in great style & sees much company within his gratings, where it is as difficult to get an audience, as if he were really an Emperor." Blennerhassett could not forget that just fifteen months earlier, Burr had inveigled him into joining his expedition with the flattering words: "Your talents and acquirements seem to have destined you for something more than vegetable life, and since the first hour of our acquaintance, I have considered your seclusion as a fraud on society."

He was now deeply in debt and unable even to afford legal counsel, having sunk $21,000 of his fortune into Burr's expedition. Counting losses from the looting of his property by the Wood County militia in December 1806 and from the forced sale months later of his household belongings and property, Blennerhassett estimated that he was $50,000 poorer than when Burr had entered his life two years earlier. He asked Joseph Alston to help him cover his losses, but Alston had his own money problems; he had underwritten up to $50,000 worth of Burr's drafts, and was now stuck with having to pay them. Nevertheless, Alston said he would try to raise money for Blennerhassett in South Carolina. Burr, promising Blennerhassett that he would one day pay him back, suggested that Blennerhassett hire a lawyer to stall his creditors.

Even though he was without cash, Blennerhassett would have legal representation. One of Burr's attorneys, Benjamin Botts, had offered his services, pro bono, saying it would be "dishonorable" to withhold them, and then Edmund Randolph had chimed in with his own pledge to help defend Blennerhassett, if it came to that.

[11]
The Trial of the Century Begins

From the citadel of the law [the Judiciary] can turn it's [sic] guns on those they were meant to defend, & control & fashion their proceeding for it's [sic] own will.
—PRESIDENT THOMAS JEFFERSON

The bias of Judge Marshall is as obvious, as if it was stamped on his forehead.
—U.S. ATTORNEY JOHN HAY

On Monday, August 3, the opening day of his treason trial, Aaron Burr walked the few blocks to the state Capitol amid a crowd of guards, friends, and admirers. Joseph Alston accompanied him into the House of Delegates, which was once again serving as a courtroom. But when everyone had assembled in the densely thronged chamber, U.S. Attorney George Hay announced that he was unready for jury selection. Scores of witnesses were still trickling into Richmond from the huge government dragnet; about 140 government witnesses would eventually assemble, from every corner of the United States. Prosecutors intended to interview each of them, hoping to find two who could attest to having seen Burr commit an overt act of treason. Burr's defense team listed seventy-one witnesses, including Andrew Jackson, War Secretary Henry Dearborn, and President Jefferson. Like every other witness, they, too, were entitled to compensation of five cents per mile if they rode to Richmond.

Hay requested a delay until Friday, August 7. As Friday neared, he asked Chief Justice Marshall for an extension until the following Monday, August 10.

The disappointed spectators returned to the taverns and the Haymarket Gardens to resume their pastimes—drinking, wagering on cockfights and horse races, reading the newspapers, and speculating about the Burr case. These were not by any means the only diversions. For the literary-minded, the *Virginia Argus* advertised a prospectus for a multi-volume narrative of the Lewis and Clark Expedition and a new map of North America. It appeared beside the current Richmond prices for tobacco, new wheat, superfine flour, fine flour, corn, hemp, iron, bacon, and whiskey. Acreage on the Severn River in Gloucester County was for sale, and so was Dr. Rees's *New Cyclopedia*—all twenty volumes—offered on the installment plan, with a volume delivered every two months, at $3.00 each. On the news pages inside were travelers' accounts of Napoleon Bonaparte's crushing defeat of the Russian army at Königsberg. Closer to home, columnists pondered America's deteriorating relations with England under headlines such as "Will There Be War?" The Washington Tavern's new owners pledged "to keep as good a table and as genteel an Inn as any in Richmond."

—m—

The following Monday, attorneys finally began selecting a jury of Virginians who, by some miracle, did not hold strong feelings about Burr or the Jefferson administration, or, at least, did not acknowledge them. From the jury pool of forty-eight men, lawyers needed to agree on twelve, and two alternates. This process had scarcely begun when Harman Blennerhassett arrived for his arraignment on charges of treason and high misdemeanor. But his lawyers were as unprepared as Hay had been a week earlier, so the arraignment was delayed until August 22, when it would again be delayed because Blennerhassett's name was misspelled on the charges.

Blennerhassett walked the mile and a half back to the prison in the sweltering high summer heat. The hot hike was no balm for his many physical afflictions, which variously included headaches, fever, a cough, "a sort of ringworm" on his face—and diarrhea, for which he took opium and calomel. When the flu went around Richmond, Blennerhassett of course caught it. Yet, except for his ailments and the oppressive heat—sometimes he would stand on a chair at night just to breathe the fresh, cool outside air through the iron grate—he acknowledged that he was permitted "every liberty . . . but those of passing from under the *roof* of this building by day, or out of *my room* at night."

Unlike the other 130 convicts in the prison, Blennerhassett did not have to work seven days a week, and he received his daily dinner, with liquor, from a Richmond tavern. Theodosia Burr Alston thoughtfully sent him oranges, lemons, and limes. An inmate barber named Vaun shaved him. "This Vaun," Blennerhassett wrote in his journal, "is only here for 18 years, merely for cutting his wife's throat with precisely the same sort of instrument with which he operates most delicately on mine, every other day." An anonymous woman left soups and jellies for Blennerhassett with the jailer. Blennerhassett later learned that his benefactress was Eliza Carrington, whose husband, Edward Carrington, was Marshall's brother-in-law and would become the Burr jury foreman. Blennerhassett worried incessantly about his family, which he had left behind in Mississippi. Each letter from his wife, Margaret, sent him into transports of joy.

—⁂—

Jefferson had escaped Washington's sauna-like heat for the cooler precincts of his Monticello estate in the Blue Ridge foothills. Postmaster Gideon Granger made sure that he continued to get his administrative mail. Couriers were also assigned to bring the president Hay's frequent reports about the trial, which went as well to nearby Montpelier, where Secretary of State James Madison was passing the "sickly season."

A letter arriving at Monticello from a Burr co-defendant, Senator John Smith of Ohio, told the president just what he did not wish to hear at the moment—that

General Wilkinson has been in Spanish pay for many years, & that the most unequivocal proofs of it are in the hands of a few designing Federalists, who are waiting with anxious hope for the time when you may have committed your reputation with the General's and then publish the evidence of his guilt.

Even more exasperating to Jefferson during August was the publication of the final volume of Chief Justice Marshall's *Life of Washington*, a book that Jefferson would resent until he drew his last breath. Not only had Marshall dared to include an unflattering history of the Republican Party, he had also devoted more space to Alexander Hamilton than to Jefferson in relating the events leading to the formation of Washington's cabinet, neglecting to even mention that Jefferson had written the Declaration of Independence. Marshall himself would later admit that the biography did not live up to his expectations, but that did not mitigate Jefferson's hatred of it. He called it a "political diatribe" and a "five-volume libel." Jefferson's feelings were so widely known that Blennerhassett mused in his prison journal that the book had inspired the president "with a more deadly hate of the Marshall faction than he has ever conceived of all the Burrites he ever heard of."

It was hard to imagine Jefferson loathing Marshall and the Judiciary more than when he had written to his son-in-law, John W. Eppes, a few months earlier: "From the citadel of the law [the Judiciary] can turn it's [sic] guns on those they were meant to defend, & control & fashion their proceeding for it's [sic] own will." The extent to which Jefferson would pillory the Judiciary depended on what happened during the Burr trial.

Marshall was not insensible to the peril facing both himself and the jury, confiding to Luther Martin, "It would be difficult or dangerous for a jury to venture to acquit Burr, however innocent they might think him."

—◇—

Presumably with Jefferson's approval, the president's allies secretly tried to persuade Blennerhassett and Burr's chief of staff, Colonel

Julien De Pestre, to betray Burr. De Pestre's brother-in-law, a clerk in the War Department, was first approached. But when he refused to implicate Burr, he was dismissed, and De Pestre himself was then told that he might be appointed to a general's rank in the Army if he testified against Burr; De Pestre refused.

While ostensibly paying Blennerhassett a friendly visit, William Duane, the editor of the pro-Republican Philadelphia *Aurora*, told him that if he would admit to having written the "Querist" essays that had appeared in the Marietta *Ohio Gazette* the previous fall—the ones that had discussed the separation of the West and a Mexican invasion—Duane would become Blennerhassett's advocate in Washington, "where nothing he should ask, would be refused him." If he did not cooperate, Duane warned, Blennerhassett's co-conspirators "would make a scape-goat sacrifice of [him] for their deliverance." Blennerhassett said that he could take care of himself.

—〰—

Jury selection proceeded so slowly that it seemed it might take weeks to seat a jury. The attorneys wrangled over whether to accept jurors familiar with the case, or with fixed opinions about Burr's guilt. Yet no self-respecting Virginia property owner—and only freeholders with assets of at least $300 could vote and serve on juries—lacked an opinion about the most sensational case in the republic's history. When asked whether he had ever asserted that Burr was guilty of treason, prospective juror Hezekiah Bucky had replied "No, I only declared that the man who acted as Colonel Burr was said to have done, deserved to be hung." And then there was Hamilton Morris, who, after being examined closely for evidence of bias, turned to courtroom spectators and said, "I am surprised that they should be in so much terror of me. Perhaps my *name* may be a terror, for my first name is Hamilton!" Burr fired back: "*That* remark is a sufficient cause for objecting to him. I challenge him peremptorily." Yet Edward Carrington, the husband of Blennerhassett's benefactress, passed Burr's test. "Have you, Colonel, any prejudice of a more settled kind and ancient date against me?" Burr asked him. "None at all," replied Carrington. "He is elected," said Burr.

The numerous challenges exhausted the entire jury pool of forty-eight; just four jurors had been seated. Hay complained acidly to Jefferson that

> the bias of Judge Marshall is as obvious, as if it was stamped on his forehead. [He is] endeavoring to work himself up to a state of feeling which will enable [him] to aid Burr throughout the trial, without appearing to be conscious of doing wrong. He [Marshall] seems to think that his reputation is irretrievably gone, and that he has now nothing to lose by doing as he pleases. His concern for Mr. Burr is wonderful.

Jefferson still stewed over the subpoena, while worrying that Marshall might send U.S. marshals to Monticello to bring him to Richmond to testify. He drafted a letter instructing Hay to order federal officers not to obey Marshall if he took such a step. "The powers given to the Exve [Executive Branch] by the consn [Constitution] are sufficient to protect the other branches from Judiciary usurpation . . . and the marshal may be assured of it's [sic] effective exercise to cover him." But Jefferson did not send the letter.

In the newspapers, prosecutors blamed defense attorneys for the depletion of the juror pool, and for the delay in the proceedings until another pool could be assembled. They gloomily predicted that Burr and his attorneys would use this tactic to stall the case indefinitely.

But then Burr surprised everyone by making a bold proposition: With Marshall's permission, he would randomly pick the rest of the jury from the new pool. With everyone having an opinion about the case, it would be otherwise impossible to seat a jury, Burr said. Hay readily consented to the unusual plan, and jury selection was swiftly completed.

The haphazard jury selection appeared to be a gallant gesture by Burr, but it was only an acknowledgment—and all the attorneys knew it—that the case's outcome would probably not be decided by the jury, but by Marshall's interpretation of treason law. "There is but one chance for the accused," Hay wrote to Jefferson,

> and that is a good one because it rests with the Chief Justice. It is already hinted, but not by himself [that] the decision of the Supreme Court [in Bollman] will not be deemed binding. If the assembly of men on [Blennerhassett] Island can be pronounced "not an overt act" [it will] be so pronounced.

—〜〜—

On Monday, August 17, George Hay addressed the jury. The government, he said, would prove that Aaron Burr had "procured" the assembly of thirty armed men on Blennerhassett Island on December 10, 1806, in order to levy war against the United States. As Marshall had secretly feared, the federal prosecutor, in his uninspiring opening statement, had immediately invoked the chief justice's assertion in the Bollman ruling that a "man may levy war against his country when not present" and thereby commit treason. In the government's view, Burr, who had left Blennerhassett Island long before December 10, had masterminded the incipient insurrection, and that was enough. Hay traced U.S. treason law back to the English Statute of 25, interpreting this ancestral connection to mean that treason could be committed in the absence of the chief suspect, and—here Hay put a bold spin on Marshall's words—even without the use of arms.

Hay stated Burr's purported aims: "To take possession of New Orleans, to excite the people there to insurrection, and to take advantage of the hostile sentiments, which prevailed to the west of the Alleghenies against the Spanish." Burr, said Hay, had spoken of seizing the U.S. government and exiling President Jefferson to Monticello. He had told Westerners "that a separation was necessary and unquestionably would take place."

When Burr had learned upon reaching Mississippi in January 1807 that Jefferson had issued a proclamation against him, he had groaned that he had been "betrayed"—and he was betrayed, said Hay, by one of America's greatest men, General of the Army James Wilkinson. In the years since the republic's founding, "no man has rendered more essential service to the people and government of the United States than General Wilkinson has done, by counteracting and defeating this project. Yet," Hay said regretfully, "for this service, eminent and important as it is, he has been as much censured, abused and calumniated as if he had joined in [the conspiracy]."

Jurors, he concluded, were duty-bound "to do justice and to decide the cause according to the evidence which will be produced before you."

Edmund Randolph, the senior attorney on Burr's defense team, afterward described Hay's opening arguments as "very weak" and confided to Harman Blennerhassett that he "had no doubt" that Burr would be acquitted.

—◊◊◊—

William Eaton strode jauntily to the witness stand, and the prosecution hit its first pothole. Burr and Luther Martin demanded that the government be required to first prove that there had been an "overt act" before being allowed to introduce collateral evidence, such as Eaton's anticipated testimony about Burr's supposed intentions. "Law and reason support us," Martin said. William Wirt retorted that that was ridiculous; testimony must be given chronologically. "Would you begin to narrate a tale at the end of it?" the prosecutor asked sarcastically. "If you were to write a history of the late Revolution, would you begin at the siege of York[town]?"

After deliberating overnight, Marshall announced the next day that he would permit collateral evidence so long as it was relevant to the "overt act." The order of presentation was unimportant, he said. William Eaton was recalled to the witness stand.

It was strange that Eaton, rather than General James Wilkinson, whose arrival from New Orleans has been so highly anticipated, should now be the government's major trial witness. Who could describe Burr's plans better than Wilkinson, merely by explaining the contents of the incriminating "cipher letter"? This undoubtedly had been the prosecution's original design—until John Randolph and the grand jury had shattered Wilkinson's credibility. Suspecting that Wilkinson's alteration of the cipher letter to conceal his previous correspondence with Burr was only the tip of the iceberg, Hay and his prosecution team were reluctant to jeopardize their case by summoning the general to the witness stand, or by even bringing up the letter.

—∿—

Because Aaron Burr was reputedly the ablest living American military leader, testified Eaton, "I should have thought it my duty to join his proposed Mexico expedition." But the more that Burr had talked, the more suspicious Eaton had become. During several meetings in Washington over the winter of 1805–1806, Burr had spoken contemptuously of the government, Eaton said, and tried to arouse his feelings against it, reminding him of the Jefferson administration's refusal to pay his Tripolitan War expenses.

If that war over tribute payments to the Barbary Powers had produced any heroes, it was Eaton. He had located the deposed brother of Tripoli's ruler amidst a civil war in Egypt, raised an army of Arab and European mercenaries and Tripolitan dissidents, and, with eight U.S. Marines, had marched 520 miles across the northern Libyan Desert and captured Tripoli's eastern provincial capital, Derna. As a direct consequence of Eaton's triumph, Tripoli's ruler had hastily signed a peace treaty with the United States. But Eaton was bitter over having to abandon his army at Derna as a condition of the peace agreement, and he had adopted the habit of denouncing the Jefferson administration at every opportunity, to anyone who would listen. While Federalists had welcomed his criticism, the Jeffersonians had not, and had retaliated by ignoring Eaton's reimbursement requests.

Eaton testified that he had pretended to agree with Burr's condemnation of the Jeffersonians so that Burr would reveal his aims, which he then did: "Revolutionizing the territory west of the

Allegheny; establishing an independent empire there, New Orleans to be the capital, and he himself to be the chief; organizing a military force on the waters of the Mississippi; and carrying conquest to Mexico." Burr's scheme reminded Eaton that Francisco Miranda, too, had offered him a command in his doomed expedition to liberate Venezuela. "He, too, was to have been an emperor; he might have been troublesome to us, and, of course, when I asked [Burr] what was to be done with him, [Burr] observed, 'Hang him.'" Eaton said that Burr also proposed "a central revolution," but Marshall interjected that this was irrelevant, and Eaton did not elaborate.

Resuming his story, Eaton said Burr had predicted that volunteers from across America would join the campaign to separate the West, drawn to it by the prospect of Mexican silver; and that New Orleans would also welcome him. Burr did not believe that the government would try to stop him from separating the West, testified Eaton, because this would be "a revolution which would rather be advantageous than detrimental to the Atlantic states; a revolution which must eventually take place; and for the operation of which the present crisis was peculiarly favorable."

Eaton was offered "the second command," behind Wilkinson, of whom Burr said "it was doubtful whether he would much longer retain the distinction and confidence he now enjoyed [as a general] and that he was prepared to secure to himself a permanency." Having known Wilkinson from their service together under General Anthony Wayne in the Ohio Territory in the 1790s, Eaton told Burr that "I knew General Wilkinson would act as lieutenant to no man in existence."

"'You are in error,'" Eaton said that Burr had replied. "'Wilkinson will act as lieutenant to me.' From the tenor of much conversation on this subject, I was prevailed on to believe that the plan of revolution meditated by Colonel Burr, and communicated to me, had been concerted with General Wilkinson, and would have his cooperation."

Alarmed by Burr's plans, Eaton went to President Jefferson and "took the liberty of suggesting to the President that I thought

Colonel Burr ought to be removed from the country." Burr inter-posed a question: Why? Eaton replied, "To remove you, as you were a dangerous man, because I thought it the only way to avert a civil war."

Eaton suggested that Jefferson appoint Burr to an embassy—in Paris, London, or Madrid. "The President, without positive expres-sion (in such a matter of delicacy), signified that the trust was too important, and expressed something like a doubt about the integri-ty of Mr. Burr." After going to such great lengths to impugn Burr's integrity, Eaton said he had then defended Burr to the president, expressing the belief that if Jefferson named him to a position of trust, he would reciprocate with loyalty. Jefferson, who might have been amused by Eaton's proposal, did not act upon it.

When Eaton reached the end of his narrative, Burr pounced. Wasn't it true that on March 1, 1807, just a few weeks after he had given a deposition damning Burr, Eaton had been paid $10,000, settling his claim against the government? And what had Eaton done after attempting to warn Jefferson? Why, he had gone home and thought no more of the matter, Burr said.

Burr's rapid-fire, badgering questions began to upset Eaton—surely Burr's intention—and when Burr asked peremptorily, "You spoke of a command?" Eaton no longer could contain himself:

> You spoke of *your* riflemen, *your* infantry, *your* cavalry. It was with the same view that you mentioned to me that that man [he point-ed to General Wilkinson behind him] was to have been the first to aid you, and from the same views, perhaps, you have mentioned *me*!

When Martin objected to Eaton's outburst, Eaton immediately bowed and apologized.

To Burr, Eaton said, "I determined to use you until I got every-thing out of you, and on the principle that 'when innocence is in danger, to break faith with a bad man is not fraud, but virtue.'"

Eaton's ceremonious departure from the witness stand was "as diverting to the whole court as it was probably beneficial to the defense," remarked Harman Blennerhassett, adding that Eaton had fallen far in everyone's esteem during his months in

> this sarcastic town, into a ridiculous mountebank, strutting about the streets—under a tremendous hat, and girt with a Turkish Sash, over coloured clothes, when he isn't tippling in the taverns, where he offers up with his libations, the bitter effusion of his sorrows....

—m—

Hot weather settled in, making the long August days almost unendurable, especially in the stuffy House of Delegates. Jurors and spectators, the lawyers, and Chief Justice Marshall, in his heavy black robe, all sweltered. Every day, temperatures climbed into the high 90s, accompanied by stultifying humidity. A violent thunderstorm provided a break in the heat wave, but then the weather turned hot and sultry again.

Among the hundreds of spectators who willingly subjected themselves to long hours of physical discomfort in order to watch the historical trial was Andrew Jackson, whose disgust with the government and its attorneys grew by the day. "I am more convinced than ever that treason was never intended by Burr, but if ever it was, you know my wishes that he may be hung.... I am sorry to say that this thing has ... assumed the shape of a political persecution." Wilkinson's betrayal of Burr inspired Jackson to remark on what was perhaps Burr's paramount weakness: "He is as far from a fool as I ever saw, and yet as easily fooled as any man I ever knew." Many people, however, did not believe that Burr had been victimized; an apocryphal, oft-repeated story that reached Blennerhassett claimed that Burr, through confederates, had tried to poison a government witness with laudanum.

Hay undoubtedly hoped that Thomas Truxtun would corroborate Eaton's damaging testimony, but the former Navy captain did not help the government's case. Truxtun testified that Burr never spoke of separating the Western states, never claimed that the government had sanctioned his expedition against Mexico. "I asked him if the executive [Jefferson] were privy to or concerned in the project. He answered, *emphatically*, that he [Jefferson]was *not*." For that reason, Truxtun declined Burr's invitation to command the expedition's naval vessels. Under Burr's cross-examination, Truxtun described their relationship: "We were very intimate. [In fact, Truxtun had given Burr a night's sanctuary at his New Jersey home after Burr had killed Alexander Hamilton.] There seemed to be no reserve on your part. I never heard you speak of a division of the Union." Truxtun said he had never doubted that Burr intended to settle lands along the Ouachita River in Louisiana. "I was astonished at the intelligence of your having different views, contained in newspapers received from the western country, after you went thither."

—∞—

Prosecutors now tried to establish that there had been an "overt act" of treason. The Blennerhassetts' gardener, Peter Taylor, whose testimony had gone a long way to persuade the grand jury to indict Burr, testified that Blennerhassett said he and Burr had purchased hundreds of thousands of acres of land in Louisiana on which to found a colony. Each colonist would receive a hundred acres and three months' provisions, while needing to bring only a blanket and rifle. But when Taylor began to question his employer about the settlement's crops and housing, he said, Blennerhassett revealed the expedition's true purpose: "I will tell you what, Peter, we are going to take Mexico, one of the finest and richest places in the whole world.'" Blennerhassett, said Taylor, asserted that

> Colonel Burr would be the king of Mexico, and Mrs. Alston, daughter of Colonel Burr, was to be the queen of Mexico, whenever Colonel Burr died. He said that Colonel Burr had made fortunes for many in his time, but none for himself; but now he was going to make something for himself.

When Taylor had asked Blennerhassett what would happen if any settler refused to join the military campaign, Blennerhassett had replied,

"O by God, I tell you, Peter, every man that will not conform to order and discipline, I will stab [them]; you'll see how I'll fix them."

However, when Burr's attorneys cross-examined Taylor, he could not recall whether the expeditioners were armed with muskets—military weapons—or with rifles for hunting and self-defense, and he admitted that he had never seen Burr on Blennerhassett Island. The men hastily left the island early on December 11, Taylor said, after "they were informed that the Kenawa [sic] militia [from Wood County, Virginia] were coming down there."

Colonel George Morgan and his sons, John and Thomas, described Burr's visit in August 1806 to Morganza, the Morgan estate outside Pittsburgh. Burr, they said, had boasted that with two hundred men he could drive the president and Congress into the Potomac River, and had predicted that in five or six years, the western states would break away from the Union, to which the elder Morgan had replied, "God forbid!" Thomas Morgan testified that Burr had tried to recruit him for a military operation; he had refused.

Then prosecutors produced a witness who they hoped would attest to having seen the all-important "overt act"—Jacob Allbright, who had been hired to build and operate a corn-drying kiln on Blennerhassett Island. Late on December 10, 1806, Allbright testified, General Edward Tupper of the Ohio militia had attempted to arrest Harman Blennerhassett, but was stopped at gunpoint by Comfort Tyler's men. As a bonfire crackled on the beach and men bustled about with armloads of provisions, Tupper had laid a hand on Blennerhassett and declared, "Your body is in my hands, in the name of the Commonwealth!" Seven or eight men quickly aimed their rifles at Tupper, who called out, "Gentlemen, I hope you will not do the like," to which one man responded, "I'd as lieve shoot as not." The confrontation ended with Tupper's departure, after wishing Blennerhassett good luck. Allbright's account seemed to furnish prosecutors with the overt act that they desperately needed.

But then Burr rose. Did Allbright know Tupper? Burr asked him. Allbright said that he did. Burr pointed to the general, who occupied a prominent seat in the courtroom, and asked whether that was he. It was, said Allbright.

Burr's implication was plain to all: Allbright might have testified to an "overt act," but why had not prosecutors asked Tupper himself to testify, when he was sitting in the courtroom? Wouldn't a militia general's testimony carry more weight than that of a workman?

Never asked to give testimony, Tupper later swore in a deposition that because he "neither had or pretended to have any authority . . . to arrest anyone," he had not attempted to do so. Tupper had instead spent a half hour on the island talking to Blennerhassett and "the people belonging to the boats"; no guns were leveled at him, "nor any incivility offered him."

When informed of Allbright's testimony, Blennerhassett sputtered that the laborer's words were "outrages upon his [Tupper's] character and feelings which he has repelled with that disgust and contempt suggested by his honour." Tupper told Blennerhassett that it was insinuated to him that if he did not corroborate Allbright's story, the government might "involve him in the pains and penalties of the conspiracy." But he had refused, while vowing that if he ever were asked to testify, he would gladly return to Richmond, "were he obliged to travel on his hands and knees."

—m—

Burr displayed a trace of impatience with the first seven witnesses' ineffectual testimony. If prosecutors were "now done with the overt act," he said, "or when they have done, I will thank them to inform me, for then we shall have some considerations to offer to the court."

Aware that "some considerations" meant that the defense was poised to challenge the prosecution's entire theory of treason, Hay summoned more witnesses in order to postpone the critical debate. Simeon Poole, sent by the Ohio governor to arrest Blennerhassett, described how, from the Ohio shore, he had observed the nighttime activity on the island and had seen armed sentinels. William Love, Blennerhassett's groom, confirmed that the men on the island were indeed armed—in self-defense, he said, against an anticipated attack by the militia from Wood County. "And to the best of my opinion, they did not mean to be killed without some return of the shot," he said. "I should be sorry if a man slapped me on my face without returning the blow." Love did not remember seeing General Tupper on the island that night, or chests of arms loaded onto the boats. The expeditioners made bullets, but Love could not say how many. "I was a servant in the house, but could not mind my own business and other people's, too," he said tartly.

Of even less consequence was the testimony of Maurice P. Belknap, an Ohio businessman who saw men cleaning rifles on Blennerhassett Island, and Edmund P. Dane, who reported that Tyler's men did not seem especially alarmed when they left the island.

Dudley Woodbridge, Blennerhassett's business partner in Marietta, Ohio, said that Burr ordered fifteen shallow-draft vessels of the "Schenectady model" employed on the Mohawk River—similar to the ones later depicted in James Fenimore Cooper's *Leatherstocking Tales*—and put in a large order for pork, whiskey, flour, and bacon. Eleven boats were completed—and seized before Burr could claim them—and of the provisions, Woodbridge said, Burr received only the pork.

Burr cross-examined Woodbridge about Blennerhassett's military abilities: "Was it not ridiculous for him to be engaged in a military enterprise? How far can he distinguish a man from a horse? Ten steps?"

"He is very nearsighted, and cannot know you from any of us at the distance [we] are now from one another," said Woodbridge [Blennerhassett, in fact, would today probably be considered legally blind; he read with his nose pressed to the page]. "He knows nothing of military affairs." Without a doubt, Blennerhassett was an educated man, Woodbridge said, and particularly learned in the arts and sciences—literature, chemistry, and music—but was not known to be a practical man.

"It was mentioned among the people in the country that he had every kind of sense but common sense. . . ."

—⁂—

Burr and his lawyers now noted that all the government's evidence was collateral, and therefore irrelevant, because no "overt act" of treason had yet been established. Prosecutors, said John Wickham, "had wholly failed to prove that an overt act of levying war had been committed on Blennerhassett's Island, and hence no evidence could be received to charge Colonel Burr, by relation, with an act which had not been proved to have been committed."

Chief Justice Marshall knew that he could not simply stop testimony. In refusing to commit Burr for treason on April 1, had he not stated that the government had failed to produce sufficient evidence? As a consequence of that finding, Jefferson had launched an unprecedented nationwide dragnet for witnesses and evidence. If Marshall now curtailed government testimony, he would be rejecting the very evidence that in April he had said was necessary, and that the government had then gone to such trouble and expense to obtain. And was it proper for him, rather than the jury, to judge the testimony's relevance?

If Marshall ended collateral testimony, Jefferson would blame him for the acquittal that almost inevitably would follow, and the judge's fate might become the one Justice Samuel Chase had barely avoided—removal from office. Marshall stalled.

"No doubt . . . that the court must hear the objections to the admissibility of the evidence; that it was a right, and [Burr's attorneys] . . . might insist on it," but the chief justice suggested postponing the motion. What did Hay think? As Marshall undoubtedly had hoped, Hay said that he had more witnesses who would speak to the question of an "overt act" of treason on Blennerhassett Island.

But Burr's lawyers had lost patience with Hay's promises to prove that there had been an overt act, and they formally requested that collateral testimony be cut off. Marshall had no choice but to announce that he would hear arguments on the disputed issue.

For months, lawyers had believed that the crucial debate that now loomed—over what constituted an "overt act," and whether the defendant needed to have been present—would decide this case.

The real Aaron Burr trial was about to begin.

[12]

Eden and the Serpent

Before an impartial jury, Burr's conduct would convict himself, were not one word of testimony to be offered against him. But to what a state will our law be reduced by party feelings in those who administer it?
—PRESIDENT THOMAS JEFFERSON

I will suppose that every man who dares to look at the accused with a smile or present him the hand of friendship should be denounced as a traitor; that his friends are persecuted and hunted down. . . .
—DEFENSE ATTORNEY BENJAMIN BOTTS

George Hay's prosecution team must have known it was in deep trouble. Its twelve witnesses had not even agreed on Burr's alleged intentions. Was it to seize New Orleans, as his treason charge contended? Was it to invade Mexico, as the high misdemeanor charge asserted? Or, as Burr claimed, did he plan to lead a band of settlers to Louisiana's Ouachita River Valley to build homes, plant crops, and raise livestock—and be ready to join any war against Spain in the Southwest? Just as disturbing from the government's standpoint, the witnesses had not described a single act of treason or war, aside from Jacob Allbright's dubious account.

Prosecutors now pinned their desperate hopes on liberal interpretations by Chief Justice John Marshall of the terms "overt act" and "levying of war," so that they might apply to a couple of dozen men armed with hunting rifles. They fervently wished that Marshall would define treason so that plotting it would be tantamount to committing it, and directing it from afar the same as being on the spot. In other words, prosecutors hoped that Marshall would invoke his Bollman opinion rather than the restrictive language of the Constitution's Article III, Section 3.

In the Bollman decision, Marshall had written that a "levying of war" was "the assemblage of a body of men for the purpose of carrying it [a treasonous plot] into execution." All participants, he had said, are traitors "who perform any part, however minute, or however remote from the scene of the action."

George Hay and his lawyers had not fully exploited this narrow passage made by Marshall through the densely restrictive language of Article III, Section 3. By failing to make the Bollman ruling the touchstone of their case, they had missed an opportunity to force Marshall to accept full ownership of it, and thus cement the ruling into law. Furthermore, prosecutors had not even proved that Aaron Burr had directed the assembly on Blennerhassett Island on December 10.

Burr and his lawyers, as they had planned from the very beginning, intended to force Marshall to distance himself from Bollman, adopt a strict interpretation of Article III, Section 3, and, in effect, decide the case from the bench. The defense was certain that the chief justice would apply a narrower Constitutional standard than the jury would—all to Burr's benefit. Treason, the Constitution clearly stated, "shall consist only in levying war," and proof of it required the "Testimony of two Witnesses to the same overt Act, or on Confession in open Court." Since Burr was not likely to confess, the government needed to produce two witnesses. It had not.

Undoubtedly with a sinking feeling, prosecutors placed their waning hopes of convicting Burr on John Marshall. Would the chief justice stand by the words he had written in the Bollman case? Had the government lawyers known of Marshall's second thoughts about the Bollman ruling, and his quiet consultations with his colleagues, they would have been more worried than they already were.

—∿∿—

Monticello's relatively temperate climate had not mitigated either Jefferson's fierce attention to the proceedings, or his rancor toward Burr and Marshall. Burr, "a crooked gun, or other perverted machine, whose aim or shot you could never be sure of," was now nearly eclipsed in Jefferson's hierarchy of villains by Marshall, who could wreck Jefferson's plan for a treason conviction with a single ruling. It wasn't fair. "Before an impartial jury, Burr's conduct would convict himself, were not one word of testimony to be offered against him," Jefferson wrote despairingly to Hay. "But to what a state will our law be reduced by party feelings in those who administer it?"

—∿∿—

On Thursday, August 20, John Wickham, forty-four, rose to argue the defense motion. Not only was Wickham the leader of the Virginia bar, but he was a highly popular figure in Richmond society, with a large circle of close friends. One of them, Chief Justice Marshall, had turned over his law practice to Wickham in 1797 when Marshall had gone to France to meet with the notorious envoys X, Y, and Z. Wickham was the only American whom Irish gentleman-writer Tom Moore, during his tour of the United States, judged to have fulfilled Moore's exacting standards for a gentleman. Wickham's sophistication, also noted by Moore, might have been due to his education in France, where he had been sent by his New York Tory parents with the idea of his embarking on a military career. This had not happened. Upon returning to America at the onset of the Revolutionary War, he had been arrested because of his parents' Loyalist sympathies, and then released into a Virginia uncle's custody. Thereafter, Virginia was his home.

As Burr watched hyper-alertly, aware that this debate could determine whether he lived or died, Wickham proved his worthiness by delivering a speech described by Littleton W. Tazewell—a lawyer who had served on the grand jury that indicted Burr, and would one day be Virginia governor—as "the greatest forensic effort of the American bar."

Throwing down the gauntlet, Wickham said, "No person can be convicted of treason in levying war, who was not personally present at the commission of the act, which is charged in the indictment as constituting the offense." From this standpoint alone, the Burr indictment should be rejected, Wickham said, because it stated that Burr was present on Blennerhassett Island and participated in the overt act, when everyone knew that he was not there. Prosecutors had tried to gloss over this huge error by pronouncing Burr guilty of "procuring" the assembly of Colonel Comfort Tyler's thirty men, thereby making him "legally present."

This reasoning conformed to English common law, but not to American Constitutional and statutory law, asserted Wickham. English treason law held that "there are no accessories . . . but that all are principals." But Congress had distinguished between "principals" and "accessories," going so far as to establish separate penalties.

Thus, Wickham said, under U.S. law,

no person can be punished for treason, or for any other offense under an act of Congress, creating such offense, unless they come within the description of the act; that no person can be said to have levied war against the United States, where it had not been levied by himself, but by others; and that no overt act of others can, under the statute, be made his overt act.

Furthermore, said Wickham, an "overt act" required an act of force.

What overt act had been proved? he asked. One witness had testified that rifles had been pointed at General Edward Tupper. But why had not Tupper, who was in the courtroom, given testimony? And if General Tupper really had tried to arrest Harman Blennerhassett, upon whose orders had he been acting? asked Wickham, noting that Blennerhassett Island was in Virginia, not Ohio, the only place where Tupper had authority as a militia leader. Where was the second witness required by the Constitution? Dismissively, Wickham said that, naturally, Comfort Tyler's men were armed; anyone going to the West would be.

Marshall interrupted Wickham to inquire whether he had encountered any case "where the court was called upon to decide, and did decide, that the evidence submitted to the jury did or did not amount to proof of the overt act?"

A tremor seemed to course through the lawyers at the prosecution table, as they frowned and made notes. Marshall was plainly considering instructing the jury about the relevance of certain evidence, and might not just disallow further witnesses, but also throw out testimony already given.

Wickham didn't miss a beat. It was the court's *duty*, he said, to make such a decision, because the defense and prosecution disagreed over what constituted "levying of war"; the government said it could be an assembly of men, while the defense argued that force must be used.

—∾—

The next day, George Hay produced two more witnesses who, he said, would describe the treasonous gathering of expeditioners on Blennerhassett Island. But Israel Miller, a member of Colonel Comfort Tyler's group, testified that the thirty-two men had only five rifles and three or four pairs of pistols among them. The other witness, Purley Howe, said that he delivered forty boat poles to two men who crossed to the Ohio shore from the island. Only after the expeditioners had departed did Howe set foot on Blennerhassett Island. The brief testimony was inconsequential.

Defense attorney Edmund Randolph declared it his duty as a citizen to combat "the pernicious doctrines of constructive treason," which, if unchecked, might be wielded against citizens who had merely entertained treasonous thoughts. At fifty-four, Randolph was the oldest attorney in the courtroom. He had served as a staff officer under George Washington during the Revolutionary War and, later, as Attorney General and Secretary of State. When President Washington discovered that Randolph was consorting with the French behind his back, Randolph was forced to resign from the cabinet. Randolph and Hay had been courtroom adversaries before, in a lawsuit over the Episcopal Church's Virginia landholdings.

The Constitution's framers, said Randolph, knew from European history that vague treason laws can become tyrants' bludgeons, and "have prevented that very evil from happening by fixing precise terms in that instrument." An "overt act," by the framers' definition, must be an act of force or violence that constitutes the "levying of war."

> How can this be reconciled with their [the government's] construction, that a bare "assemblage of men, met for a treasonable purpose," is sufficient to constitute the crime of levying war? . . . It proves most clearly the fallacy of the doctrine for which these gentlemen contend.

Randolph then attacked the heart of the government's case: The Dr. Justus Bollman ruling, he said, was unimportant and should not be considered binding on future cases:

> What were Bollman and Swartwout charged with? They were charged with treason generally; but it was well ascertained, that there was no evidence of actual force in levying war, and therefore it was unnecessary to pay any attention to that subject. The decision on this point, if there were any such, was *extrajudicial* [author's italics].

In making this assertion, Randolph had for the first time deployed the defense's primary argument. If Marshall agreed with Randolph that his Bollman decision had been extrajudicial, prosecutors might just as well concede the case to Burr.

When Randolph had finished, George Hay said the government was unready to argue the motion and requested a recess until Monday, August 24. Burr and his attorneys were immediately on their feet, loudly objecting that the prosecutors should have been ready to present their arguments, and that it was unfair to jurors to unnecessarily extend their confinement in the summer heat.

Hay said that the defense's half-dozen skilled lawyers had prepared arguments that had taken two days to deliver. How could three government attorneys be expected to reply to this onslaught with only one day's preparation? The defense motion was so critical, said Hay, that if it were granted, the government's case would be at an end.

Marshall gave Hay the extra time he requested.

—✕✕—

Perhaps with the idea of deploying the least of his legal team first and saving the best for last, on Monday, August 24, Hay permitted Alexander McRae, who also was Virginia's lieutenant governor, to open the government's argument against halting testimony. The acid-tongued Scotsman stated that the testimony of Eaton, the Morgans, Taylor, and Allbright had already proven Burr's guilt. As if to demonstrate the truth of this naked assertion, McRae acknowledged that they had, in fact, convinced him. In a regretful tone, he said, "I wish, sincerely wish, that no motion had been made, which would impose on me, as this does, the necessity of . . . expressing my belief that he has committed the offense for which he is indicted." Having unburdened himself of this unsurprising personal revelation, McRae declared that Burr's absence from Blennerhassett Island on December 10 did not excuse him as a principal, or necessarily make him an accessory. "He is the first mover of the plot; he planned it, he matured it; he contrived the doing of the overt acts which others have done. He was the alpha and omega of this treasonable scheme, the very body and soul, the very life of this treason."

—✕✕—

The following day, thirty-five-year-old William Wirt was poised to augment his rising reputation as a gifted orator. Orphaned as a boy, Wirt had developed a knack for making friends; it was a way to get along in a world of strangers. Extremely popular, renowned for his wit, singing, and violin playing, Wirt had many friends. While his childhood sorrows had shadowed him into adulthood—his first wife had died—they did not prevent him from enjoying life. During the Burr trial, Wirt, who ordinarily lived alone, was the guest of the Gamble family at Gray House, which overlooked the James River near the penitentiary. Gray House rang with song and laughter, as Wirt reveled in the company of the elder Gambles; their daughter, Agnes, and her husband, Governor William Cabell; and the Gambles' other daughter, Elizabeth—who would soon become Mrs. Wirt.

The Bollman decision, Wirt now said in court, was the basis for the government's prosecution of Burr as the mastermind of the plot to seize New Orleans. This ruling meant that Burr's absence from Blennerhassett Island on December 10 did not excuse him from the crime committed there. Edmund Randolph was wrong, he said, in asserting that because Dr. Justus Bollman and Samuel Swartwout were never arraigned for treason, the Bollman ruling was "extrajudicial" regarding treason. Quite the contrary, said Wirt. "It is a direct adjudication of a point immediately before the court."

Ridiculing the defense's implication that Burr's absence from Blennerhassett Island made him only an accessory, and Harman Blennerhassett the principal, because of his presence for the overt act, Wirt asked:

> Who is the most guilty of treason, the poor, weak, deluded instruments, or the artful and ambitious man who corrupted and misled them? There is no comparison between his guilt and theirs; and yet you secure impunity to him, while they are to suffer death!

The Supreme Court's declaration in the Bollman case—that the prime mover's absence during the commission of a treasonous act did not excuse him—was morally correct: "If treason ought to be repressed, I ask you, who is the most dangerous and the most likely to commit it? The mere instrument who applies the force, or the daring aspiring elevated genius who devises the whole plot, but acts behind the scenes?" Compare Aaron Burr and Harman Blennerhassett, he told the court, and see what you make of them.

Wirt now rewarded the gallery for its long forbearance with the delays and postponements and cramped lodgings, and for enduring the scorching summer heat. He gave them everything they had come to hear; he related the story of Burr and Blennerhassett as a parable on the order of man's fall from grace, with Blennerhassett—an Adam in his Eden—succumbing to the serpent Burr's blandishments.

Who is Blennerhassett? A native of Ireland, a man of letters, who fled from the storms of his own country to find quiet in ours. His history shows that war is not the natural element of his mind. If it had been, he never would have exchanged Ireland for America. So far is an army from furnishing the society natural and proper to Mr. Blennerhassett's character, that on his arrival in America, he retired even from the population of the Atlantic States, and sought quiet and solitude in the bosom of our western forests. But he carried with him taste and science and wealth; and lo, the desert smiled! Possessing himself of a beautiful island in the Ohio, he rears upon it a palace and decorates it with every romantic embellishment of fancy. A shrubbery, that Shenstone might have envied, blooms around him. Music, that might have charmed Calypso and her nymphs, is his. An extensive library spreads its treasures before him. A philosophical apparatus offers to him all the secrets and mysteries of nature. Peace, tranquility and innocence shed their mingled delights around him. And to crown the enchantment of the scene, a wife, who is said to be lovely even beyond her sex and graced with every accomplishment that can render it irresistible, had blessed him with her love and made him the father of several children. The evidence would convince you that this is but a faint picture of the real life. In the midst of all this peace, this innocent simplicity and this tranquility, this feast of the mind, this pure banquet of the heart, the destroyer comes; he comes to change this paradise into a hell.

The "destroyer," of course, was Aaron Burr.

The conquest was not difficult. Innocence is ever simple and cred-
ulous. Conscious of no design itself, it suspects none in others. It
wears no guard before its breast. . . . Such was the state of Eden
when the serpent entered its bowers. The prisoner, in a more
engaging form, winding himself into the open and unpracticed
heart of the unfortunate Blennerhassett, found but little difficulty
in changing the native character of that heart and the objects of its
affection. By degrees he infuses into it the poison of his own ambition. He breathes into it the fire of his own courage; a daring and
desperate thirst for glory; an ardor panting for great enterprises, for
all the storm and bustle and hurricane of life.

Soon after Burr's arrival, Blennerhassett ceased to enjoy his
books and music; he grew bored with family life.

His imagination has been dazzled by visions of diadems, of stars and
garters and titles of nobility. He has been taught to burn with restless emulation at the names of great heroes and conquerors. His
enchanted island is destined soon to relapse into a wilderness; and in
a few months we find the beautiful and tender partner of his bosom,
whom he lately permitted not the winds of summer to visit too
roughly, we find her shivering at midnight, on the winter banks of the
Ohio and mingling her tears with the torrents, that froze as they fell.

Wirt held the courtroom audience spellbound. His speech,
when published, became an instant classic. For the next century, in
fact, American schoolchildren would memorize Wirt's "Who is
Blennerhassett?" speech, which outlived the memory of Burr's trial
and probably single-handedly did more than anything else to fix
Burr's villainy in the public memory. In the Richmond courtroom
that day, Wirt's metaphorical trip to Eden and the Fall impressed
nearly everyone—except Burr and his defense team, who adopted

the habit of launching into mock recitations of Wirt's speech as a standing joke. Burr amused his friends for the rest of his life by reciting passages from Wirt's speech, and then sometimes describing Blennerhassett as he really was.

—ⱳⱳ—

The formidable task of rebutting Wirt's melodramatic soliloquy fell to youthful, witty, loquacious Benjamin Botts. "I cannot promise you, sir, a speech manufactured out of tropes and figures. Instead of the magnificent image of Bonaparte ascending to quench the stars, so fitted for the dry law question in debate," he said with heavy irony, "my humble efforts will be altogether below the clouds . . . I am compelled to plod heavily and meekly through the dull doctrines of Hale and Foster." Botts's deft puncturing of Wirt's high-flown rhetoric drew loud laughter.

He scoffed at the government's assertion that Colonel Comfort Tyler's thirty men had "levied war" and committed an overt act of treason by assembling on Blennerhassett Island: "They had some arms with ammunition. They watched their property at the boats. They prepared provisions for descending the river; and at a place contiguous to the island, they killed some squirrels." The men, he said, might have owned six or seven guns among them.

"As to their presenting guns at General Tupper, it ought not to be believed," Botts said. "If believed, it was only an act of violence to a private individual, or at most it was but resistance to an officer. But Tupper was not in office. He was out of the state of Ohio."

And what did the force on Blennerhassett Island plan to attack? he asked. New Orleans, twenty-two hundred miles away? Wood County, Virginia? "I apprehend that the people of Wood meditated war on the people of the island, not that the islanders meditated war against the militia. And accordingly we find that the people of the island fled silently in the night from those of Wood. And because they *fled*, it seems they were *guilty of acts of war!*"

Botts suggested an analogy:

If I run away and hide to avoid a beating, I am guilty and may be convicted of assault and battery! . . . I think it must have struck you, that such an overt act, as fits the definition and principles which Mr. Hay has furnished, would be common to all men alive. There would be no difficulty in proving an overt act on any human being who has ever been in an assemblage; and who has not been in an assemblage of men? . . . On Blennerhassett's Island, from what you have heard from the witnesses, there was nothing but peace and innocence; no acts of war.

Grand juries in Kentucky and the Mississippi Territory could not find any acts of war either, said Botts. With cutting sarcasm, he said:

They were so stupid as not to perceive in a collection of men without arms, without any possible means of annoyance, without any hostile disposition and without the possibility of getting away their women and families, anything criminal, much less any aptitude to overturn two mighty empires. It remained for us, the members of the Virginia bar, to come out and astonish the world with the profundity of our learning in matters of war.

They have ascertained that there was a terrible war. I ask you, what manner of war was it? We have had a much more serious war here than was on the island. We have had here a carnage of breaths, sour looks and hard words and the roaring of vocal cannon. . . . Is it not a mockery to speak of the war on Blennerhassett's Island?

he asked, when the Wood County militia was responsible for the violence that did occur:

There was indeed on the island a dreadful war of sympathy and sorrow. A mother in tears with her children around her, driven from their home by a mob, the windows of their house broken, their property destroyed and the lives of the family endangered. . . . It was said that they were the regular militia of Wood County.

But they were not under orders from either the governor of Virginia, or the president—the only two officials who had the authority to deploy the militia.

Botts condemned the government's attempts to silence Burr's supporters. "I will suppose that every man who dares to look at the accused with a smile or present him the hand of friendship should be denounced as a traitor; that his friends are persecuted and hunted down," he said disgustedly.

> It is difficult and inconvenient for the accused to procure evidence; that those who dare to show a disposition to give evidence for him are discouraged, censured, intimidated, but on the other, a liberal treasury of the United States, the patronage of the government and all the offices of the government, over an extensive territory, are enlisted in getting evidence to be exhibited against one man; and that man imprisoned and without property and without the ordinary means of obtaining testimony or information, by the obstruction of the mail.

He described how government agents had plundered post offices in New Orleans and other cities.

"I will say," Botts said mockingly, "that if while we have such a virtuous president, an administration so distinguished for talents and virtue, such enormous offenses be committed, if such atrocious practices take place with impunity under such an administration, nothing can save the Constitution."

[13]

"Will o' the Wisp Treason"

Will the court take away the power from the jury, because the prisoner asks it to do so?

—U.S. Attorney George Hay

We labor against great prejudices against my client, which tend to prevent him from having a fair trial. I have with pain heard it said that such are the public prejudices against Colonel Burr, that a jury, even should they be satisfied of his innocence, must have considerable firmness of mind to pronounce him not guilty.

—Defense attorney Luther Martin

On Wednesday, August 26, George Hay looked like a sick man as he stood before the hot, crowded courtroom. Although it was generally believed that he had the flu, he did not; he was simply exhausted. The demanding job of prosecuting the highest-profile case in the nation's history had exacted a steep price in frayed nerves, lost sleep, and battered self-confidence. Moreover, Hay had been thrust into the wilting national spotlight of the Aaron Burr treason case just a week after his wife's death.

Regarded by his peers in the Richmond bar as a competent but uninspired attorney, Hay had tried valiantly to hold his own against some of the nation's top trial lawyers—Aaron Burr and Luther Martin, and their galaxy of brilliant associates—and to keep his footing amid the torrent of advice and complaints issuing from the pen of President Thomas Jefferson.

Every time he entered the Virginia House of Delegates, Hay must have been nagged by a sense of losing a little more ground to Burr and his efficient team. Inexorably, the defense lawyers had siphoned the initiative away from prosecutors and put the government on the defensive.

If inspirational words were ever needed, it was when Hay rose to deliver the final government argument in favor of permitting testimony to continue. But as he began speaking, it became painfully clear that it was not going to be his day. Aware that his eloquence would never match William Wirt's, or even Benjamin Botts's, Hay attempted to turn his plainspokenness to his advantage.

> I cannot instruct you by my learning, amuse you by my wit, make you laugh by my drollery, nor delight you with my eloquence. All I can do is to express to you in plain language the convictions perhaps of a mistaken judgment; but such as they are I shall deliver them to you with as much brevity as possible.

His modesty might have initially won him the audience's sympathy, but his listless delivery soon extinguished it.

And then, five minutes into his presentation, Hay blundered badly. In discussing the treason trial of John Fries, the "Hot Water Rebellion" leader, Hay noted that the judge, Supreme Court Justice Samuel Chase, had been later impeached "for his arbitrary and irregular conduct at the trial. . . . He attempted to wrest the decision from the jury, and prejudge the case before hearing all the evidence in it; the identical thing which this court is now called on by these gentlemen themselves to do."

Hay had everyone's attention as he quoted from the first article of impeachment, in which Chase's conduct was declared to be "highly arbitrary, oppressive and unjust . . . in delivering an opinion in writing on the question of law . . . tending to prejudice the minds of the jury against the cause of the said John Fries. . . ." After citing other impeachment articles in Chase's case that he considered relevant, Hay said:

Well, sire, what is the thing which the gentlemen concerned in this defense are calling on the court to do? The identical thing which Judge Chase did.... All their arguments are to prove that this court has a right to decide that an act has or has not been proved. Will the court take away the power from the jury, because the prisoner asks it to do so?

It appeared that Hay had just threatened Chief Justice Marshall with impeachment if the judge were to grant Burr's motion to halt testimony. Burr and his attorneys feverishly jotted down notes for their rebuttal. Marshall may have inwardly shuddered, for the very outcome that he had feared—his impeachment and subsequent trial before Congress—now appeared to be at hand.

Yet, Hay's statements might also be read as a provocative argument of the question of whether a judge should prevent a jury from hearing testimony that he believed to be irrelevant. It was "a most dangerous proposition," he said, for a judge to deny a jury its duty to weigh all the evidence in a case; this was a cornerstone of the right to a trial by jury. Hay said:

> I consider this principle of the trial by jury preserved in its utmost purity and independence, as connected with the best principles of the human heart. It ought to be viewed and approached with the utmost reverence and caution; and when a judge is called on to do what may lead him to encroach on this principle, he will advance with the utmost circumspection and awe.

If a judge took it upon himself to decide when evidence was relevant and when it was not, and he decided that an overt act was proved, what point was there in allowing collateral evidence to be introduced? "If the court say it is proved, why require more evidence?" he asked. But if a judge found that the overt act was unproven, why prohibit secondary evidence that might prove the overt act?

Hay quoted to Marshall from his Bollman decision the defining words for the "levying of war":

War can only be levied by the employment of actual force. What is meant by the words the employment of actual force? Not fighting a battle; but preparing the means to make war. The meaning is explained in the next sentence: troops must be embodied, men must be assembled, in order to levy war. Do not these words amount to a declaration, that when troops are embodied, and men assembled, the war is levied?

In the same way that force need not be used in order to levy war, a traitor need not be present in order to commit an overt act of treason, Hay argued: "If the assemblage on Blennerhassett's Island were an overt act of levying war, the person who procured that assemblage, by whom its movements to and from the island were directed, is emphatically guilty of levying war against the United States."

In closing, he warned that cutting off testimony would imperil the sacred doctrine of trial by jury, which then, like the toppling of the first domino, could precipitate the eventual collapse of Constitutional government. "If it be impaired, the whole edifice may totter to its base. It is the first column of our free Constitution and government. If you undermine it, the whole may fall into ruins."

<hr>

When Hay finally sat down on Thursday, August 27, Charles Lee, who had so far played a minor role in Burr's defense, pounced on Hay's ineptly drawn parallel between the impeached Justice Chase and Chief Justice Marshall.

"It was very kind in the gentleman to remind the court of the danger of a decision of the motion in favor of the prisoner; a decision like that, which had already produced the impeachment of another judge," he said.

Hay was on his feet. "It was innocently said and compatible with the highest respect for the court; not with the design which the gentleman—I will say not very candidly—insinuates."

Unwilling to make an issue of what was of such grave concern to him, Chief Justice Marshall said to Hay, "I did not consider you as making any personal allusion, but as merely referring to the law."

But having pinned Hay down, Lee was unwilling to let him off so easily:

> The gentleman plainly insinuated the possibility of danger to the court, from a favorable opinion to the prisoner; because he said that the opinion which we claimed for him was the same in substance, as had occasioned the impeachment of one judge already. It certainly would not be unfair to infer, that it was intended to show that the same cause might again produce the same effect.

Having made his point, Lee then argued that the government had misinterpreted the Bollman decision. An assembly of men *alone* did not constitute an overt act of war; it was just one ingredient. A forcible act was also needed, he said, yet none had occurred on Blennerhassett Island on December 10, nor was Burr even present. Since his indictment alleged that he was, Lee said, Burr was therefore innocent of the charge.

Time still remained on August 27 for Luther Martin—whom Harman Blennerhassett described as "the rearguard of Burr's forensic army"—to begin his presentation. But Martin was not in the courtroom, and defense lawyers would not send for him. Martin was not yet ready to speak, they said.

—◊◊◊—

During a recent visit to Blennerhassett's prison apartments, the loquacious, hard-drinking Martin had summarized for him the main arguments of the past week, embellished with long, verbatim excerpts. At one point during Martin's thirty-five-minute performance—Blennerhassett timed him—the Irishman placed a tumbler of brandy before Martin. "No ceremonies retarded the libation." Nor did the libation interrupt the effusion of information from the great lawyer; he recited from papers that he had written, caricatured Jefferson, and related his own history with Burr, interspersing his commentary with praise and criticism for several other people as well.

Blennerhassett's obvious admiration for Martin's superior mnemonic powers was leavened by more prosaic observations, such as Martin's "preternatural secretion or excretion of saliva, which embarrasses his delivery," and his rude manner and ungrammatical language. In his habits, noted Blennerhassett, Martin was "gross and incapable of restraint, even upon the most solemn public occasions."

—◊◊◊—

The following day, Luther Martin turned his heavy, red butcher's face to the jury and solemnly pledged to make no

> apology for any length of time I may occupy in the discussion of the question. When we are defending the life of a human being, and discussing principles of such vast importance to the interests of the community and posterity, time ought not to be regarded.

Martin demonstrated his absolute devotion to this principle by speaking all day Friday and Saturday—a total of fourteen hours.

"It is the duty of the court to prevent the introduction of any evidence in any case before it, which is irrelevant to the issue," he said. But because the defense had objected to superfluous testimony, it had been "denounced throughout the United States, as attempting to suppress the truth and encroaching upon the exclusive rights of the jury." Yet, for all the censure and abuse aimed at him, Martin still felt only the "sincerest gratitude to heaven, that my life has been preserved to this time" in order to rescue his friend, Burr, from "the fangs of his persecutors." If Martin's efforts were rewarded by Burr's vindication, and

> in healing the deep wounds inflicted on the breast of [Theodosia], by the envenomed shafts of hatred and malice hurled at the heart

of the father—if our efforts shall succeed in preserving youth, innocence, elegance and merit from a life of unutterable misery, from despair, from distraction—it will be to me the greatest pleasure. What dear delight will my heart enjoy!

He then began his frontal assault on the government case, which, he said, was wrongly grounded upon British treason law, under which a man could be convicted and hanged for merely imagining the king's death. But there are no kings in the United States, Martin said, and there are only two kinds of treason: in which war is levied against the United States, and in which aid and comfort are given to America's enemies. Buttressing his arguments with long excerpts from English and American case law, he displayed his staggering legal scholarship by analyzing British treason trials all the way back to 1300 and the reign of Edward I. In one case, Martin read aloud most of the arguments and part of the evidence—thirty pages of text.

We see what a system of oppression, persecution and tyranny was formerly adopted in Great Britain by the means of constructive treason, and corrupt and pliant judges. The doctrine of constructive treasons, the rule that all are principals in treason, and that whatever in case of felony would render a man an accessory will in case of treason make him a principal, originated in the worst of times, in the most tyrannical reigns, and when the most corrupt and wicked judges sat in the English courts.

Martin's meaning was unmistakable.

—∽—

Those not yet numbed by the rumble of Martin's voice—saved from hoarseness by frequent sips of rum from a stone mug—returned the next morning to hear him discourse on the Bollman ruling. The government had misread the opinion, he said. Dr. Justus Bollman and Samuel Swartwout were set free because

there was no proof that treason had been committed by Colonel
Burr or any other person; . . . that if there were any proof, it was no
more than of an expedition intended against the Spanish provinces;
an expedition which, as it depended on a war with Spain—of
which there was then the greatest probability—would have been
honorable if the war took place, and no treason if the war did not
take place: a war in which if he succeeded, he would have acquired
honor and glory; and which in any event would have been but a
misdemeanor, by which neither his honor nor reputation could
have been sullied.

All other issues addressed by the court in the Bollman decision,
aside from the question of whether Bollman and Swartwout should
be held for treason, were "extrajudicial"—beyond the scope of the case
and deserving "no credit as binding on this court," Martin said. "As a
binding judicial opinion, it ought to have no more weight than the
ballad or song of Chevy Chase. . . . There has been nothing but a mere
dictum that has no sort of authority as a legal decision."

Having reduced the Bollman ruling to irrelevancy, Martin now
marshaled his arguments on the question of what actually did constitute a "levying of war." Levying war, he said, "must be an act of
such notoriety, that every one sees it. When troops are levied and
when they march through the country, and etc., the people behold
them; and the knowledge of the fact is universal." But this was not
the case with Burr's expedition, said Martin.

If I were to name this, I would call it the will o' the wisp treason.
For though it is said to be here and there and everywhere, yet it is
nowhere. It exists only in the newspapers and in the mouths of the
enemies of the gentleman for whom I appear; who get it put into
the newspapers.

An act of war cannot be a private conversation that may or may
not have occurred; it would be too easy for people to accuse their
enemies of conspiracies that never existed. "If open deeds, notorious

facts are not to be the only evidence, confessions must be received," he said. But the accused's supposed avowals should not be regarded as evidence of treason, "for they can be easily feigned against him by an enemy to gratify his resentment." The Constitution's framers "would not expose the life of any man to the hazard of being destroyed by perjury incapable from its nature of being disproved." Nor did they intend for the term "levying of war" to carry

> an unnatural and dangerous construction, unknown in common parlance and unusual in history or judicial proceedings. . . . If they had intended that merely to enlist men, to raise and embody troops, to raise an army without anything more, should constitute treason, they would have expressed it in such plain terms as to defy misconstruction.

And so it went, hour after hour. When prosecutors complained that Martin had shifted the entire basis for halting testimony, John Wickham stepped forward with an elucidation that was as refreshing as a drink of ice water would have been on this broiling-hot day:

> We say that there is no evidence of the presence of Mr. Burr with the persons who committed the acts on Blennerhassett's Island. We call on them to prove it if they can. If they cannot prove it, we say that there is not a single tittle of evidence that can affect him; that those acts of others on the island are not treasonable; they do not amount to an overt act of levying war; and if they were treasonable, he is but an accessory before the fact; and therefore they must prove the guilt of the principal by the record of his conviction before they can charge the accessory.

Wickham sat down, and Martin resumed his outpouring of case studies, observations, and declarations; but finally, as the afternoon shadows lengthened, he resurrected Hay's fumbling allusions to Justice Samuel Chase's impeachment, and discoursed on the subject of the intimidation of witnesses, judges, and juries:

We labor against great prejudices against my client, which tend to prevent him from having a fair trial. I have with pain heard it said that such are the public prejudices against Colonel Burr, that a jury, even should they be satisfied of his innocence, must have considerable firmness of mind to pronounce him *not guilty*. God in heaven! Have we already under our form of government—which we have so often been told is best calculated of all governments to secure our rights—arrived at a period when a trial in a court of justice, where life is at stake, shall be but a solemn mockery, a mere idle form and ceremony to transfer innocence from gaol to the gibbet, to gratify popular indignation excited by bloodthirsty enemies?

After exhorting judge and jury alike to be courageous, the Bulldog of Federalism took his seat.

No one understood better than Chief Justice Marshall the momentousness of the decision that he faced. Granting the defense motion would be tantamount to declaring that prosecutors had not proven an overt act of treason. The government's case would be lost. Would Jefferson then follow through with Hay's thinly veiled threat to impeach him?

Marshall's future on the bench, as well as the fate of the Judiciary, might well depend on the decision he would make during the forty hours to come.

[14]

Marshall's Ruling for the Ages

The opinion of the Chief Justice is too voluminous to be generally read, and on the great question about the overt act of levying war too obscure and perplexed to be understood.
—U.S. ATTORNEY GEORGE HAY

His first and last determination, with the morning and the night, should be the destruction of those enemies who have so long and so cruelly wreaked their malicious vengeance upon him.
—HARMAN BLENNERHASSETT ON AARON BURR

On Saturday, August 29, when the day's sweltering heat began to subside, John Marshall sat down with quill and paper at his desk in his Shockoe Hill home.

Working until late Saturday night and through Sunday, the chief justice ordered his thoughts on treason from the nearly hundred thousand words that he had heard spoken in his courtroom during the previous week. Troubled by Jefferson's obsessive pursuit of Burr, and alarmed at how easily treason law could be forged into a weapon of repression, he defended individual rights, but balanced them with society's welfare.

Midnight Sunday found him toiling with the desperate energy of a man who knows that he dare not fail.

He was still scratching away with his quill during the early hours of Monday, August 31.

Sometime before dawn, Marshall finished and then slept for a few hours.

The forty-four-page decision cited more authorities and references than any other Marshall opinion.

Although composed rapidly, it addressed every issue argued during the previous week: the Bollman decision's relevance; what constituted an "overt act" of treason and a "levying of war"; and whether the "prime mover" in a treasonous design remained culpable even if absent from the scene of an overt act.

At twenty-five thousand words, the opinion was easily Marshall's longest, and arguably his most important.

—∽∾—

While the chief justice was shut away in his study, worshippers attended Sunday services at the Capitol. Catholics went to a Mass celebrated by the Abbe du Bois, a French exile, in the second-floor courtroom, while directly beneath them, in the House of Delegates, Episcopalians and Presbyterians were led in a joint service by their respective parsons, John Blair and John Buchanan. Blair and Buchanan were close friends, not rivals; in fact, the more affluent Buchanan routinely gave his wedding and funeral fees to Blair, whose congregation was small and who had a large family to support. Because the Reverend Blair's congregation had no church, and the Reverend Buchanan's St. John's Presbyterian Church was distant from the westward-growing city, they held services in the Capitol on alternate Sundays. But this Sunday, as they sometimes did, the parsons held a joint service, with one of them delivering the sermon.

An eye-catching advertisement appeared in the *Virginia Gazette* on Monday, August 31:

> The Gentleman—who while I was on St. [Saturday] last addressing the court, TOOK MY CANE from the seat behind me and carried it away—is respectfully requested to send it when he was done with it, to the Bar of the Swan Tavern. Luther Martin.

There is no record of whether the cane was ever returned.

The crowd spilled out of the House of Delegates on Monday morning, August 31, as it had on the trial's opening day. Inside, every spot where one could stand, sit, or perch was taken, and although the hour was early and the August heat had not yet begun its fiery assault, the makeshift courtroom was already stuffy from the hundreds of people tensely awaiting John Marshall's arrival. Then a hush fell over the room. The black-robed chief justice strode through the press of bodies to take his customary seat on the bench.

Marshall laid the sheaf of paper covered with his handwriting before him and surveyed the assemblage of planters, lawyers, doctors, merchants, frontiersmen, river men, writers, and politicians. Washington Irving had returned to New York, and Winfield Scott was with his militia unit, but Theodosia Burr Alston and her husband, Joseph Alston, were present, as was Andrew Jackson—all eager to witness the next act of the unfolding drama.

Judge Marshall started to read his opinion. It would take four hours for him to get through all of it.

He began by praising the attorneys for their exhaustive debate of the motion. "A degree of eloquence seldom displayed on any occasion has embellished a solidity of argument and a depth of research by which the court has been greatly aided in forming the opinion it is about to deliver."

The lawyers listened intently, eyeing the stack of handwritten text, as thick as a man's finger, as though it might furnish clues as to how Marshall would rule. Would he require prosecutors to prove an overt act of treason before they would be permitted to introduce other evidence? Would he uphold the Bollman ruling's assertion that a person might participate in a treasonous act committed hundreds of miles distant?

Marshall led his listeners back to the origins of the term "levying of war"—the English Statute of 25 of Edward III, familiar ground to those who had sat through the previous week's arguments. But he did not find useful any of the major English court rulings regarding "a person who performs no act in the prosecution of the war, who counsels and advises it, or who being engaged in the conspiracy fails to perform his part"—in other words, Aaron Burr. And the English doctrine, stating that an accessory to treason is no different than the principal, was inapplicable in the United States, the chief justice said, removing one of the pillars of the government's case.

Marshall then betrayed his doubts about the applicability of the Bollman decision—the basis for the grand jury indictments and the government's entire case. He singled out the passage:

> If a body of men be actually assembled for the purpose of effecting by force, a treasonable purpose, all those who perform any part, *however minute or however remote from the scene of the action* [author's italics], and who are actually leagued in the general conspiracy, are to be considered as traitors. But there must be an actual assembling of men for the treasonable purpose, to constitute a levying of war.

Bollman's and Swartwout's participation in the assembly on Blennerhassett Island was never an issue, Marshall said, because they were never there. Thus, the Bollman opinion's assertion that an accused traitor was blameworthy even if he were absent during the commission of an overt act was extrajudicial—as defense attorneys had insisted all along. "The court is therefore required to depart from the principle there laid down," he said.

Furthermore, the Bollman ruling may not have even been a majority opinion, said Marshall. While four of the seven justices had concurred in the unanimous decision, one of the four had missed some of the debate, and might, in fact, have not agreed with the decision. If the three absent justices dissented, and the one judge changed his mind, the decision could be overturned. While he considered the opinion "perfectly correct," Marshall said that if the outcome of this trial depended on *Bollman*, it might be prudent to bring the case before the entire Supreme Court a second time.

But neither Burr's whereabouts on December 10 nor Marshall's own misgivings about the Bollman ruling would determine whether the court should stop testimony. This issue, the chief justice said, rested squarely upon the question of whether the overt act claimed by the government—the assembly on Blennerhassett Island—constituted a "levying of war."

English judges had declared that a "levying of war" must "be a warlike assemblage, carrying the appearance of force, and in a situation to practice hostility." But American judges have set a higher threshold, Marshall said, citing the John Fries treason case and others. "It is to be observed that these judges are not content that troops should be assembled in a condition to employ force. According to them, some degree of force must have been actually employed."

But did not the Supreme Court's Bollman ruling lower the bar for an overt act, so that it might consist of the mere assembly of armed men, without the use of force? Marshall asked.

George Hay must have begun to get a headache when Marshall, once again siding with Burr's attorneys, said that too much had been read into the Bollman decision on this particular issue. It might be expected, said Marshall,

> that an opinion which is to overrule all former precedents, and to establish a principle never before recognized, should be expressed in plain and explicit terms. . . . Had the intention been entertained to make so material a change in this respect, the court ought to have expressly declared that any assemblage of men whatever, who had formed a treasonable design, whether in force or not, whether in a condition to attempt the design or not, whether attended with warlike appearances or not, constitutes the fact of levying war.
>
> Yet no declaration to this amount is made. Not an expression of the kind is to be found in the opinion of the Supreme Court.

The point of the Bollman ruling never was to extend the definition of treason to an assembly of men, Marshall said. The court did not hear evidence on this question because it was tangential to the case. It was "sufficient for the court to say that unless men were assembled, war could not be levied." The government had constructed its argument upon scraps such as this, as well as upon an *omission* from the Bollman ruling, the chief justice said, then supplying the omitted last two words: "That the assemblage which constitutes the fact of levying war ought to be *in force* [author's italics]."

When Colonel Comfort Tyler's 30 men embarked from Blennerhassett Island to descend the Ohio River, Burr was not present, the chief justice said the evidence showed.

> It is then the opinion of the court that this indictment can be supported only by testimony which proves the accused to have been actually or constructively present when the assemblage took place on Blannerhassett's [sic] Island. . . . It is further the opinion of the court that there is no testimony whatever which tends to prove that the accused was actually or constructively present when that assemblage did take place; indeed the contrary is most apparent.

If this were a statutory felony case, "admitting the crime to have been completed on the island, and to have been advised, procured, or commanded by the accused, he would have been uncontestably an accessory and not a principal." But an accessory to a crime cannot be prosecuted before the principal, because the accessory's guilt depends on the principal's. "It would exhibit a monstrous deformity indeed in our system if B might be executed for being accessory to a murder committed by A, and A should afterwards upon a full trial be acquitted of the fact."

Did treason differ from a felony in this respect? Marshall asked, and then obliterated any faint hopes that George Hay and his prosecutors might have still have nurtured:

> The legal guilt of the person who planned the assemblage on Blannerhassett's [sic] Island depends not simply on the criminality of the previous conspiracy, but on the criminality of the assemblage. If those who perpetrated the fact be not traitors, he who advised the

fact cannot be a traitor. . . . His guilt therefore depends on theirs; and their guilt cannot be legally established in a prosecution against him. The law of the case being thus far settled, what ought to be the decision of the court on the present motion?

—The indictment charged Burr with levying war against the United States, alleging that an overt act of levying war occurred. But the overt act "is not proved by a single witness."

—The indictment stated that Burr was present on Blenner-hassett Island when overt acts were committed, "but the fact of his absence is not controverted."

—"The Constitution and law require that the [overt act] should be established by two witnesses; not by the establishment of other facts from which the jury might reason to this fact."

If that was not clear enough, Marshall also declared that "no testimony relative to the conduct or declarations of the prisoner elsewhere and subsequent to the transaction on Blennerhassett's island can be admitted . . . until there be proof of the overt act by two witnesses."

Marshall then drew a deep breath and plunged into the thorny issue that had nagged at him since it became a certainty that he—not the prosecution and its 140 witnesses, not the defense attorneys, and not even the jury—would decide this trial's outcome.

It was the matter of his survival on the bench:

That this court dares not usurp power is most true. That this court dares not shrink from its duty is not less true. No man is desirous of placing himself in a disagreeable situation. No man is desirous of becoming the peculiar object of calumny. No man, might he let the bitter cup pass from him without self-reproach, would drain it to the bottom.

But if he have no choice in the case, if there be no alternative presented to him but a dereliction of duty or the opprobrium of those who are denominated [as] the world, he merits the contempt as well as the indignation of his country who can hesitate which to embrace.

Until World War II, Marshall's analysis of treason and its elements served as the foundation of American treason law.

—∽∾∽—

Turning to the jurors, the chief justice instructed them to commence deliberations and reach a verdict.

Hay, somber and weary-looking, rose to his feet to seek a reprieve, be it ever so brief, from the inevitable. The government needed time, Hay said, to review the decision—time for prosecutors to hunt through Marshall's twenty-five thousand words for a reason to believe that their case was not utterly lost, and that 140 witnesses had not been summoned to Richmond across vast distances to no purpose.

Marshall granted the delay, and adjourned the court until the next day.

There is no record of it, but Burr and Luther Martin that afternoon must have enjoyed a particularly gay dinner in their lodging, surely in the company of Theodosia and Joseph Alston.

—∽∾∽—

Hay's parsing of Marshall's decision yielded only cranky complaints: "The opinion of the Chief Justice is too voluminous to be generally read, and on the great question about the overt act of levying war too obscure and perplexed to be understood," he grumbled to Jefferson. "The explanation of the opinion of the Supreme Court in the case of Bollman and Swartwout renders it very difficult to apprehend what was before perfectly intelligible."

On Tuesday, September 1, Hay announced to the court that he had no further evidence to present to the jury.

Marshall sent the jury from the courtroom to deliberate.

In just minutes, the jurors brought back a verdict.

The jury foreman, Colonel Edward Carrington, read the decision: "We of the jury say that Aaron Burr is not proved to be guilty under this indictment by any evidence submitted to us. We therefore find him not guilty."

Burr and Luther Martin sprang to their feet, protesting. The jury's language was irregular and informal, they said, talking over one another.

Burr asked Chief Justice Marshall to direct the jury to revise its verdict so that it read simply, "Not guilty." Hay argued that the verdict should stand as written; its form, he said, did not change its meaning. If the verdict went on the record this way, countered Martin, it would imply the jury's disapproval of Marshall's decision to suppress irrelevant testimony. The jury, he said, should only be permitted to pronounce Burr's guilt or innocence.

Carrington volunteered to rewrite the verdict if the court wished, but another juror, Richard E. Parker, insisted that the language remain.

With Solomon-like impartiality, Marshall said the verdict could stand as written, but would be entered in the court record as "not guilty." He thanked the jurors and discharged them.

—⁘—

As a result of the verdict, the treason charges against the remaining six defendants began to unravel. John Wickham asked that Burr's co-defendant, Jonathan Dayton, be permitted to post bail, since he, too, was absent from Blennerhassett Island on December 10, 1806. Hay glumly announced that the government would drop its prosecution of Dayton for treason, and agreed to $10,000 bail for him on the high misdemeanor charge. The next day, treason charges were also dropped against Harman Blennerhassett, Ohio Senator John Smith, Comfort Tyler, and Israel Smith. They all posted bond and went free.

Davis Floyd, the seventh defendant, had not been brought to Richmond to stand trial, but he was tried later in the Indiana Territory for treason and high misdemeanor. Although he was convicted of both charges, Floyd's crimes were so lightly regarded in Indiana that he was fined just $20 and spent three hours in jail. Not long afterward, he was appointed clerk of the Territorial Legislature, and later became a circuit judge.

On President Jefferson's instructions, Hay requested a new treason trial for Burr in either Ohio, Kentucky, Tennessee, or the
Mississippi Territory—wherever the charges might stick. But
Marshall said Burr must first stand trial for the high misdemeanor
charge that he still faced: allegedly violating the Neutrality Act by
planning to invade the Spanish Southwest and Mexico. The
lawyers debated whether Burr should even be allowed to post bail,
since the government intended to bring a new treason charge.
Again, prosecutors lost; Marshall set Burr's bail at $5,000. Two sup-
porters immediately put up the money.

After spending the last two months in prison or under house
arrest, Burr was now free.

—⁓—

Burr enjoyed his liberty by taking long, relaxing walks around
Richmond with Theodosia, as if to show off his beautiful, brilliant
daughter to the admiring city. Theodosia Burr Alston was prouder
than ever of her notorious father. "The knowledge of my father's
innocence, my ineffable contempt for his enemies, and the eleva-
tions of his mind have kept me above any sensations bordering on
depression."

Creditors descended upon Burr after his acquittal—within
weeks, lawsuits against him totaled $36,000—yet Burr was buoy-
ant and full of plans. Harman Blennerhassett and Senator John
Smith listened in amazement as he confidently predicted that in six
months he might well revive his schemes. "We could now new-
model them in a better mold than formerly, having a clearer view of
the ground, and a more perfect knowledge of our men."

"We were silent," Blennerhassett wrote of his and Smith's
stunned reactions to this possibility, after everything they had just
been through. If Burr possessed "sensibility of the right sort,"
Blennerhassett noted dryly, "his first and last determination, with
the morning and the night, should be the destruction of those enemies who have so long and so cruelly wreaked their malicious
vengeance upon him."

Now free himself to roam the city, Blennerhassett sampled the pleasures of Richmond society, which embraced him as it had Burr. At Burr's urging, he attended a concert by the Richmond Harmonic Society and was even invited to participate; if he had thought to bring his spectacles, he could have played violin. After all the years on his river island, he savored the fellowship and musical entertainments. He made the acquaintance of Catherine Gamble, the Gamble family matriarch who had sent him baskets of food while he was in prison, and Mrs. David Randolph of the ubiquitous Randolph clan. Mrs. Randolph, who managed a boarding house, had devised a "cold box" that became a prototype for one of the first refrigerators in the United States.

Mrs. Randolph's brother was Jefferson's son-in-law, yet she was unrestrained in her criticism of the president. Blennerhassett wrote in his journal:

From this lady, the near relation of the President . . . I heard more pungent strictures upon Jefferson's head and heart, because they were better-founded than any I had ever heard before: and she certainly uttered more treason than my wife ever dreamed of. . . . She cordially hoped, whenever Burr or anyone else again attempted to do anything, the Atlantic States would be comprised in the plan.

Knowing that the president's avenging spirit had animated the prosecution throughout the trial, Blennerhassett admired Chief Justice Marshall's courage. "I suspect . . . Mr. Marshall early perceived his course lay between Scylla and Charybdis, tho' he equally disregarded the dangers that menaced him on either side."

Blennerhassett's delight with again being at liberty soon became tinctured by his financial problems; he was $50,000 poorer than before the expedition, and his beloved island and possessions had been sold to satisfy creditors. While Joseph Alston had indemnified the $21,000 Blennerhassett had advanced to Burr, the South Carolina planter would only make good on one-fourth of it. From Burr, Blennerhassett got only promises. After one exasperating financial discussion with Burr, he angrily wrote that "this American Chesterfield . . . is fast approaching the limits of that career he has so long run thro' the absurd confidence of so many dupes and swindlers." Full of self-recriminations as he was, Blennerhassett undoubtedly was beginning to count himself among the former.

[15]

"A Sort of Drawn Battle"

The most unpleasant case which has ever been brought before a Judge in this or perhaps any other country.
—CHIEF JUSTICE JOHN MARSHALL

Congress must determine whether the defect has been in the evidence of guilt, or in the law, or in the application of the law.
—PRESIDENT THOMAS JEFFERSON

George Hay was dejected, and Harman Blennerhassett was becoming more cynical by the day about Burr and the government, but Burr's acquittal upset no one more than President Thomas Jefferson. He had declared a national emergency and state militias had been placed on alert. He had pronounced Burr's guilt "beyond question" and had then supervised the unprecedented dragnet for witnesses and evidence. Throughout the Richmond proceedings, President Jefferson had been in nearly daily contact with Hay.

And it had all come to nothing.

"The event has been what was evidently intended from the beginning of the trial, that is to say, not only to clear Burr, but to prevent the evidence from ever going before the world," the president complained to Hay. As the words poured from Jefferson's pen, one could almost watch his malice, like a shadow, shift from Aaron Burr to Chief Justice John Marshall and the Judiciary. Because of

Marshall, Burr was now able to leisurely stroll along Richmond's streets, arm in arm with Theodosia. If Jefferson could not see Burr to the gallows, he would see Marshall removed from office, and the Judiciary made answerable to Congress and the president.

Hay stoked the president's anger toward Marshall by reporting that his co-counsel, William Wirt, "who has hitherto advocated the integrity of the chief-justice, now abandons him. This last opinion has opened his eyes, and he speaks in the strongest terms of reprobation."

Because Marshall would not permit the evidence to be heard in court, Jefferson said, it was imperative that he and Hay lay it before Congress. "It is now, therefore, more than ever indispensable that not a single witness be paid or permitted to depart until his testimony has been committed to writing," he instructed Hay. Prosecutors must record the statements of the more than a hundred and twenty government witnesses who had not testified. Then, after reviewing all of the evidence, Congress could judge "whether the defect has been in the evidence of guilt, or in the law, or in the application of the law." Clearly, in Jefferson's view, Burr's acquittal meant that there had been a "defect."

"This criminal is preserved to become the rallying point of all the disaffected and worthless of the United States, and to be the point on which all the intrigues and the conspiracies which foreign Governments may wish to disturb us with are to turn." The president and Secretary of State James Madison, who was at his Montpelier home, agreed that Hay should vigorously prosecute the high misdemeanor charge against Burr; whatever the outcome, either Burr or Marshall would pay a price. "If defeated, it will heap coals of fire on the head of the Judge; if convicted, it will give time to see whether a prosecution for treason against him can be instituted in any, and what other court"—preferably a western jurisdiction in which Burr had actually accompanied the expedition.

The president and Madison also wanted new treason charges to be filed against Burr's co-defendants, wherever the government could win convictions. Hay was instructed how to proceed.

"We [Jefferson and Madison] are inclined to think it may be best to send Blennerhassett and Smith (Israel) to Kentucky to be tried both for treason and misdemeanor. The trial of Dayton for misdemeanor may as well go on at Richmond."

Burr added to Jefferson's vexation by asking Chief Justice Marshall to issue a second subpoena duces tecum to Jefferson, demanding that he hand over another letter sent to him by General of the Army James Wilkinson. Dated November 12, 1806, this letter warned that Burr was descending the Mississippi River to New Orleans with seven thousand men. As Marshall granted Burr's motion for the second subpoena, Burr reminded him that the president had not yet produced Wilkinson's October 21, 1806, letter, the object of Marshall's previous subpoena.

When Jefferson learned of the new subpoena, he exploded:

As I do not believe that the district courts have a power of *commanding* the executive government to abandon superior duties & attend on them, at whatever distance, I am unwilling, by any notice of the subpoena, to set a precedent which might sanction a proceeding so preposterous.

But upon cooler reflection, he instructed Hay to give Burr both letters. Having already sent Hay the October 21 Wilkinson letter, Jefferson now dispatched the second letter by courier, after first deleting passages that he considered to be confidential.

The defense lawyers grumbled about the omissions, but neither they nor Marshall formally demanded the expunged material, and there the matter of presidential privilege rested.

Burr and his lawyers may not have pressed the issue because they might already have gotten unexcised copies through other sources. Burr had somehow managed to obtain the depositions and evidence presented to the grand jury—documents usually kept under lock and key. As a lawyer familiar with the sacrosanctity of grand jury evidence, Harman Blennerhassett could only express admiration for Burr's resourcefulness: "It must be confessed that

few other men in his circumstances could have procured these documents out of the custody of offices filled by his inveterate enemies," Blennerhassett wrote in his journal. "I have long been at a loss
to imagine the means he used. . . ."

—∞—

Burr's second trial, which began September 9 on the misdemeanor
charge of violating Spain's neutrality, was anticlimactic after the
high drama of his treason trial. Prosecutors argued as vigorously as
before for Marshall to allow collateral testimony, but they had no
new evidence, and the large crowds that had flooded into the
House of Delegates like an August high tide now ebbed along with
the summer heat. Thousands of suddenly bored courtroom
habitues packed their belongings, loaded their wagons and saddled
their horses, and went home.

The government's seven-count misdemeanor indictment against
Burr rapidly encountered the same insoluble problems that had
stopped testimony during the treason trial: An overt act had to be
proven, as did Burr's presence on Blennerhassett Island. When five
days of testimony failed to establish either fact, the defense asked
Chief Justice Marshall to halt the admission of secondary evidence.
As Marshall had ruled previously, he ruled once more: The government must first prove that there had been an overt act in which
Burr participated before it could introduce evidence of Burr's supposed intentions.

Hay gave up. Now, in fact, suffering from the flu that he had
been rumored to have contracted weeks earlier, on September 15 he
moved to discharge the jury. But Burr and his attorneys insisted on
a verdict and, therefore, Marshall instructed the jury to deliberate.

The jurors briefly did, then pronounced Burr "not guilty."

—∞—

After this second setback, Jefferson wrote in frustration to William
Thomson, a writer friend. "The scenes which have been acting at
Richmond are sufficient to fill us with alarm. We supposed we

possessed fixed laws to guard us equally against treason and oppression; but it now appears we have no law but the will of the judge." To
General of the Army Wilkinson, the president said that Marshall's
rulings were tantamount to "a proclamation of impunity to every traitorous combination which may be formed to destroy the Union...."

Wilkinson and Jefferson's other allies and supporters commiser-
ated with the president. "The disgraceful and dishonorable scenes
which have been passing in review here are drawing to a close,"
wrote Wilkinson, audaciously suggesting that Marshall's "enterprise
and hardihood almost justify the suspicion that he has been a party
to the conspiracy." Attorney General Caesar Rodney said the government attorneys had "acquitted themselves with honor. But it is
in vain to struggle against wind & tide. The current on the bench
was irresistible."

—∞—

Marshall convened a new hearing on the government's motion to
file new treason charges against Burr. Unlike the two previous trials, when Marshall had thwarted the government's wish for a broad
airing of its evidence, he now placed no restrictions on testimony.
From September 15 to October 19, Marshall served as a hearing
magistrate—a most lenient one, at that—who permitted the government to interview more than fifty witnesses at length. Perhaps
the chief justice believed that by mollifying prosecutors now, he
could avoid impeachment.

But the failed Chase prosecution in 1805 had convinced Jefferson
that impeachment was an ineffective brake on the Judiciary.
"Impeachment is a farce which will not be tried again," he told
Congressman William Branch Giles. Jefferson's new plan of attack
was a constitutional amendment that would permit the Executive
and Legislative branches to remove federal judges for misconduct.
The idea had ripened after Burr's second acquittal, which Jefferson
had predicted would lead to "an amendment to the Constitution
which, keeping the judges independent of the Executive, will not
leave them so, of the nation."

"Removal by address," as it was called, had been debated by the Constitution's framers—and rejected, because of its potential for abuse. The provision had been adopted in 1701 England, where judges could be removed by an "address," or appeal, by Parliament to the king or queen. But the Constitution's authors believed that adopting "removal by address" would tempt the Executive Branch and Congress to subordinate the Judiciary, upsetting the balance of power.

Now reprised by either Jefferson and Madison, or at least with their approval, the proposal found favor with Jefferson loyalists. "The period has arrived when this colossal power, which bestrides the Legislative & Executive authorities, should be reduced to its proper limits," wrote Caesar Rodney.

—∽∽—

While Jeffersonians searched for the right tool to clip the Judiciary's wings, the hearing in Richmond ground on day after day, week after week, with Marshall, more referee than judge, interceding only when absolutely necessary. Dozens of witnesses who had had no chance to testify during Burr's two trials now told their stories. Others, like William Eaton, expanded upon earlier testimony that had been cut short by the defense's insistence that all evidence had to bear on an overt act.

A Blennerhassett neighbor, Alexander Henderson, affirmed what had become apparent during Burr's treason trial—that the talkative Harman Blennerhassett was not one to keep a secret. During a visit to Henderson's home in Wood County, Virginia, in early September 1806, Blennerhassett had told Henderson and his brother, John, that Burr planned to separate the western states and territories, and then seize New Orleans, its banks, military stores, and fifty French cannons. Blennerhassett had invited Henderson to join the expedition, but Henderson said he was in such poor health that he could scarcely walk from his house to his mill. Blennerhassett told Henderson that Burr "had made the fortunes of hundreds without at all advancing his own; he mentioned, as an instance, the Manhattan Bank and Company," one of Burr's greatest triumphs as a New York political operator, and which later fell under the Clinton family's control. "Mr. Blennerhassett said, if Mr. Jefferson was any way impertinent," Henderson said, "that Colonel Burr would tie him neck and hands, and throw him into the Potomac." Blennerhassett had also proudly claimed authorship of the inflammatory essays that appeared in Ohio newspapers under the name "Querist."

William Eaton testified that Burr had taken the same tone with him when speaking of Jefferson and his administration, describing how "he would turn Congress neck and heels out of doors, assassinate the President—or what amounted to that—and declare himself the protector of an energetic government." Burr had said he would "hang him," "throw him into the Potomac," said Eaton, and "send him to Carter's mountain," the promontory on which Monticello rested. Eaton said that he had tried to discourage Burr by predicting that he would never find men "who would support him in projects of such a treasonable, and, I think I said, murderous nature." But Burr had brushed off Eaton's objections, professing to know the mind of the American people, to which Eaton said that he had replied, "The people were not prepared for his usurpations, that the very name of *usurper* would put him down."

During his cross-examination of Eaton, Burr dredged up a court-martial proceeding that had been brought against Eaton in 1797, when he was an Army captain in Georgia. He summoned Eaton's superior officer from that time, Colonel Henry Gaither, and swore him in as a witness.

"I have been taken by surprise!" Eaton angrily interjected. "I did not suppose that the tombs were to be ransacked, to establish things which happened beyond the flood."

However, Gaither's testimony was more dud than bombshell: The War Department had destroyed all pre-1801 court-martial records, and Gaither had only a vague recollection of what the charges against Eaton had alleged; he thought it had something to do with selling rations for profit. Eaton asserted that the charges had been thrown out, and that they were trumped up anyway— retaliation by Gaither for Eaton having corresponded directly with

War Secretary Timothy Pickering, and refusing to join Gaither in a land speculation scheme.

—∿—

To far better effect did Burr, Luther Martin, Benjamin Botts, and John Wickham bludgeon General James Wilkinson's credibility. Wilkinson had not testified since his calamitous grand jury appearance in June. Now he found himself anchoring the government's attempt to bring a treason charge against Burr in another jurisdiction. The defense, however, possessed crippling weapons: the altered cipher letter and evidence of Wilkinson's ties to Spain.

Littleton Tazewell testified that after he and other grand jurors had mastered the code employed by Burr in his July 22, 1806, letter to Wilkinson, they decoded the letter themselves, and discovered that Burr had received a May 13 letter from Wilkinson. Wilkinson had omitted this from his translation. Besides contradicting Wilkinson's assertion that he had not corresponded with Burr, the May 13 reference had also controverted his affidavit swearing that he had sent Jefferson an accurate translation. When Samuel Swartwout had subsequently remembered a line from Wilkinson's May 13 letter—the words "I am ready"—the grand jury had nearly indicted Wilkinson, Tazewell said.

On the witness stand, Wilkinson admitted that he had written a letter to Burr on May 13, but said its purpose was to draw out Burr's plans. While he said he could not recall most of what he had written, he distinctly remembered the damaging words quoted by Swartwout—and they were taken out of context, Wilkinson said. He had actually written, "I fancy Miranda has taken the bread out of your mouth, and I shall be ready for the grand expedition before you are."

Major James Bruff, an Army artillery officer, testified that Burr and Wilkinson had met in St. Louis during the late summer of 1805, when Wilkinson also had sounded out Bruff about joining what he would describe only as a "large enterprise." When Bruff displayed no enthusiasm for it, Wilkinson turned resentful and sarcastic, refusing to discuss his plans further. Not only was Wilkinson corresponding often with Burr at the time, said Bruff, but also with Senators John Adair, John Smith, and John Brown.

Bruff said he tried to warn his superiors in Washington that Wilkinson was a Spanish spy and in league with Burr, but his reports were ignored. He had then personally presented his information to Caesar Rodney. The attorney general's response stunned him:

> What would be the result if all your charges against General Wilkinson should be proven? Why just what the Federalists and all the enemies of the present administration wish—it would turn the indignation of the people from Burr on Wilkinson. Burr would escape and Wilkinson would take his place.

Wilkinson indignantly denied that he had ever suggested an enterprise to Bruff, turning his eyes heavenward and placing both hands over his heart. "Before God," he said, "his [Bruff's] whole narrative is either a vile fabrication or a distortion of facts." The general said he was ringed by tormenters dedicated to ensuring that "every art is employed, and witnesses are raked and scraped from every quarter to rip up the remotest transactions of my life, to affect my credibility, to wound my fame and rob me of my reputation."

Burr, he acknowledged, had indeed visited him in St. Louis in September 1805, and had complained of

> the imbecility of the government, said it would molder to pieces, die a natural death, or words to that effect, adding that the people of the West country were ready for revolt. To this I recollect replying that if he had not profited more by his journey in other respects, he had better have remained in Washington or Philadelphia; for surely, said I, my friend, no person was ever more mistaken.

Luther Martin launched a fresh attack on Wilkinson: "We wish to show that General Wilkinson is interested in the destruction of

Colonel Burr; that he has placed himself in such a situation that he must hang Colonel Burr, or be himself eternally detested." Martin summoned Thomas Power, a Spanish subject who lived in New Orleans. A treatise to Congress then being written by Congressman Daniel Clark, the wealthy New Orleans merchant, would claim, among other things, that Power had delivered Spanish pension payments to Wilkinson. After completing the treatise, Clark, in 1809, would then publish *Proofs of the Corruption of Gen. James Wilkinson and of his Connexion with Aaron Burr*, a well-documented condemnation of Wilkinson that would detail his relationship with Power.

But on the witness stand, Power refused to answer when Burr's attorneys asked him whether Wilkinson had corresponded frequently with the former Spanish governor of Louisiana, Baron Francisco Luis Hector de Carondelet (it one day would be shown that Carondelet was Wilkinson's paymaster). Power knew that if he denounced Wilkinson, he would have to answer to unhappy Spanish officials; but if he did not, American officials might deport him. Marshall ordered Power to answer the question. After a short delay, Power, clearly discomfited, acknowledged grudgingly that Wilkinson and Carondelet had carried on a correspondence, using a complicated cipher. Wilkinson's aura of patriotism and virtue flickered. Soon, it would vanish altogether.

—m—

For five long days, without letup, General Wilkinson was by turn questioned and cross-examined, fed easy questions and mercilessly grilled, placated and accused by insinuation. Wilkinson blustered and ranted; he was wary, defensive, fearful, blunt, and meandering. The general's contradictions, admissions, and slips began to add up. He admitted having written at least two other letters to Burr, besides the one on May 13; they were sent during the fall of 1805, possibly in early 1806. But Wilkinson said he had only intended to draw out Burr's "grand enterprise." Burr sent him six letters, Wilkinson said, smoothly adding, in case any of them should unexpectedly surface, that they were all of "an ambiguous aspect, speaking of some enterprise without designating any and were calculated to inculpate me, should they be exposed."

He had sent Jefferson an unfaithful translation of the cipher letter, he said, because Burr had deliberately salted it with incriminating phrases; he was thereby justified in striking them out. He blamed his attorney, A. L. Duncan, to whom he had delegated the task of omitting Burr's damning words, for making too many deletions. By the time Wilkinson discovered what Duncan had done, he said, it was too late to make corrections. Duncan, however, testified that Wilkinson, not he, made the erasures.

Wilkinson's long correspondence with Carondelet proved that he was a Spanish spy, and therefore a traitor to the United States, said Burr and his lawyers. Wilkinson had admitted tampering with the cipher letter, they said, and he had changed his story at least once about the nature of his correspondence with Burr.

Wilkinson's ordeal by cross-examination continued. He acknowledged sending agents in civilian clothes to arrest Burr in Mississippi, even though he had no authority to do so. The defense lawyers pressed him to answer accusations that, while in New Orleans, he had ordered the post office rifled and mail addressed to others brought to him for examination. Wilkinson refused.

Samuel Swartwout, who had delivered the letter to Wilkinson in Natchitoches, accused Wilkinson of lying about their conversation. He had never told the general, as Wilkinson had contended, that Burr planned to overthrow New Orleans or seize its banks. "I first heard of such a project from Wilkinson. I never heard anything of the kind from Burr," he said. He had not even known that there was a bank in New Orleans. "Wilkinson said that he had been told that Burr intended to separate the Union—that he wished it were so, that he should like to be in his empire. I replied that I knew nothing of it. I never heard Burr say any such thing." Burr had only discussed settling the Ouachita River Valley in Louisiana if there were no war with Spain. "He [Burr] invited me to go there and plant cotton with him," Swartwout said.

John Wickham's withering cross-examination of Wilkinson on September 29, Blennerhassett noted, "so embarrassed Hay as well as the General, that it would be impossible to say, which of them, most heartily welcomed a sudden adjournment in which Hay hastily sought the only retreat that was left to his confusion."

The accumulated admissions, lies, accusations, and denials undermined the prosecution's case, eroded Wilkinson's credibility, and even deflated the general's customary pompousness. "General Wilkinson exhibited the manner of a sergeant under a Ct. Martial rather than the demeanor of an accusing Officer confronted with his Culprit," observed Blennerhassett.

Swept away with Wilkinson's arrogance was Hay's faith in the general. "My confidence in him [Wilkinson] is shaken, if not destroyed," Hay wrote to Jefferson. "I am sorry for it, on his own account, on the public account, and because you have expressed opinions in his favor. But you did not know then what you will soon know, and what I did not know until after, long after, my declaration above mentioned."

—⁓—

Federalist newspapers acidly suggested that the interminable hearing be called "King Tom's Puppet Show" or "Much Ado About Nothing." The Federalist *Virginia Gazette* was even harsher: "History will hardly furnish an example of such oppressive tyranny as has been practised under the administration of Mr. Jefferson."

When Chief Justice Marshall upheld the president's right to withhold portions of a letter that he had written to Wilkinson, Luther Martin also lashed out at Jefferson's involvement in every aspect of the case.

> And is Mr. Jefferson to be the judge of the relevancy of evidence, in a prosecution in which he has taken so active a part against the accused? Mr. Jefferson, sir, is a man of no legal knowledge. He was of no celebrity as a lawyer before the Revolution, and he has since been so much engaged in political pursuits that he has had time enough to unlearn the little law he ever knew.

Blennerhassett deplored the government's efforts to "ruin [Burr], by dragging him thro' every other District in the Union" until it found a venue in which it could win a treason conviction. Only a "persecuting and vindictive Govt." would order its lawyers "to har-rass [sic] an obnoxious but innocent victim of its wrath."

The Republican Richmond *Enquirer* was just as outraged as Blennerhassett—but over the defense attorneys' rough treatment of Wilkinson, who, in the newspaper's view, had been slandered by

> a host of enemies whetted by disappointment and stimulated by revenge. . . . We have seen witnesses of almost every country and denomination, the avowed enemies of General Wilkinson, hunted up from the remotest extremes of the union, to violate the seal of confidence and rip up the private transactions of his life!

As the testimony continued, week after week, the attorneys indulged their growing testiness by occasionally sniping at one another. Prosecutor William Wirt lampooned Luther Martin's affin-ity for rum during a tedious debate about admitting as evidence part of a letter rather than all of it.

"This is only an extract," Martin observed.

"I had no other," replied General Wilkinson.

"We take no extracts," Martin said, returning the document.

"Unless it be of molasses," Wirt was heard to say.

—〰—

On October 10, Chief Justice Marshall issued his final decision in *United States v. Aaron Burr.* Just one-tenth the length of his epic rul-ing of August 31, the decision did not break new legal ground, but it ended President Jefferson's crusade against Aaron Burr.

The government had failed to justify the need for new treason charges against Burr, in any jurisdiction, Marshall wrote. "Weighing the whole of this testimony, it appears to me to preponderate in favor of the opinion that the enterprise was really against Mexico.

"But there is strong reason to suppose that the embarcation [sic] was to be made at New Orleans, and this, it is said, could not take place without subverting for a time the Government of the Territory, which it is alleged would be treason." However, Marshall did not believe that New Orleans would have been necessarily overthrown if Burr had staged a Mexican invasion force there. "An embarcation [sic] of troops against a foreign country may be made without revolutionizing the Government of the place and without subverting the legitimate authority."

Blennerhassett sarcastically noted, "Mr. Marshall, at last, has delivered an elaborate opinion, purporting that he cannot commit any of us for treason; not because we had none in our hearts, but because we did none with our hands."

Yet, Marshall did commit Burr and Blennerhassett to the federal court in Chillicothe, Ohio, to face new high misdemeanor charges of conspiring to violate Spain's neutrality. Hay announced that he would advise against further prosecution, and Burr and Blennerhassett were released on $3,000 bond each. Neither would ever appear in court on the charges.

Burr succinctly expressed his mixed feelings about the outcome to Theodosia: "After all, this is a sort of drawn battle."

—⁓—

Aaron Burr's enemies were apoplectic; once again, Chief Justice Marshall had placed Burr beyond their reach. It was the second time that Marshall had prevented prosecutors from filing a treason charge against the former vice president, and two of his other rulings had directly resulted in Burr's acquittal.

William Duane's Philadelphia *Aurora* and Thomas Ritchie's Richmond *Enquirer* set upon Marshall with the righteous fury of avenging angels. "Let the judge be impeached!" cried the *Enquirer*. Both newspapers published a series titled, "Letters to John Marshall," by "Lucius," a nom de plume adopted by Jefferson's friend William Thomson. The letters pronounced Marshall "a disgrace to the bench of justice" who had "prostrated the dignity of the chief justice of the United States. . . . You are forever doomed to blot the fair page of American history, to be held up [with Burr] as examples of infamy and disgrace, of perverted talents and unpunished criminality. . . ."

Marshall had not only infuriated his and Burr's enemies; but his decision to try Burr and Blennerhassett in Ohio had upset Burr, his lawyers, and the Federalists who had stood by the chief justice during the arduous months in Richmond.

"This opinion was a matter of regret and surprise to the friends of the chief justice, and of ridicule to his enemies—all believing that it was a sacrifice of principle to conciliate Jack Cade [Jefferson]," Burr observed to Theodosia. Blennerhassett agreed with Burr, writing in his journal: "He [Marshall] is a good man, and an able lawyer, but timid and yielding under the fear of the multitude, led . . . by the vindictive spirit of the party in power."

—∾∾—

Marshall left Richmond for a needed vacation in the Blue Ridge Mountains. In a letter to a friend, Judge Richard Peters of Philadelphia, the chief justice took a moment to reflect on the judicial cyclone that had just passed—including being hanged and burned in effigy by a Baltimore mob, beside effigies of Burr, Blennerhassett, and Luther Martin. The Burr case he said, was "the most unpleasant case which has ever been brought before a Judge in this or perhaps any other country."

But Marshall seemed to take quiet pride in having refused to compromise his principles:

> It was most deplorably serious & I could not give the subject a different aspect by treating it in any manner which was in my power. I might perhaps have made it less serious to myself by obeying the public will instead of the public law & throwing a little more of the sombre on others.

—∾∾—

Joseph Hamilton Daviess, the former Kentucky U.S. attorney and Marshall's brother-in-law, wrote a pamphlet, *A View of the President's Conduct, Concerning the Conspiracy of 1806*, that excoriated Jefferson's actions. Still burning over his dismissal by Jefferson after his failure to indict Burr, Daviess criticized the president for ignoring his

many warnings about Burr. Besides displaying all of their correspondence, including Daviess's January 1806 assertion that Wilkinson
was on Spain's payroll, *A View* was also spiced with Daviess's barbed
commentary about the president. In one passage, Daviess wrote
that while Jefferson had once been a patriot, "he has long since made
his judgment play the whore to his ambition. . . ."

Blennerhassett described the pamphlet as "a hasty, passionate
performance . . . bearing hard upon Jefferson's hypocricy [sic] and
neglect of the author, and the early information he gave him of
Burr's designs and first movements."

—᙭᙭—

Jefferson, who would never be reconciled to Burr's acquittal, now
took his first step toward punishing Marshall for letting him go
free. In his Seventh Annual Message to Congress on October 25,
he promised to lay before Congress all of the evidence gathered by
prosecutors from testimony and depositions—and then did so on
November 23. In the message, he said:

> From the whole you will be enabled to judge whether the defect was
> in the testimony, in the law, or in the administration of the law; and
> wherever it shall be found, the legislature alone can apply or origi-
> nate the remedy. . . .
>
> The framers of our Constitution certainly supposed they had
> guarded, as well as their government against destruction by trea-
> son, as their citizens against oppression under pretence of it; and if
> these ends are not obtained it is of importance to enquire by what
> means, more effectual . . . they may be procured.

Excised from an early draft of Jefferson's address, probably at the
urging of the president's trusted adviser, James Madison, were
words tinged with the president's bitterness: "And truth & duty
alone extort the observation that whenever the laws were appealed
to in aid of the public safety, their operation was on behalf of those

only against whom they were invoked." But even with the deletion of those words, it was clear that the president believed that Chief Justice John Marshall personified the "defect."

Blennerhassett, for one, understood what Jefferson wanted: for Congress to consider sanctions against Marshall

> by signifying a doubt—whether we have not still the use of our necks, thro' the misconduct of the judge.—Should the latter suffer as it were penance for that timidity of conduct which was probably as instrumental in keeping him from imbruing [sic] his hands in our blood.

Jefferson's congressional allies attempted to make it easier to prosecute treason and to impose judicial term limits. Jefferson asked Congressman John Randolph to draft a bill to punish conspirators who are absent when an overt act of treason is committed; Randolph's bill was never debated. The Senate approved a similar bill, introduced by Virginia Senator William Branch Giles. It died in the House. Ohio Senator Edwin Tiffin proposed a Constitutional amendment that would have eliminated lifetime tenure for federal judges, setting term limits instead. The amendment also authorized the president to remove a judge if two-thirds of both houses of Congress concurred. It was the very "removal by address" proposal that the framers of the Constitution had rejected. The Senate, too, rejected it.

As these reform efforts waxed and waned, a congressional committee recommended the expulsion of Ohio Senator John Smith, one of Burr's alleged co-conspirators. The committee concluded that even though charges against Smith had been dropped, he had still conspired against "the *peace, union* and *liberties* of the people of the United States." Only the government's vigilance had prevented "a war of the most horrible description." The Senate voted 19–10 to remove Smith—one vote less than the two-thirds needed. Smith, however, resigned.

—⁂—

Left to restore his tarnished reputation, Wilkinson adopted the dubious strategy of challenging John Wickham and John Randolph to duels. Wickham, whom Wilkinson accused of having called him a perjurer in open court, flatly refused, but invited the general to sue him for slander if he believed he had been wronged. Wilkinson did not sue. The general then called out Randolph, who had nearly persuaded the grand jury to indict him. Randolph scornfully replied: "In you, sir, I can recognize no right to hold me accountable for my public or private opinion of your character . . . I cannot descend to your level."

Rather than duel Wilkinson, Randolph rose in the House and requested that Congress investigate the general. In support of his motion, he read two letters given to him by Congressman Daniel Clark that detailed Wilkinson's covert dealings with the Spanish. Clark had obtained the letters from Thomas Power, the reluctant witness who had confirmed Wilkinson's secret correspondence with Baron de Carondelet. In one of the letters, dated January 1796, Carondelet had informed a subordinate that he was sending $9,640 to Wilkinson in two sugar barrels. Randolph asserted that the letter proved that Wilkinson had "corruptly received money from the Government of Spain or its agent" while serving as a U.S. Army officer.

Feeling his pursuers' hot breath on his neck, Wilkinson asked his Spanish patrons for help. They did not let Spy No. 13 down. In a letter to Congress, Vicente Folch, the governor of Spanish West Florida, said that he possessed no documents indicating that Wilkinson was ever in Spain's service. The $9,640 sent to the general in the sugar barrels a decade earlier, Folch said, was payment for an old tobacco contract.

In a separate letter to Wilkinson, Folch assured the general that he had taken the precaution of forwarding to Havana for safekeeping every document that might incriminate Wilkinson. Consequently, the full extent of Wilkinson's treachery was not known until nearly a century later, when American forces occupied Havana during the Spanish–American War and seized Spanish documents there.

Indebted to Folch for lying to Congress on his behalf, Wilkinson arranged for him to receive fifteen hundred barrels of flour, despite the trade embargo that Jefferson had imposed in response to English aggression.

—∽—

Jefferson headed off Randolph's embryonic Congressional investigation of Wilkinson by announcing that War Secretary Henry Dearborn had already begun an inquiry.

Conducted by three military officers loyal to Wilkinson and the Jefferson administration, the investigation found no evidence that Wilkinson had received money from Spain for "corrupt purposes."

Epilogue

The great object of my fear is the federal judiciary.
—THOMAS JEFFERSON, 1821

Every check on the wild impulse of the moment is a check on his own power, & he is unfriendly to the source from which it flows. He looks, of course, with ill will at an independent judiciary.
—CHIEF JUSTICE JOHN MARSHALL ON JEFFERSON, 1821

There! You see? I was right! I was only thirty years too soon. What was treason in me thirty years ago, is patriotism now.
—AARON BURR, IN 1836,
UPON LEARNING OF TEXAS INDEPENDENCE

Amazingly, after all that had happened, Aaron Burr had not given up on his scheme to invade Mexico. He only wanted money, he believed. With his designs laid bare during his treason trial, Spain would certainly not underwrite him. In England, however, Burr believed that he might find fresh support, as well as new investment opportunities.

Burr asked Harman Blennerhassett, who had connections in England, for the names of English friends who might introduce Burr to rich prospective patrons. Willing to try anything that might advance his financial claims ahead of Burr's many other creditors, the Irish exile named three noblemen who might assist Burr, if Blennerhassett gave him letters of introduction. Blennerhassett described Burr's reaction to his offer:

The effect of this communication . . . was rapture. The whole man changed. With all his studied reserve, he could not restrain his transports, which agitated his countenance and his movements far more than the news of a capital prize in the lottery could have done.

Blennerhassett and Burr both desperately needed something on the order of a lottery prize to liberate them from debt and public disgrace. In Baltimore, fifteen hundred angry citizens, along with fifers and drummers playing "The Rogue's March," had pursued them through the streets to Luther Martin's home, where Martin's law students and friends stood guard with swords, pistols, and rifles. Mounted police interceded before blood was shed, so the mob hanged and burned effigies of Burr, Martin, Blennerhassett, and Marshall. Burr and Samuel Swartwout slipped away in a police escort to the stage station and fled to Philadelphia, with Blennerhassett following later.

Blennerhassett and Burr argued about money; Blennerhassett wanted a written pledge from Burr that he would repay what he owed, and Burr refused to give it. Blennerhassett withdrew his offer to recommend Burr to his English friends. "I feel that I could not solicit their attentions to you as my friend," he informed Burr. With that, their friendship ended, leaving Blennerhassett to try to salvage what remained of his former life, perhaps recalling Attorney General Caesar Rodney's description of Burr all those months ago—"this wandering meteor . . . which now has suddenly fallen among us, as if from the skies"—and feeling that it had landed on top of him.

Reflecting on all that had happened over the past year, Blennerhassett remembered that acting Mississippi Governor Cowles Meade had said that Burr had seemed "at *times* deranged." While Blennerhassett believed that this might be "the only means of accounting for his occasional rashness in his assertions," he did not think it altogether explained Burr's paradoxes. "No two persons of his acquaintance will ever understand him alike, and yet all who still adhere to him, profess a unity of confidence in him."

In Philadelphia, Burr's habitual stoicism crumbled under the accumulated setbacks of the past year. He was maligned and hated; his reputation was irretrievably ruined. And there was no respite from the creditors who harried him whenever he showed his face on the streets. His friend Charles Biddle found him shut up in a boarding house, looking "pale and dejected . . . generally alone," and talking about committing suicide. As he always did, though, Burr recovered his optimism and by the spring of 1808, he was preparing to sail to England.

On June 9, the packet *Clarissa Ana* departed New York. Burr was aboard, registered as H. E. Edwards.

—⁓⁓—

The attack on the frigate *Chesapeake* in June 1807 had excited a nationwide clamor for war, but Navy Secretary Robert Smith and Treasury Secretary Albert Gallatin urged Jefferson not to act rashly. Going to war with England might well plunge America into the interminable, bloody Anglo–French war on the European mainland—the very outcome Jefferson did not want. Hadn't he condemned "foreign entanglements" in his 1801 inaugural address? With its resounding victory at Trafalgar in 1805, the Royal Navy now ruled the seas, but Napoleon's armies dominated the mainland, encouraging Jefferson in the hope that England might negotiate with America—and England did, to a point. While Britain was willing to apologize for the *Chesapeake* attack and discuss reparations, it would not consent to stop boarding U.S. ships to impress American seamen.

During the early 1790s, Jefferson and Madison had recommended trade sanctions to counteract England's trade restrictions, but were blocked by Alexander Hamilton. Now, encouraged by Smith and Gallatin, the Virginians dusted off their 15-year-old plan, while recognizing that targeting English imports exclusively would be tantamount to declaring war.

Their modified plan was an across-the-board trade embargo of all nations. All imports and exports were prohibited; only coastal trading was permitted. The Embargo Act of December 1807, its advocates believed, would deprive Europe of essential U.S. food products without a commensurate loss to America. British leaders would be forced to forswear impressment, a bloodless triumph for the Jefferson administration. But England found other markets and did not renounce impressment. Deprived of imports and foreign markets, the American economy nosedived into a deep depression. The Embargo's one lasting achievement—unrealized for years—was the creation of new American industries to make the finished goods that were no longer arriving from Europe.

—∿—

Even with America and Great Britain on the brink of war, Burr still tried to find English backers for his plan to invade Mexico. Unsurprisingly, he was rejected at every turn. But the trip wasn't entirely in vain; Burr made a lifelong friend of the famed philosopher and economist Jeremy Bentham, and he met Sir Walter Scott, Charles Lamb, and other distinguished Britons. American diplomats kept Jefferson and Madison informed of Burr's activities, and perhaps also whispered to their British counterparts that Burr's continuing presence in England might retard future negotiations. Whatever the reason, British immigration officials began deportation proceedings. Burr blamed "Mr. Jefferson, or the Spanish Juntas, or probably both." At one point, Burr, hoping to avoid deportation, tried to claim British citizenship, advancing the specious argument that because he was born in British-governed colonial America, he was, in fact, a British subject according to the adage "once an Englishman, always an Englishman." But he evidently had second thoughts about becoming a British citizen, for he dropped the matter. In 1809, Burr was expelled from England.

He sailed to Sweden, then to Denmark, and from Denmark to Germany. In Weimar, he became acquainted with the royal family, Schopenhauer's mother, the poet Wieland, and Goethe, and he nearly married the dazzling Mademoiselle de Reizenstein; but, as with his dalliance with British citizenship, Burr did not follow through to the wedding.

In February 1810, Burr was in Paris, offering to help Napoleon conquer Mexico. (Napoleon Bonaparte only dreamed of Mexican conquest; his nephew, Louis Napoleon, or Napoleon III, unfortunately acted on this impulse, with the result that his surrogate, the Austrian archduke Maximilian, was overthrown by Mexican rebels and executed in 1867.) Burr also advanced other proposals, such as drawing the United States into a war with England so that France, with Burr's assistance, could seize Canada, Florida, Cuba, and Mexico.

For months, the French, as they had with John Marshall in 1797, rebuffed him and feigned interest, ignored him and procrastinated. Burr was granted an audience with Napoleon's brother, Jerome Bonaparte, who had married the former Elizabeth Patterson of Baltimore and enjoyed a brief celebrity in Washington in 1805. All of Burr's lobbying came to nothing; all of his proposals were rejected. Louis Roux, a French functionary who made notes of the meetings with Burr, wrote that while Burr tried to enlist the French in his schemes against the Spanish colonies, he drew the line at breaking up the United States, despite the European powers' obvious interest in seeing the republic dissolved. "Mr. A. B. does not see these powers as having had any object other than the odious one of putting the country in disarray. . . . He had none himself, nor has he any desire to see one carried out."

Burr was ready to go home, but he discovered that the malice of the Virginians continued to shadow him. French officials, refusing him a passport, sent him to the U.S. consul—Alexander McRae, one of the government lawyers who had prosecuted Burr in Richmond. McRae curtly declined to help Burr unless he surrendered and agreed to stand trial in Ohio for the high misdemeanor charge pending against him there. The consul may only have been following the instructions of U.S. minister John Armstrong, a DeWitt Clinton follower who was probably adhering to the policy of President James Madison. After having encouraged French officials to continue blocking Burr's departure, McRae wrote to Secretary of State Robert Smith, the former Navy

Secretary, that he hoped his actions met Smith's "approbation and that of the President."

Destitute and barred from returning home, Burr shivered in a freezing little attic room in Paris, afflicted with headaches, piles, and chronic diarrhea, the result of his subsistence diet of rice and potatoes. To obtain money for food, he played whist and translated books published in English into French. One such book, he discovered, was a slanderous screed directed against him. Burr translated it anyway, needing the money.

—⟿—

For Theodosia's edification, Burr kept a journal and wrote letters. Composed with an air of determined cheerfulness, they made light of his tribulations and described with surprising frankness the many women whom he bedded. His shorthand for this was *muse*, a French hunting expression meaning "the beginning of the rutting time." He wrote of strolling for an hour "during which mus. mauv [bad *muse*]," then, upon returning to his hotel, encountering "the chambermaid, fat, not bad; *muse* again."

But Theodosia, reading between the lines, recognized her father's growing desperation. "Tell me that you are engaged in some pursuit worthy of you," she wrote to him.

When Burr's exile extended to two years and then three, Theodosia began appealing to well-connected former friends to assist her father. To Treasury Secretary Albert Gallatin, she wrote, "Must he ever remain . . . excommunicated from the participation of domestic enjoyments and the privileges of a citizen . . . ?" Receiving no reply from Gallatin, she tried First Lady Dolley Madison. Surely Mrs. Madison remembered that when she was a young widow, she had designated Aaron Burr in her will to be her son's guardian, and that it was Burr who had introduced her to his old Princeton classmate, James Madison, all those years ago.

Why . . . is my father banished from a country for which he has encountered wounds & dangers & fatigue for years? Why is he driven from his friends, from an only child, to pass an unlimited time in exile, and that, too, at an age when others are reaping the harvest of past toils?

Mrs. Madison could not assist her father. "She expresses great affection for me, calling me her *precious friend*,'" Theodosia told her half-brother, Frederick Prevost, "pays me some compliments badly teared & regrets that Mr M. finds it impossible to gratify my wishes & c."

In 1811, the French finally issued Burr a passport to leave the country, and he booked passage on a ship to New York. As the ship sailed to Amsterdam he wrote in his journal, "My windows look over the ocean; that ocean which separates me from all that is dear. With what pleasure I did greet it after three year's absence. . . ."

His happiness was soon dashed; a British privateer captured his ship in the North Sea, and Burr and the other passengers were unceremoniously dumped in London. Stranded and nearly penniless, Burr struggled just to survive during the winter of 1811–1812.

In March 1812, Burr borrowed money for passage on the *Aurora*, bound for Boston. Traveling under the assumed name of Monsieur Adolphus Arnot, he arrived in Boston on May 5, 1812, and disembarked without attracting any notice—he was wearing a wig and had grown out his whiskers. A month later, he was in New York City, trying to stay out of sight at the home of his loyal friends Samuel and Robert Swartwout.

—✳—

While Burr was away in Europe, a fire had destroyed the new Richmond Theatre on Academy Square on December 26, 1811, killing seventy-two people, including Burr's former lawyer, Benjamin Botts, and his wife. John Wickham's daughter, Julia, narrowly escaped; a rescuer dragged her by the hair from the burning building. The fire erupted in the stage scenery during the first act, and spread so rapidly that the victims were trapped inside the theater and incinerated. The entire nation mourned them. John Marshall, aided by Wickham, headed the committee that was organized to raise money for a monument to the dead. So much money was collected that instead of a monument being built, an interdenominational church, Monumental Church, was raised in 1814 on the ashes of the theater and the victims.

—∽—

Burr's homecoming in 1812 coincided with Congress's declaration of war on Great Britain. General James Wilkinson remained in command of the U.S. Army, despite numerous courts-martial, hearings, and inquiries into his conduct. Persevering and lucky, Wilkinson emerged without a single judgment against him, and still in the government's good graces, thanks to his loyal patron, Thomas Jefferson. In 1813, Wilkinson's surprise seizure of West Florida from the Spanish during an uncharacteristically rapid march to Mobile raised expectations that he would shake off all the rumors and scandals and prove himself to be a fighting general after all. But when he took command of seven thousand troops in upstate New York, his usual slowness and caution reasserted themselves. Eight hundred British troops repulsed his tentative thrust into Canada at Chrysler's Farm in November 1813. His disgusted officers requested a new commander, one who would not dose himself so liberally with whiskey and laudanum. But Wilkinson was not removed.

During the harsh winter of 1813–1814, Wilkinson's men suffered needlessly because he neglected to ensure delivery of food and clothing that was warehoused nearby. In the spring of 1814, he led four thousand troops on a new Canadian offensive, only to be stopped by 180 British troops in a stone mill. Wilkinson was court-martialed. But his great luck held one more time; he was acquitted of all charges. This time, however, he was not given another command, and with reluctance, he retired from the Army to his plantation south of New Orleans. He died in Mexico City in 1825 while waiting to receive a land grant in present-day Texas.

—∽—

The war rehabilitated the becalmed military careers of Winfield Scott and Andrew Jackson, who were both punished by Jefferson and Madison for publicly denouncing Wilkinson as the mastermind of the Burr conspiracy. Suspended for one year from the Army because he pronounced Wilkinson guilty of treason, Scott was a lieutenant colonel on the Canadian frontier when the war began. He soon proved that he was a capable combat officer, leading the successful attack against Fort George on Lake Ontario in May 1813, and, in July 1814, decisively defeating a brigade of British regulars on Chippewa Plain. By the end of the war, Scott was a brigadier general. In 1847, during the Mexican–American War, General Scott's army landed at Vera Cruz and marched into Mexico City, a textbook-perfect campaign that would have pleased Burr.

President Madison remembered Andrew Jackson's tirades against Jefferson and Wilkinson from the Virginia Capitol steps, and he may also have recalled how Jackson had supported James Monroe during the 1808 presidential campaign. For whatever reason, when new Army generals were appointed in 1812, Jackson was not among them. But Tennessee chose Jackson to command its fifteen hundred volunteers, even though he was forty-six and had scant military experience. Jackson made up for his inexperience with aggressiveness. While the U.S. Army fought the British regulars in Canada, the Tennessee volunteers met a British-incited threat in the Deep South—an uprising of young Creek Indians known as the Red Sticks, who had allied themselves with the British in hopes of blocking American expansion into their homeland. In a series of sharp, bloody battles in Alabama in 1813 and 1814, Jackson's Tennesseans defeated the Red Sticks.

Grudgingly recognizing Jackson's talents as a military leader, the Madison administration in 1814 commissioned him a major general in the regular U.S. Army. With the British aiming one last blow at the South in the hope of forcing a renegotiation of the Treaty of Ghent, which ostensibly had ended the war, Jackson, his Tennesseans, and a scratch force of the pirate Jean Lafitte's men and six hundred slaves dealt the British their worst land defeat of the war in January

1815 outside New Orleans, killing or wounding two thousand of the five thousand British regulars.

In 1816, Burr quietly lobbied for Jackson to be the Republicans' presidential candidate rather than James Monroe. The time had come, said Burr, to break up the Virginia "junto, this vile combination which rules and degrades the United States," even though, as Burr sarcastically observed, Monroe was "exactly suited" to the Virginians' purposes. "Naturally dull and stupid; extremely illiterate; indecisive to a degree that would be incredible to one who did not know him; pusillanimous, and, of course, hypocritical; has no opinion on any subject." The Virginians' grip on the President's House, however, remained as strong as ever; Jackson would have to wait twelve more years. In the meantime, General Jackson would complete the forcible acquisition of Spanish Florida begun in 1813 by Wilkinson—by defeating the Seminole Indians and forcing Spain to cede the rest of Florida to the United States.

—m—

Jefferson and Madison rewarded George Hay and William Wirt for their loyal pursuit of Burr, fruitless though it was. Hay was appointed a federal judge in Virginia and married James Monroe's daughter Eliza; Wirt became U.S. Attorney General, but is better remembered for his acclaimed biography of Patrick Henry.

Of Burr's attorneys, only John Wickham enjoyed a long, prosperous life; his wealthy Virginian clients made him one of Richmond's richest men. At the time of his death in 1839, he had fathered nineteen children, bred famous racehorses, built a grand neoclassical home that later became a National Historic Landmark, and had written what is believed to be the first biographical sketch of his good friend John Marshall. Benjamin Botts perished in the 1811 theater fire, and Edmund Randolph died in 1813 at the age of sixty. Luther Martin's health and solvency both collapsed, and he became an embarrassment in Baltimore. Always true to his friends, Burr brought Martin to New York and cared for him in his home until Martin's death in 1826 at the age of eighty-one.

—〰—

Jefferson devoted his post-presidency to his lifelong passion, Monticello; to helping establish the University of Virginia in nearby Charlottesville (Jefferson monitored the work's progress with a telescope from his Monticello veranda); and to his mechanical contrivances and farming experiments, the latter carried out by his hundred slaves and their overseers. He continued to meticulously record his mounting debts in his account books. Sixty-six years old when he left Washington, Jefferson, although a touch arthritic, was still lean and fit enough to ride daily. He stayed mentally agile by dabbling in philosophy, reading omnivorously, collecting books—which later helped launch the Library of Congress—tinkering with his gadgets, and sustaining a massive correspondence. He wrote hundreds of letters to his successors, Madison and Monroe, and to John Adams, his former political foe and latter-day friend.

Jefferson never forgave John Marshall, who continued to preside over the Supreme Court even after Jefferson's death in 1826. In 1821, Marshall and the Judiciary could still rile Jefferson, as evidenced by his letter to Judge Spencer Roane of the Virginia Court of Appeals, written after Roane, in the Richmond *Enquirer*, criticized Marshall's extension of federal power.

> The great object of my fear is the federal judiciary. That body, like gravity, ever acting, with noiseless foot, and unalarming advance, gaining ground step by step, and holding what it gains, is ingulphing [sic] insidiously the special governments into the jaws of that which feeds them.

—〰—

Marshall was equally uncharitable in his few recorded statements about his great nemesis, having taken to derisively calling Jefferson the "great Lama of the mountains." But the publication of Jefferson's letter to Roane inspired Marshall to pen his most barbed evaluation of the former president since the Burr trial. In August 1821, he wrote to his friend Joseph Story:

> He [Jefferson] is among the most ambitious &, I suspect, among the most unforgiving of men. His great power is over the mass of the people & this power is chiefly acquired by professions of democracy. Every check on the wild impulse of the moment is a check on his own power, & he is unfriendly to the source from which it flows. He looks, of course, with ill will at an independent judiciary.

When Jefferson died on July 4, 1826, only hours before his faithful correspondent, John Adams, Marshall did not publicly comment on the passing of his cousin and fellow Virginian.

Marshall presided over the Supreme Court until his death on July 6, 1835, at the age of seventy-nine. By then, the great era of the court's consolidation of power had passed, as had the period known as "The Marshall Court." But Marshall's contributions would stand, rock-like, for centuries: He had affirmed the Constitution's primacy and established the Judiciary as an independent branch of government. Between 1801 and 1835, he wrote 519 of the court's 1,106 opinions, and 36 of the 62 decisions that were devoted to constitutional questions.

Marshall was pessimistic about "the sovereign will of the people" that elected Andrew Jackson president in 1828. The following year, at the Virginia Constitutional Convention—held in the same room as Burr's treason trial—Marshall and the aged remnants of the Revolutionary War's old guard—former Presidents James Madison and James Monroe, John Randolph, and William Branch Giles—arose one last time to block changes that they feared would damage the instrument they had helped create all those years ago.

—∽∾—

Harman Blennerhassett rejoined his family in Mississippi in 1808, bought a thousand acres near Port Gibson, and started a cotton plantation, "La Cache." However, the Irishman's business ineptitude and lucklessness spoiled his fresh start. La Cache steadily lost money, and the Embargo and the War of 1812 closed off markets for the Blennerhassetts' crops.

In a desperate attempt to raise funds, Blennerhassett tried to blackmail Joseph Alston, who was running for governor of South Carolina. Blennerhassett warned Alston that unless he repaid the $15,000 that Blennerhassett had advanced to the Burr expedition and that Alston had indemnified but not repaid, he would expose Alston's connection to the Burr conspiracy. Alston didn't send the money, and Blennerhassett didn't publish anything. Blennerhassett renewed the threat two years later, in 1813—when Alston was governor—with the same result.

The Blennerhassetts sold La Cache and moved to Montreal, where Harman had been promised a court position by an old school friend, the Duke of Richmond, the new governor-general of Canada. But some of Harman's unluckiness must have rubbed off on Richmond; he was bitten by a rabid fox and died. Harman's promised job went to someone else. He practiced law in Montreal until poor health and age forced him to return with his family to England, where he moved in with his spinster sister, Avice, in Bath. Later, the family moved again, to the Channel Islands.

Harman died on Guernsey in 1831 at the age of 66. He never again saw his island, now Blennerhassett Island State Park, West Virginia. His surname is well known in the mid-Ohio Valley, gracing a nearby town, an historic Parkersburg, W. Va., hotel, and the ferry that brings visitors from Parkersburg to Harman's and Margaret's island.

Margaret was left penniless and lived with relatives the rest of her days. In 1842, she returned to the United States to petition Congress to reimburse her for the fifteen boats the government had seized near Marietta, Ohio, thirty-six years earlier. Henry Clay presented her petition to the Senate. Before the Senate could act, however, Margaret died, heart-broken over her many disappointments.

Never reconciled to the loss of her beautiful Ohio River island, Margaret had written:

There rose the seat, where once, in pride of life,
My eye could mark the queenly river's flow,
In summer's calmness, or in winter's strife,
Swollen with rains, or battling with the snow.
Never, again, my heart with such joy shall know.
Havoc, and ruin, rampant war, have pass'd
Over that isle with their destroying blast.

—∽∽—

A month after returning to New York, fifty-six-year-old Aaron Burr reopened his law practice. His four-year exile and the war with England might have persuaded some people to forgive Burr, but not Burr's creditors; upon learning that he had returned, they immediately began badgering him for payment. Burr knew that in order to keep them at bay, he had to start making money; his law practice, in its first twelve days, generated $2,000 worth of trade. When the novelty wore off and there were fewer clients, Burr, still buried in debt, resigned himself to working for the rest of his life.

But he was often able to forget his financial troubles in the happy anticipation of soon being reunited with Theodosia and his beloved grandson, Aaron Burr Alston, nicknamed "Gampy." During his exile, Burr had tried to hoard trinkets, coins, and books for Gampy. For years, he had imagined handing the gifts to the ten-year-old and giving Theodosia the journal to which he had confided his private thoughts and observations in the hope that his beloved daughter might one day read them.

But just as fate had robbed Burr of his parents and grandparents in the span of a year, so now did it again conspire against him.

Two letters arrived that caused the normally stoical Burr to sink into despair.

A few miserable days past, my dear father, and your late letters would have gladdened my soul; and now I rejoice at their contents as much as it is possible for me to rejoice at any thing; but there is no more joy for me; the world is a blank.

I have lost my boy. My child is gone forever. He expired on the 30th of June. My head is not now sufficiently collected to say anything further. May Heaven, by other blessings, make you some amends for the noble grandson you have lost.

Burr tore open the second letter, from his son-in-law, Governor Joseph Alston. It was equally heart-rending. "That boy, on whom all rested . . . he who was to have redeemed all your glory, and shed new luster upon our families—that boy, at once our happiness and our pride, is taken from us—*is dead.*"

Twenty-nine-year-old Theodosia's constitution, frail in the best of times, buckled under the shock of her son's death. By turn feverish, lethargic, and depressed, she wasted away. Fearing that they might now lose Theodosia in addition to young Aaron, Burr and Joseph Alston, whose duties as governor and state militia commander prevented him from leaving South Carolina, arranged for her to travel to New York. They hoped that her native city's bracing northern air and her father's company would restore her health. Rather than expose her to the rigors of a long overland trip by coach, Burr and Alston decided that she would instead travel by ship, a journey of just five or six days.

Theodosia was bringing her father a trunk filled with his papers, which he had left with her when he sailed to Europe in 1808, and her baggage might have also contained a new portrait of herself. As her embarkation date neared, her spirits noticeably improved; she appeared to be looking forward to the change of scene. But Dr. Timothy Greene, a family friend whom Burr had sent to watch over his daughter, warned, "You must not be surprised to see her very low, feeble, and emaciated. Her complaint is an almost incessant nervous fever."

In Georgetown, South Carolina, Theodosia, Dr. Greene, and Theodosia's maid boarded the schooner *Patriot*, which had just returned from a privateering cruise against the British. Governor Joseph Alston handed the captain a note requesting his wife's safe passage to New York, to be presented to British warship officers should they stop the *Patriot* during her cruise.

The *Patriot* sailed on December 31, 1812, and vanished without a trace.

—∿—

For weeks, Burr, a lonely-looking figure, haunted the Battery, seeking any news of his daughter's ship, but there was none. To his shattered son-in-law, who had lost his entire family in seven months, Burr confided that he was now "severed from the human race." As he later said, "When I realized the truth of her death, the world became a blank to me, and life had then lost all its value." Unlike Burr, who believed it a sign of weakness to regret what was gone, Alston was unable to go through the motions of living; he died three years later at the age of thirty-seven.

—∿—

The mysterious disappearance of the *Patriot* and Aaron Burr's daughter caused a nationwide sensation. The ship's fate would never be known with certainty but was the subject of rumors and speculation for more than half a century.

While she probably sank in a gale that British warship logs report to have struck Cape Hatteras when the schooner would have been sailing through the "Graveyard of the Atlantic" off North Carolina, other stories have persisted down through the years. The most enduring, which launched a dozen variations, originated with the confessions of two pirates before their execution on a U.S. naval vessel in 1820. Jean Desfarges and Robert Johnson claimed to have signed on the *Patriot* as sailors. After a few days at sea, they said, they locked the passengers and crew below, looted the ship, and then scuttled it with everyone aboard. The pirates' confession, however, suffered from two major factual errors: They said the *Patriot* sailed from Charleston, instead of Georgetown; and they said they enjoyed continuous fair weather.

Another popular version had the *Patriot* running aground on North Carolina's Outer Banks, where the notorious "wreckers" who inhabited the area murdered everyone aboard. The wrecker story

was revived decades later when a woman's portrait, possibly Theodosia's, which she might have been bringing to her father, turned up
in the humble hut of a wrecker's ill, seventy-year-old widow in
Nags Head, North Carolina. The portrait's subject was fashionably
dressed, frail, dark-haired, and dark-eyed—in other words, the very
image of Theodosia Burr Alston. The widow, Mrs. Polly Mann,
told the physician attending her, Dr. William Gaskins Pool of
Elizabeth City, North Carolina, that her late husband had found it
on a grounded, empty ship in a cabin littered with women's belongings. Besides claiming the portrait, her husband had also taken a
trunk packed with black silk dresses and a black lace shawl. Mrs.
Mann gave the trunk and the portrait to Pool and, years later, it
became part of the collection of the Lewis Walpole Library at Yale
University. The identity of the portrait subject has never been
determined. While Burr descendants believe that the woman is
Theodosia, Alston descendants disagree.

—◊◊◊—

Bereft of children and grandchildren, Burr became a foster parent
and guardian to a brood of children. He was a natural teacher, as
his rearing of Theodosia had demonstrated, and children loved
him. As he entered his seventies, his willingness to take responsi-
bility for feeding, clothing, and educating young children belied his
assertion that he was now severed from the human race.

His avocation as a guardian began with his litigation of the
estate of Mecdef Eden, a wealthy New York brewer who, upon his
death in 1798, had left his considerable property to two sons, who
had then squandered it in just a few years. After one of the sons
died, Burr took up the survivor's quest to recover some of the property, and even moved the son's impoverished family into his own
home. With occasional assistance from Daniel Webster and Martin
Van Buren (rumored to be Burr's illegitimate son), Burr recovered
a former Eden farm, followed by more valuable plots of land owned
by corporations inside the city, restoring the estate to solvency. By
degrees, he also took charge of educating the surviving son's three

stepdaughters, Sally Ann, Elizabeth, and Rebecca, and became their guardian when their father died in 1819.

Burr began taking in other children as well—the sons and daughters of his late wife's relatives, after they had lost their families; and children sent to him by former paramours who claimed they were his. He fed, clothed, and educated them all, either in his home, in homes that he found for them in other cities, or in boarding schools.

Absorbed as he was with his law practice and his growing family, Burr was enjoying "a green old age" when George W. Johnson visited him in 1832. The Buffalo lawyer described meeting "a cheerful, fine-looking gentlemanly old man."

—◊◊◊—

When he was seventy-seven, Burr married Eliza Bowen Jumel, believed to be the richest woman in America. Better known as Madame Jumel, she was the daughter of a streetwalker and was reputedly once a courtesan herself. She was the widow of Stephen Jumel, a wealthy French-born wine trader, to whose fortune she had added considerably by making shrewd investments. After their marriage, Burr promptly moved into her enormous Manhattan home (the Morris–Jumel Mansion on Washington Heights) and began happily spending her money, going through thousands of dollars in months. This was more intolerable than any infidelity would have been to Burr's mercenary bride; she filed for divorce after just a year of marriage, in July 1834. As they traded adultery accusations, Madame Jumel got a court order keeping Burr away from her property.

—◊◊◊—

Months later, Burr suffered a major stroke, and friends moved him into the old Jay Mansion, which had been converted into a boarding house. When it was condemned, he was taken to the Hotel St. James at Port Richmond, Staten Island. There he died, at the age of eighty, on September 14, 1836, the very day that his divorce from Madame Jumel became final.

During the last year of his life, Burr became excited when he learned of the revolution in Texas. "There! You see? I was right! I was only thirty years too soon. What was treason in me thirty years ago, is patriotism now."

Aaron Burr was buried with honors in Princeton Cemetery, in the President's Plot, beside the graves of his father and grandfather. The members of the College of New Jersey's Cliosophic Society, which Burr had supported all his life, followed his remains to the cemetery. For thirty days, they observed his passing by wearing strips of black crepe on their left arms.

Today, yellowwood and white pine trees shade Aaron Burr's final resting place, and the inscription on his modest headstone is weathered and difficult to read. Yards away, traffic grinds by on a busy residential street.

In the first decade of the twentieth century, when Woodrow Wilson was president of Princeton College, he visited Burr's grave with Walter Flavius McCaleb, that era's leading scholar on the Burr conspiracy.

The men removed their hats, and Wilson murmured, "How misunderstood, how maligned."

—⁓—

Indeed, the name Aaron Burr remains a byword for underhandedness, disloyalty, and mischief of every kind, from personal licentiousness to dirty politics, from dueling to treason. The *New York Review of 1838* wrote of Burr: "a monster of licentiousness, a reckless trifler with feminine hearts, a traitor to his country . . . Machiavelli, Don Juan and Benedict Arnold rolled into one . . . a festering mass of moral putrefaction." *Harper's Magazine* in 1857 began a story with:

> There never was a greater villain than Aaron Burr—never! What is written of him—what has become history and world talk—is nothing to the unwritten, untold deeds of darkness that he was ever perpetrating. His whole life was intrigue. Woman was his spoil. . . .

While much was made during his lifetime and afterward of
Burr's countless dalliances with women—and Burr was sexually
active, even hyperactive—he was generally faithful to his wife while
she was alive, more than can be said for many public men. When he
was a widower, his mistresses were usually single women or
widows, and he condemned exploitative relationships with young,
vulnerable women.

Burr also lived by a strong personal code of asceticism in eating
and drinking, and habitual politeness and courtliness toward
women; he forbore any show of dismay or unhappiness, and tried
to be unfailingly loyal, discreet, and generous. All praiseworthy
attributes, they were better suited to a gentler, bygone era, as were
Burr's habits of never speaking ill of others or defending himself
against slander. His adherence to this code handicapped him in the
ruthless, rough-and-tumble politics of the early nineteenth century.
His rapport with children, his willingness to personally guarantee
their welfare, and his belief that girls deserved the same education
as boys—in Burr's time, a radical view—all bespoke a generosity of
spirit for which he is rarely credited.

Yet he was prone to a singular weakness, a politician's failing:
telling people what he thought they wanted to hear, either to win
their friendship or their support. While there is no evidence that
Burr actually made any effort to separate the West, he certainly
spoke of it—possibly encouraged by men like George Morgan and
William Eaton, who had something to gain by running to Jefferson
with stories about Burr: for Eaton, reimbursement for his Tripoli
expedition; for Morgan, the speedy settlement of his Indiana land
claims. Significantly, none of the men implicated with Burr stated
in their correspondence or journals that he ever contemplated a
separatist scheme, even when, as in the case of Harman Blennerhassett, they were offered amnesty for such testimony. Once, when
asked by his friend and biographer, Matthew L. Davis, whether he
had planned to detach the West, Burr is said to have replied, "No, I
would as soon have thought of taking possession of the moon, and
informing my friends that I intended to divide it among them."

—m—

But what if Burr *had* invaded the Southwest and Mexico? The Civil War might have occurred earlier if Burr, an abolitionist, had ruled Texas and Mexico. He would have barred the westward migration of slavery; tensions between North and South might have come to a boil long before 1861. But without the Southwest's resources, the South would have been defeated quicker. General Ulysses S. Grant's 1863 victory at Vicksburg exposed the Confederacy's dependence on the Southwest for food, cotton, and men. Burr's triumph, however, would not necessarily have spared Texas the bloodlettings at the Alamo and San Jacinto. The proud, independent Texans would have bridled at any sort of Mexican dominion—whether Burr's or Antonio Lopez de Santa Anna's—and would have rebelled. Inevitably, America would have been drawn into a war with Mexico, with the same outcome.

The one certainty of the Burr Conspiracy is that Burr planned an expedition against the Spanish Southwest and Mexico—a filibuster in the spirit of those attempted by George Rogers Clark, William Blount, and Francisco de Miranda. He turned to this sketchy plan only when its success was practically assured by General James Wilkinson, and when other avenues for his ambition were closed to him: politics, by Jefferson, the Virginians, and the Republican press; and the law, by the duel with Alexander Hamilton that made Burr a wanted man in New York and New Jersey.

Burr's reputation, blackened by his unwillingness to respond to his enemies until it was too late, might have eventually recovered, if his most important papers had not vanished in 1813 with his daughter and her ship. As a result, the prevailing accounts of the 1800 election, the Hamilton duel, and the Burr conspiracy overwhelmingly reflect the opinions of Thomas Jefferson, his allies, and the Republican newspapers.

Yet reputation appeared to matter little to Burr, even in old age, when slanderous stories still surfaced occasionally. Once, when shown an especially biting newspaper attack, Burr shrugged and said,

"I don't care what they say of me. They may say whatever they please. I let them alone. I only ask to be let alone." Another time, when accosted by a woman who said to him, "Why, colonel, if they were to accuse you of murder, I don't think you'd deny it," Burr responded:

> What good would it do? Every man likes his own opinion best. He may not have a hundred thousand dollars, but he has his opinion. A man's opinion is his pride, his wealth, himself. As far as I am concerned, they may indulge in any opinion they choose.

After his first meeting with Burr, George W. Johnson, the Buffalo lawyer, wrote of him:

> A great man, and perhaps as good as the average of our statesmen. A victim of circumstances. Had another vote made him president instead of Jefferson, their destinies might have been exchanged. He was a brave man. If it is ever right to kill in a duel, he was right to kill Hamilton. . . . He was fond of women, but was always decent: worse offenses than that. Not by any means a model man—a good man; but not so bad as it is the fashion to paint him.

—∾—

In orchestrating the destruction of Aaron Burr's political fortunes, Thomas Jefferson had developed habits of mind that account for his sometimes obsessive pursuit of his former vice president in 1807. Jefferson had so often pronounced Burr a rogue politician, for the sake of eliminating him as a rival, that he finally came to believe it as fact, and thus was able to justify any action against him: character assassination, political muggings, even rewriting history. After Republican newspapers reported that Burr, and not Jefferson, had welcomed the Federalists' overtures in February 1801—an amazing statement, since the Federalist vote swing benefited Jefferson, not Burr—the president had watched contentedly as his vice president's political star sank out of sight. Then he denied Burr a second term as vice president. To drive a stake through Burr's hopes of becoming New York governor and, perhaps, rebuilding his political base, Jefferson first pledged to not take sides in the race, then quietly let Republicans know that he favored Burr's opponent, Morgan Lewis. As a result, Burr thought it safe to run, and then lost. Finally, to make certain that history judged the 1800 election the way that Jefferson wished it to be remembered, he committed his version of it to the *Anas*.

In his *History of the United States of America During the First Administration of Thomas Jefferson*, Henry Adams described the forces that coalesced to destroy Burr: "Never in the history of the United States did so powerful a combination of rival politicians unite to break down a single man as that which arrayed itself against Burr. . . ."

From habits of thinking acquired during this systematic eradication of Burr's political hopes, Jefferson was able to contrive treason out of a slipshod filibuster and, without a shred of solid evidence, fix it thus in the public mind—as well as in history. In reaching this conclusion, the president had to ignore Joseph Hamilton Daviess's warnings about James Wilkinson and the newspaper reports that claimed that the General of the Army was a Spanish spy. He had to overlook Wilkinson's puzzling dilatoriness—insubordination, really—in shifting his command from St. Louis to New Orleans in 1806. Jefferson's malice toward Burr made it easy for him to believe—or profess to believe, anyway—Wilkinson's wild stories about Burr's army of thousands descending the Mississippi River, and to declare a national emergency, pronounce Burr guilty of treason in a message to Congress, and launch an unprecedented dragnet for testimony that would convict him.

Had a more pliable judge than Chief Justice John Marshall presided over Burr's treason trial, the Judiciary might have evolved into an instrument of repression, as it is in other nations. Rather than being interpreted as the Constitution's framers wished, the charge of treason might have become a means of silencing political opponents. The president and his official papers might today be immune from subpoena, and lie concealed behind a curtain of unassailable secrecy—rather than the more amorphous barrier of executive privilege established by Jefferson's refusal to appear in court and his excision of confidential material from the documents that he produced. Another judge might not have interfered with Jefferson's fervent wish to see his former vice president convicted of treason and sentenced to the gallows.

But would Jefferson have allowed Burr to hang? Most assuredly, no. Jefferson, the most accomplished politician of his era, would have known that executing Burr would have handed a galvanizing issue to Burr's infuriated supporters, to the Federalists, and to the disgruntled elements of Jefferson's own party, jeopardizing Jefferson's cherished plans for a Virginia dynasty in the President's House that would last until 1825. By commuting the death sentence, Jefferson would have washed away the traces of his own pathological pursuit of Burr in the healing waters of clemency.

John Marshall's refusal to compromise Constitutional protections thwarted Jefferson's attempt to indulge in political license. By defining treason in strictly Constitutional terms, Marshall removed it from the domain of "constructive" interpretations, and placed it beyond the reach of politics. His principled stubbornness placed the chief justice squarely in Jefferson's sights, just as he had foreseen. But his dignified impartiality, aided by the diversion provided by the HMS *Leopard*'s attack on the *Chesapeake,* shielded him from removal and the Judiciary from being subordinated to the Executive and Legislative branches.

The pursuit of Aaron Burr and his alleged co-conspirators dominated America's public life for a full year, and resulted in no convictions and no jail sentences. The defendants went free because of four pivotal decisions by Chief Justice Marshall. The attempts made to then punish him and the Judiciary failed; Marshall kept his job for 28 more years. By any measure, Jefferson's crusade against Aaron Burr, John Marshall, and the Judiciary was a debacle.

But the trial and its aftermath scarred all three men: Jefferson's libertarian reputation was tarnished, Burr's life was irreparably ruined, and Marshall's public standing suffered.

Jefferson's actions during 1807 marred an otherwise superlative presidential record. Jefferson, who rarely admitted his mistakes, did not this time, either. And he never wavered in his support of General James Wilkinson, although he must have believed that Wilkinson had been a Spanish agent. Jefferson's hatred of Marshall remained immutable, but he found Burr, as always, to be problematic; the former vice president kindled in Jefferson a mixture of admiration, fear, jealousy, and vindictiveness. Jefferson's thoughts on Burr were sometimes even tinged with regret over Burr's wasted potential—without any recognition of his own indispensable role in that result. In one of these reflective moments, Jefferson wrote:

"No man's history proves better the value of honesty. With that, what might he [Burr] not have been!"

Bibliography

Abernethy, Thomas Perkins. *The Burr Conspiracy*. New York: Oxford University Press, 1954.

Adams, Henry. *History of the United States of America During the First Administration of Thomas Jefferson*, Vol. II. New York: Antiquarian Press, 1962.

Adams, John. *The Works of John Adams*. Freeport, N.Y.: Books for Libraries Press, 1969.

Alexander, Holmes Moss. *Aaron Burr: The Proud Pretender*. New York: Harper and Brothers, 1937.

Ambrose, Stephen E. *Undaunted Courage: Meriwether Lewis, Thomas Jefferson, and the Opening of the American West*. New York: Touchstone, 1997.

American Historical Review, Vols. X, XIX. London: Macmillan, 1905, 1914.

American State Papers. Documents, Legislative and Executive, of the Congress of the United States. Washington: Gales and Seaton, 1832.

Beirne, Francis F. *Shout Treason: The Trial of Aaron Burr*. New York: Hastings House, 1959.

Beveridge, Albert J. *The Life of John Marshall*. Boston, New York: Houghton Mifflin, 1919.

Blennerhassett, Margaret. *The Widow of the Rock and other Poems*. Montreal: E. V. Sparhawk, 1824.

Boyer, Paul S. (ed). *The Oxford Companion to United States History*. Oxford, New York: Oxford University Press, 2001.

Brady, Joseph P. *The Trial of Aaron Burr*. New York: Neale, 1913.

Bruce, William Cabell. *John Randolph of Roanoke, 1773–1833*. New York: Octagon, 1970.

Brunson, B. R. *The Adventures of Samuel Swartwout in the Age of Jefferson and Jackson.* Lewiston, N.Y.: Edwin Mellen, 1989.

Burr, Aaron, Matthew L. Davis (ed.). *Memoirs of Aaron Burr.* Freeport, N.Y.: Books for Libraries Press, 1970.

———, Mary-Jo Kline (ed.). *Political Correspondence and Public Papers of Aaron Burr.* Princeton, N.J.: Princeton University Press, 1983.

Chernow, Ron. *Alexander Hamilton.* New York: Penguin, 2004.

Christian, W. Asbury. *Richmond, Her Past and Present.* Richmond: L. H. Jenkins, 1912.

Clark, Daniel. *Proofs of the Corruption of Gen. James Wilkinson, and of his Connexion with Aaron Burr.* Freeport, N.Y.: Books for Libraries Press, 1970.

Clark, Thomas D., and John D. W. Guice. *Frontiers in Conflict: The Old Southwest, 1795–1830.* Albuquerque: University of New Mexico Press, 1989.

Concise Dictionary of American Biography. New York: Charles Scribner's Sons, 1964.

Constitution of the United States, with the Declaration of Independence and the Articles of Confederation. New York: Barnes & Noble, 2002.

Côté, Richard N. *Theodosia Burr Alston: Portrait of a Prodigy.* Mount Pleasant, S.C.: Corinthian Books, 2002.

Cowley, Robert (ed). *What Ifs? of American History: Eminent Historians Imagine What Might Have Been.* New York: G.P. Putnam's Sons, 2003.

Cox, Isaac Joslin. *American Historical Review.* London: Macmillan, 1914.

Dabney, Virginius. *Richmond: The Story of a City.* Garden City, N.Y.: Doubleday, 1976.

DeConde, Alexander. *This Affair of Louisiana.* New York: Charles Scribner's Sons, 1976.

Duke, Maurice, and Daniel P. Jordan (eds). *A Richmond Reader, 1733–1983.* Chapel Hill, N.C.: University of North Carolina Press, 1983.

Elliott, John Carroll, and Ellen Gale Hammett. *Charged With Treason: Jury Verdict, Not Guilty.* Parsons, W. Va.: McClain, 1986.

Ellis, Joseph J. *American Sphinx: The Character of Thomas Jefferson.* New York: Alfred A. Knopf, 1997.

Ellis, Richard E. *The Jeffersonian Crisis: Courts and Politics in the Young Republic.* New York: Oxford University Press, 1971.

Elsmere, Jane Shaffer. *Justice Samuel Chase.* Muncie, Ind.: Janevar, 1980.

The Examination of Col. Aaron Burr. Richmond: Seaton Grantland, 1807.

Fitch, Raymond E. (ed). *Breaking With Burr: Harman Blennerhassett's Journal, 1807.* Athens: Ohio University Press, 1988.

Fleming, Thomas J. *Duel: Alexander Hamilton, Aaron Burr, and the Future of America.* New York: Basic Books, 1999.

Frazier, Ian. "Route 3." *The New Yorker,* February 16 & 23, 2004.

Funk & Wagnalls New Encyclopedia. Funk & Wagnalls, 1983.

Gallatin, Albert. *Selected Writings of Albert Gallatin.* Indianapolis, New York: Bobbs-Merrill, 1967.

Gerber, Scott Douglas (ed.). *Seriatim: The Supreme Court before John Marshall.* New York, London: New York University Press, 1998.

Gilbert, Felix (gen. ed.). *The Norton History of Modern Europe.* New York: Norton, 1970.

Hamilton, Alexander. *The Papers of Alexander Hamilton.* New York: Columbia University Press, 1977.

Hay, Thomas Robson, and M. R. Werner. *The Admirable Trumpeter: A Biography of General James Wilkinson.* Garden City, N.Y.: Doubleday, Doran, 1941.

Heidler, David S., and Jeanne T. Heidler (eds.). *Encyclopedia of the War of 1812.* Santa Barbara, Denver: ABC-CLIO, 1997.

Hollon, W. Eugene. *The Lost Pathfinder: Zebulon Montgomery Pike.* Norman: University of Oklahoma Press, 1949.

Irving, Pierre M. *The Life and Letters of Washington Irving.* New York: G.P. Putnam, 1863.

Irving, Washington. *Life of George Washington.* New York: A. L. Burt, 1855.

Jackson, Andrew, Harold D. Moser (ed.). *Papers of Andrew Jackson.* Knoxville: University of Tennessee Press, 1984.

Jacobs, James Ripley. *Tarnished Warrior: Major-General James Wilkinson.* New York: Macmillan, 1938.

James, James Alton. *The Life of George Rogers Clark.* Chicago: University of Chicago Press, 1928.

Jefferson, Thomas. *The Autobiography of Thomas Jefferson.* New York: Capricorn, 1959.

————. *The Complete Anas of Thomas Jefferson.* New York: Round Table Press, 1903.

————, John P. Foley (ed.). *The Jeffersonian Cyclopedia.* New York: Russell & Russell, 1900.

————. *The Papers of Thomas Jefferson.* Princeton, Oxford: Princeton University Press, 2000.

————, Paul Leicester Ford (ed.). *The Writings of Thomas Jefferson.* New York, London: Putnam, 1897.

————. *Writings of Thomas Jefferson.* Washington: Thomas Jefferson Memorial Association, 1903.

Jenkinson, Isaac. *Aaron Burr: His Personal and Political Relations with Thomas Jefferson and Alexander Hamilton.* Richmond: Cullaton, 1902.

Kennedy, Roger G. *Burr, Hamilton, and Jefferson: A Study in Character.* New York: Oxford University Press, 2000.

King, Charles R. *The Life and Correspondence of Rufus King.* New York: Putnam, 1897.

Letters in Relation to Burr's Conspiracy, Library of Congress Web Site.

Levy, Leonard W. *Jefferson and Civil Liberties: The Darker Side.* Cambridge: The Belknap Press of Harvard University Press, 1963.

Lomask, Milton. *Aaron Burr.* New York: Farrar, Straus, Giroux, 1982.

Loth, David Goldsmith. *Chief Justice: John Marshall and the Growth of the Republic.* New York: Norton, 1949.

Madison, James. *James Madison Papers.* Presidential Papers Microfilm. Davis Library, University of North Carolina, Chapel Hill.

Malone, Dumas. *Jefferson the President.* Boston: Little, Brown, 1974.

Marshall, John. *The Papers of John Marshall.* Chapel Hill: University of North Carolina Press, 1993.

Masterson, William H. *William Blount.* Baton Rouge: Louisiana State University Press, 1954.

McCaleb, Walter Flavius. *The Aaron Burr Conspiracy.* New York: Argosy-Antiquarian, 1966.

————. *A New Light on Aaron Burr.* New York: Argosy-Antiquarian, 1963.

Melton, Buckner F., Jr. *Aaron Burr: Conspiracy to Treason.* New York: Wiley, 2002.

————. *The First Impeachment: The Constitution's Framers and the Case of Senator William Blount.* Macon, Ga.: Mercer University Press, 1998.

Minnigerode, Meade. *Lives and Times: Four Informal American Biographies.* New York, London: Putnam, 1925.

Mordecai, Samuel. *Richmond in By-Gone Days.* Richmond: George M. West, 1856.

Morison, Samuel Eliot. *The Oxford History of the American People.* New York, Scarborough, Ontario: New American Library, 1972.

Munford, Robert Beverley, Jr. *Richmond Homes and Memories.* Richmond: Garrett and Massie, 1936.

Mushkat, Jerome. *Tammany: The Evolution of a Political Machine, 1789–1865.* Syracuse, N.Y.: Syracuse University Press, 1971.

Nettels, Curtis P. *The Emergence of a National Economy, 1775–1815.* New York, Evanston, London: Harper & Row, 1962.

The Norton Anthology of American Literature. New York, London: Norton, 1979.

The Oxford Dictionary of Quotations. Third Edition. Oxford, New York, Toronto, Melbourne: Oxford University Press, 1980.

Parmet, Herbert S., and Marie B. Hecht. *Aaron Burr: Portrait of an Ambitious Man.* New York: Macmillan, 1967.

Parton, James. *The Life and Times of Aaron Burr.* New York: Mason Brothers, 1858.

Pickett, Albert James. *History of Alabama, and Incidentally of Georgia and Mississippi, from the Earliest Period.* Charleston, S.C.: Walker and James, 1851.

Political Graveyard Web site. http://politicalgraveyard.com.

Reardon, John J. *Edmund Randolph: A Biography.* New York: Macmillan, 1974.

Remini, Robert V. *Andrew Jackson and the Course of American Empire, 1767–1821.* New York, Hagerstown, San Francisco, London: Harper & Row, 1977.

Richmond *Enquirer.* Microfilm. Library of Virginia.

Robertson, David. *Reports of the Trials of Colonel Aaron Burr . . . in the Circuit Court of the United States . . . in the District of Virginia.* Philadelphia: Hopkins and Earle, 1808.

Rogers, James A. *Theodosia and Other Pee Dee Sketches.* Columbia, S.C.: R. L. Bryan, 1978.

Rogow, Arnold A. *A Fatal Friendship: Alexander Hamilton and Aaron Burr.* New York: Hill and Wang, 1998.

Safford, William H. *The Blennerhassett Papers.* Cincinnati: Moore, Wilstach & Baldwin, 1864.

Schachner, Nathan. *Aaron Burr, A Biography.* New York: A.S. Barnes, 1961.

———. *Alexander Hamilton.* New York, London: Thomas Yoseloff, 1946.

———. *Thomas Jefferson, A Biography.* New York, London: Thomas Yoseloff, 1951.

Scott, Lt. Gen. Winfield. *Memoirs.* Freeport, N.Y.: Books for Libraries Press, 1970.

Shevory, Thomas C. (ed.). *John Marshall's Achievement: Law, Politics, and Constitutional Interpretations.* New York, Westport, Conn., London: Greenwood Press, 1989.

Simon, James F. *What Kind of Nation: Thomas Jefferson, John Marshall, and the Epic Struggle to Create a United States.* New York: Simon & Schuster, 2002.

Stanard, Mary Newton. *Richmond: Its People and Its Story.* Philadelphia, London: Lippincott, 1923.

Stites, Francis N. *John Marshall, Defender of the Constitution.* Boston, Toronto: Little, Brown, 1981.

Swick, Ray. *An Island Called Eden: The Story of Harman and Margaret Blennerhassett.* Parkersburg, W.Va.: Parkersburg Printing Co., 2000.

———. "Theodosia Burr Alston," *The South Atlantic Quarterly,* Autumn 1975, Vol. 74, No. 4.

Thomas, Evan. *John Paul Jones: Sailor, Hero, Father of the American Navy.* New York: Simon & Schuster, 2003.

Tucker, Glenn. *Dawn Like Thunder: The Barbary Wars and the Birth of the U.S. Navy.* Indianapolis: Bobbs-Merrill, 1963.

Ubbelohde, Carl, Maxine Benson, and Duane A. Smith. *A Colorado History.* Boulder: Pruett, 1988.

Vidal, Gore. *Burr: A Novel.* New York: Random House, 1973.

Virginia Argus. Microfilm. Library of Virginia.

Walters, Raymond, Jr. *Albert Gallatin: Jeffersonian Financier and Diplomat.* New York: Macmillan, 1957.

Wandell, Samuel H., and Meade Minnigerode. *Aaron Burr.* New York, London: The Knickerbocker Press, G. P. Putnam's Sons, 1925.

Wheelan, Joseph. *Jefferson's War: America's First War on Terror, 1801–1805.* New York: Carroll & Graf, 2003.

Whitney, David C., and Robin Vaughn Whitney. *The American Presidents.* New York: Prentice Hall, 1993.

Notes

Prologue

1. "Eight dusty riders": Pickett, vol. 2, p. 227; Parton, p. 449; Beirne, p. 31.
2. "The onlookers' interest sharpened": Abernethy, pp. 221–222; Parton, pp. 444–445; Schachner 1961, p. 383.
3. "About 10 P.M. on February 18, 1807": McCaleb 1966, p. 277; Pickett, vol. 2, pp. 216–218.
4. "Early in the morning": Richmond *Enquirer*, April 17, 1807.
4. "Perkins borrowed a canoe": DeConde, p. 217.
4. "The young lieutenant": Perkins, vol. 2, pp. 218–220; McCaleb 1966, p. 277; Beirne, p. 121.
4. "He played chess": Parton, pp. 447–448.
4. "Fearing that Spanish troops": Richmond *Enquirer*, April 17, 1807.
5. "Burr, Perkins, and the": Pickett, vol. 2, pp. 221–223; Parton, p. 448.
5. "The riders followed": Schachner, p. 385; Pickett, vol. 2, pp. 223–225.
5. "To everyone's astonishment": Pickett, vol. 2, p. 227.
6. "Perkins returned to Chester": Melton 2002, pp. 164–165; Pickett, vol. 2, p. 227.
6. "The Eagle sprawled": Melton 2002, pp. 166–167; Beirne, p. 31.
6. "Marshall, his wife Polly": Stites, p. 88.
7. "Marshall's presence in the": Beirne, pp. 45, 196.
7. "Bollman, a thirty-seven-year-old": Schachner 1961, pp. 325, 173; Kennedy, pp. 338–340.
8. "Wilkinson had promptly arrested": Beveridge, vol. 3, p. 343.
8. "President Jefferson had issued": Jefferson 1897, vol. 9, pp. 14–20.

8. "John Adams complained": Schachner 1961, p. 390.

8. "Federalist Senator William Plumer": Ibid., p. 388.

9. "Article I, Section 9": *Constitution of U.S.*, p. 46.

9. "Amid a hurricane of criticism": *Virginia Argus*; Beveridge, vol. 3, pp. 358–360.

9. "'The P. assured him'": Madison, series 1, reel 9.

10. "At Jefferson's request": Burr 1970, vol. 2, pp. 387–391.

10. "And it forcefully stated": Marshall, vol. 6, pp. 488–495.

11. "Other judges released": McCaleb 1966, pp. 248–249.

11. "A hush fell over": *Examination*, p. 1; Beveridge, vol. 3, pp. 370–372.

11. "If they had not": Beirne, p. 34.

12. "Then, before adjourning": *Examination*, pp. 1–3; Schachner 1961, p. 401.

CHAPTER 1: THE "HAND OF MALIGNITY"

13. "The Virginia Capitol's Federal": *Examination*, pp. 4–5.

13. "The prosecution team": Lomask, vol. 2, p. 230; Beirne, pp. 42, 33.

14. "Hay, not known for": *Examination*, p. 6.

14. "For Burr to be held": Ibid., pp. 7–8, 10.

15. "Prosecutors read from": Ibid., pp. 10–11.

15. "Burr and his attorneys": Ibid., pp. 23–24.

15. "Burr and his followers: Ibid., p. 22.

15. "Attorney General Rodney": Ibid., pp. 25–26.

16. "John Wickham derided": Ibid., pp. 13–14.

16. "Knowing that Marshall": Ibid., p. 29.

16. "The prosecution, declared Wickham": Ibid., pp. 15–16.

16. "If the government": Ibid., pp. 18–20.

17. "Jefferson, suffering from": Malone, p. 291.

17. "To Jefferson's vast irritation": Schachner 1951, pp. 851, 834–836.

18. "On October 22, 1806, Jefferson": Jefferson 1903, pp. 246–247.

18. "Disgusted with Jefferson's apparent": Lomask, vol. 2, p. 126; Beveridge, vol. 3, pp. 315–317.

18. "Strangely, only two months": Plumer letter to Jeremiah Mason, January 4, 1807, Beveridge, vol. 3, p. 338.

19. "In a letter to George Morgan": McCaleb 1963, p. 110.

19. "Prosecutors had neither proved": Marshall, vol. 7, pp. 13–21; Malone, p. 300.

20. "Government lawyers, naturally enough": *Examination*, p. 36, footnote; Beveridge, vol. 3, p. 377, footnote.

21. "Marshall set a $10,000": *Examination*, p. 38; Christian, pp. 65–66.

21. "'The judges here have'": Jefferson 1897, vol. 9, p. 41.

21. "'As if an express'": Jefferson to Giles, April 20, 1807, Ibid., pp. 42–43.

21. "Yet Jefferson had begun": Schachner 1951, p. 852; Jefferson 1903, p. 258.

22. "Burr's trial would give": Jefferson 1897, vol. 9, pp. 42–43.

Chapter 2: The Political Maestro

23. "L'Enfant had haughtily withdrawn": Morison, vol. 2, pp. 84–85.

24. "Notably absent was President Adams": Lomask, vol. 1, p. 297.

25. "When Jefferson arrived": Ibid.; Schachner 1951, p. 661; Burr 1983, vol. 1, p. 519.

26. "New York's importance became": Burr 1983, vol. 1, p. 420.

26. "Smart and energetic": Schachner 1961, pp. 1–14; *Norton Anthol.*, pp. 245, 205–206.

26. "And then, as though": Schachner 1961, pp. 17–19.

27. "At eleven years of age": Burr 1983, vol. 2, p. 1057.

27. "Moderating his severe": Schachner 1961, pp. 21–22; Burr 1983, vol. 1, p. lxix.

28. "Graduating at age sixteen": Schachner 1961, pp. 24–28.

28. "In September 1775": Ibid., pp. 36–37.

28. "Sixteen years earlier": Morison, vol. 1, pp. 229–230.

28. "At Quebec, though": Schachner 1961, pp. 41–42.

29. "Burnished in the nineteenth-century": Kennedy, p. 45.

29. "Promoted to major": Lomask, vol. 1, pp. 43, 57–60; Schachner 1961, pp. 44–48, 51.

30. "A satisfying assignment": Schachner 1961, pp. 49–50.

31. "Burr's excellent reputation": Boyer, p. 800; Schachner 1961, pp. 54–58.

31. "In Westchester County": Fleming, pp. 85, 150; Davis, vol. 2, p. 271.

31. "The bride was": Schachner 1961, p. 55; Côté, p. 47; Burr 1983, vol. 1, p. lxvi.
32. "Burr and Hamilton often": Schachner 1961, pp. 77–80; Fleming, p. 100.
32. "But it wasn't long": Schachner 1961, pp. 94–102.
32. "Theodosia was already suffering": Côté, p. 55; Burr 1983, vol. 1, p. lxvi; Minnigerode, p. 108; Fleming, p. 90; Schachner 1961, pp. 120–121.
33. "Wollstonecraft's 1792 book": Swick 1975, p. 499; Chernow, pp. 59–60, 97, 101, 108, 234.
34. "As he once declared": February 8, 1793, letter to Mrs. Theodosia Burr, Burr 1970, vol. 1, pp. 361–362.
34. "Burr believed that women's": Lomask, vol. 2, pp. 370–371.
34. "To inculcate self-sufficiency": Swick 2000, p. 496; Minnigerode, pp. 103–104.
34. "Nearly every distinguished": Schachner 1961, pp. 130–131; Rogers, pp. 7–8; Burr letter to Theodosia, February 23, 1805, Burr 1970, vol. 2, p. 355.
34. "Theodosia's friends included": Schachner 1961, p. 479; Fleming, p. 106.
35. "During the summer of 1791": Fleming, p. 37; Burr 1983, vol. 1, p. lxx.
35. "For Burr, politics": Burr letter to Aaron Ward, January 14, 1832, Burr 1983, vol. 2, p. 1211; Lomask, vol. 1, p. xv.
35. "Early in the 1792": Burr 1983, vol. 1, pp. 105–117.
36. "Warned by Rufus King": Jenkinson, pp. 78–79.
36. "Devoting himself to his": Schachner 1961, pp. 138–139; Morison, vol. 2, pp. 65–66.
37. "Hamilton continued trying": Schachner 1961, pp. 145, 148; Morison, vol. 2, p. 74.
37. "Burr also made": Schachner 1961, pp. 135–137; Burr 1983, vol. 1, pp. 267–269.
38. "As the election of 1800": Fleming, p. 88; Schachner 1961, p. 173.
38. "A keystone of the": Mushkat, p. 1; Schachner 1961, pp. 174–176; Burr 1983, vol. 1, pp. 400–402; Fleming, p. 214.

39. "During Burr's meeting": Burr 1983, vol. 1, pp. 420–421; Jefferson to Madison, January 12, 1800, Jefferson 1897, vol. 7, pp. 401–402.

39. "Rather than campaign himself": Burr 1970, vol. 2, pp. 52–56; Burr 1983, vol. 1, p. 422.

40. "Bending over their maps": Parmet and Hecht, pp. 149–150.

40. "The law barred propertyless": Schachner 1961, pp. 174–176.

40. "Burr's organizational skills": Burr 1983, vol. 1, p. 425.

40. "Gallatin, in charge of": Burr 1983, vol. 1, pp. 431–434; Simon, p. 120.

Chapter 3: "The Man Whom His Country Delights to Honor"

43. "That morning, in a letter": Marshall, vol. 6, p. 89.

44. "While Marshall admired neither": Ibid., pp. 46–47.

44. "Jefferson's letter had referred": Schachner 1951, p. 578.

45. "It had the opposite": Stites, p. 51.

45. "The Jay Treaty and the": Morison, vol. 2, pp. 67–68.

46. "After naming Marshall": Ibid, pp. 70–72; Schachner 1951, pp. 589–590.

46. "The Directory, however": Morison, vol. 2, pp. 70–72.

46. "After months of futile": Ibid., p. 72; Stites, pp. 64–65.

46. "During endless rounds": Beveridge, vol. 2, p. 348; Stites, p. 65.

47. "Like Jefferson, Marshall was": R. Ellis, p. 119.

47. "Marshall's popularity once caused": Jefferson 2000, vol. 28, p. 539.

48. "Overwhelmed by impossible": Schachner 1951, pp. 200–202, 214–216.

48. "Marshall received his baptism": Stites, pp. 7–12; Schachner 1951, p. 593.

49. "Elected to the": Stites, pp. 18–43; Mordecai, p. 188.

50. "The Washington administration offered": Morison, vol. 2, p. 57; Stites, pp. 44–54.

50. "To prepare for war": Morison, vol. 2, pp. 73–74; Schachner 1951, pp. 602–603.

51. "Nearly alone among Federalists": Simon, pp. 56–57.

51. "George Washington had persuaded": Ibid., pp. 67–68.

51. "Marshall led the funeral": Ibid., p. 90.

51. "Against his party's wishes": Boyer, p. 640.

52. "Alexander Hamilton and other": Simon, pp. 87, 134.

52. "Marshall, however, stood by": Ibid., pp. 101–103; Morison, vol. 2, p. 70.

52. "The ten-year-old Supreme Court": Simon, pp. 138–139.

53. "For the third time": Ibid., p. 134.

53. "He left his mark": Ibid., pp. 151–152.

54. "John Adams would later": Stites, p. 79.

CHAPTER 4: THE REVOLUTION'S INSPIRED WORDSMITH

56. "'All will, of course'": Schachner 1951, pp. 662–663.

56. "Marshall's relief upon": Marshall, vol. 6, p. 89.

56. "Burr's comparatively bland": Burr letter to Caesar A. Rodney, Burr 1983, vol. 1, p. 518.

56. "Nowhere in the inaugural": Jefferson letter to John Dickinson, Jefferson 1897, vol. 9, pp. 201–202.

57. "Federalists did nothing": Simon, pp. 51–52.

57. "The Southern states, wrote": Schachner 1951, p. 605.

57. "Jefferson gloomily predicted": Jefferson letter to Virginia Senator Stevens Mason, Jefferson 1897, vol. 7, p. 283.

57. "Nullification supporters reasoned": Simon, pp. 58–59; Levy, pp. 58–59; Schachner 1951, pp. 610–612.

58. "John Breckenridge introduced": Schachner 1951, pp. 617–618.

58. "In the meantime": Elsmere, pp. 93–98, 82.

58. "Chase and District Judge Cyrus Griffin": Ibid., pp. 114–116, 124; Christian, p. 49.

59. "The harshest sedition penalty": Simon, p. 53.

59. "A popular Republican toast": Elsmere, pp. 123–125.

59. "Soon after taking office": Simon, p. 150; Fleming, pp. 43, 166–167.

59. "The Federalists initially made overtures": Burr 1983, vol. 1, pp. 456–457, footnote; Lomask, vol. 1, pp. 257–258.

60. "'Know that I should'": Burr 1983, vol. 1, p. 471.

60. "On December 23": Ibid., pp. 473–474.

60. "This new approach was evident": Ibid., pp. 478–479.

60. "Jefferson alerted Burr": Ibid., p. 469.

61. "A snowstorm enveloped Washington": Schachner 1951, p. 203.

62. "'Burr loves nothing but'": Fleming, p. 96.

62. "Adams objected to": Adams letter to Elbridge Gerry, J. Adams, vol. 9, pp. 577–578.

62. "'Burr is not a Democrat'": Burr 1983, vol. 1, p. 482.

62. "'Mr. Burr would not'": Jenkinson, pp. 105–107.

62. "Bayard was even more": Hamilton, vol. 6, p. 522.

63. "The conditions to which": Schachner 1951, p. 1019 footnote, 203; Jenkinson, pp. 105–108, 111–114.

63. "The very day that": Jefferson 1897, vol. 7, p. 491.

63. "On Monday, February 17": Burr 1983, vol. 1, p. 486.

64. ". . . the United States' 5,308,000 inhabitants": Nettels, p. 383, Table 1.

64. "During the presidential": Schachner 1951, pp. 640–643.

64. "Regarding Daniel Shays's 1786": J. Ellis, p. 99; Oxford Dict., p. 272.

65. "He once espoused": J. Ellis, p. 111.

65. ". . . the federal debt": Gallatin, pp. 208–209.

65. "Jefferson moved into": Schachner 1951, pp. 720–721; Fleming, p. 150.

66. "At home, he could": Tucker, p. 137.

66. "At the President's House": J. Ellis, pp. 24–25.

66. "Known as a good": Fleming, p. 107; Schachner 1951, p. 720.

66. "Jefferson's father, Peter": Jefferson 1959, pp. 19–21.

67. "The following year": J. Ellis, p. 27.

67. "'. . . a silent member'": Ibid., p. 44.

67. "Posterity-conscious even in": Ibid., pp. 107–108.

68. "In 1778, Jefferson wrote": Levy, pp. 34–36.

68. "Known as 'the Hair Buyer'": Thomas, p. 172.

68. "He ordered Hamilton kept": Schachner 1951, pp. 182–184.

68. "'. . . a colossus to the'": Jefferson 1897, vol. 9, pp. 309–310.

68. "Their enmity developed": Simon, p. 31: Schachner 1951, pp. 440–443.

69. "The Judiciary Act had": Stites, pp. 78–81, 84; Simon, p. 149.

69. "Jefferson chopped seventeen": Stites, p. 84.

70. "The Judiciary, Republicans were certain": Simon, p. 148.

70. "But when a repeal bill": R. Ellis, pp. 43–45, 48–50; Jefferson 1897, vol. 8, p. 128; Elsmere, pp. 142–144; Stites, p. 86.

70. "Charles Lee, the brother": *Political Graveyard* Web site.

70. ". . . his lawsuit, taking its": Simon, pp. 173–174.

71. "Marshall denied Lee's request": Marshall, vol. 6, pp. 165–185; Stites, p. 89; Elsmere, pp. 154–155.

71. "A Republican newspaper shrewdly": Elsmere, pp. 156–157.

71. "Jefferson could not have": Levy, p. 79.

71. ". . . an effective weapon: impeachment": Elsmere, pp. 191–192.

72. "Impeachment's origins can be": Ibid., pp. 181–183.

72. "The Republicans' first target": Elsmere, p. 159; Fleming, pp. 191–193.

73. "Chase defiantly accused Jefferson": Elsmere, pp. 200, 175–176; Marshall, vol. 6, pp. 347–348.

73. "Senators and congressmen murmured": Beirne, pp. 3–5; Burr 1970, vol. 2, pp. 356–357; Elsmere, pp. 225–226.

73. "Shaky from a recent": Elsmere, p. 217; Kennedy, p. 229.

73. "Justice Chase was charged": H. Adams, p. 229.

73. ". . . in the grand jury's presence": Elsmere, p. 162.

73. "Upon reading newspaper accounts": Jefferson 1897, vol. 10, pp. 387–390.

74. "On February 4, when": Elsmere, pp. 263–264; Schachner 1961, p. 266.

74. "But in the weeks": Simon, p. 280; Schachner 1961, p. 263.

74. "The vice president presided": Burr 1970, vol. 2, p. 360.

74. "Congressman John Randolph": Simon, p. 200.

75. ". . . as did Philip Barton Key": *Political Graveyard* Web site.

75. "Martin argued that Chase's": Elsmere, p. 292.

75. ". . . he began sobbing": H. Adams, vol. 2, pp. 236–237.

75. "It failed to muster": Ibid., pp. 239–240; Elsmere, pp. 301–302.

75. "Impeachment, he now believed": Elsmere, p. 303.

CHAPTER 5: THE EMBATTLED VICE PRESIDENT

77. "In an entry dated February 12, 1801": Jefferson 1903, p. 209.

78. "Jefferson restated Burr's supposed": Ibid., pp. 222–223.

78. "In April 1806": Ibid., pp. 239–241.

78. "This entry coincided": Schachner 1961, p. 234.

78. "Of seven major appointments": Ibid., p. 217.

78. "In Connecticut and South Carolina": Ibid., p. 675; Kline, vol. 1, pp. 534–542.

78. "One of the snubbed": Fleming, pp. 119–120.

79. "During the Senate debate": Jenkinson, p. 100; Schachner 1961, pp. 221–224.

79. "Burr then compounded": Beveridge, vol. 3, p. 279.

79. "As Republican newspapers assailed": Burr 1983, vol. 2, p. 622; Jefferson 1903, vol. 8, p. 94.

80. "Burr's final rupture with": Burr 1983, vol. 2, pp. 641–646; Burr 1970, vol. 2, pp. 86–89.

80. "The scathing attacks on Burr": Fleming, pp. 81–84; Schachner 1961, p. 231.

81. "'It is not worth while'": Burr 1970, vol. 2, p. 205.

81. "As a result of": Schachner 1961, p. 230.

81. "But the scurrilous attacks": Burr 1983, vol. 2, pp. 641–646, 724–728.

81. "By the end of 1802": King, pp. 192–193, 160–161.

82. "'I fear I have'": Parton, vol. 1, p. 276.

82. "*An Examination* sold more": Schachner 1961, p. 232; Fleming, p. 125; Burr 1983, vol. 2, p. 822.

82. "Irving's *Morning Chronicle* was": Burr 1983, vol. 2, p. 840.

82. "On January 26, 1804": Burr 1983, vol. 2, p. 822.

83. "Jefferson's intense dislike": Ibid., p. 822.

83. "Clinton, in fact, was": Ibid., pp. 822–823.

83. "Known as 'The Old Incumbent'": Fleming, pp. 33–35.

83. "But Clinton did": Burr 1983, vol. 2, p. 827.

83. "One of his first actions," Ibid., p. 829.

84. "Fearing that the recent": Morison, vol. 2, pp. 94–95.

84. "At a dinner with Burr": Fleming, p. 146.
84. "The mere threat": Morison, vol. 2, pp. 94–95.
84. "He could not permit": Fleming, pp. 198–200.
84. "Moreover, the president was": H. Adams, vol. 2, p. 192; Kennedy, pp. 209–210.
85. "But Lansing withdrew": Fleming, pp. 161–162.
85. "Lansing's replacement, State Supreme": Ibid.
85. "Burr tried to distinguish": Burr 1983, vol. 2, pp. 833–834; Schachner 1961, pp. 241–243.
85. "As Jefferson recounted their": Burr 1983, vol. 2, pp. 852–853.
85. "When he first learned": Jefferson 1897, vol. 9, p. 455.
86. "According to Cheetham": Burr 1983, vol. 2, p. 853.
86. "The Burr campaign never": Ibid., vol. 1, p. 248, vol. 2, pp. 833–835.
86. "Morgan Lewis was so": Ibid., vol. 2, p. 842.
86. "To no one's surprise": Schachner 1961, p. 245.
86. "Aaron Burr, seated at": Fleming, pp. 309–310.
87. "A few weeks before": Burr 1983, vol. 2, p. 877.
88. "In 1797, Burr had": Ibid, vol. 1, pp. 301–311; Schachner 1961, p. 146.
88. ". . . Hamilton adopted an": Burr 1970, vol. 2, pp. 295–297.
88. "No more than a": Lomask, vol. 2, p. 28; Vidal, pp. 268–269. Ian Frazier, in his feature story, "Route 3," in the February 16 & 23, 2004, issue of the *New Yorker* magazine, reports that the spot was virtually obliterated by a nineteenth-century road and railroad tracks.
89. "Hamilton and Burr had": Kennedy, p. 83; Burr 1983, vol. 1, p. 410.
89. "In 1801, his nineteen-year-old": Fleming, pp. 8–9.
89. "They were .544 caliber": Rogow, p. 248.
89. "Burr's second, William P. Van Ness": Fleming, pp. 314–326; Burr 1970, vol. 2, pp. 309–317.
90. "Stricken New York Federalists": Fleming, pp. 302–303; Lomask, vol. 2, p. 27; Schachner 1961, p. 252.
90. "Pressured by New York": Fleming, pp. 340–357.
90. "Mayor Clinton closed down": Ibid., pp. 335–339.
91. "Treasury Secretary Albert Gallatin": Walters, pp. 166–167.
91. "Burr was not reviled": Fleming, p. 361; Schachner 1961, pp. 254–255; Burr 1983, vol. 2, p. 881.

91. "A blunt bit of": Schachner 1961, p. 255.

91. "There, he slipped aboard": Kennedy, p. 202.

91. "In a note to Theodosia": Burr 1970, vol. 2, pp. 331–332.

92. "He even managed some": Ibid., pp. 351–352.

92. "Jefferson and George Clinton": Whitney and Whitney, p. 484; H. Adams, vol. 2, pp. 201–204.

92. "Looking for business opportunities": Lomask, vol. 2, p. 41.

92. "While Burr was on": Burr 1970, vol. 2, pp. 339, 359.

92. "He was forced to": Ibid., p. 349.

92. "A former fur trader": Fleming, p. 357.

92. "Still $8,000 in debt": Schachner 1961, pp. 259–261.

93. "Senators had previously": Fleming, p. 79.

93. "On March 2, 1805": Burr 1983, vol. 2, pp. 909–910.

93. "Speaking without notes": from John Quincy Adams's notes, Ibid., pp. 912–913.

93. "'Every gentleman was silent'": Ibid., p. 910.

94. "The *Washington Federalist* called": Burr 1970, vol. 2, p. 361.

CHAPTER 6: THE GRAND JURY CONVENES

95. "Richmond had fallen under": Christian, p. 61; Beirne, p. 30.

96. "The Federalist-leaning upper": Elsmere, pp. 116–117.

96. "In less turbulent times": Christian, p. 64.

96. "In 1807, between one-third": Dabney, p. 63.

96. "The shipments were landed": Beirne, p. 57.

96. "In their leisure time": Christian, pp. 62–63; Lomask, vol. 2, pp. 236–237.

97. "The *Enquirer's* habitual bias": *Enquirer*, Microfilm 23A.

97. "The medley of front-page": Ibid., March 31, May 26, and April 7, 1807.

98. "The walkers and riders": Stanard, pp. 98–101; Lomask, vol. 2, pp. 236–237; Mordecai, pp. 71–73.

98. "The House of Delegates": Lomask, vol. 2, p. 228.

98. "The crowd spanned": Beveridge, vol. 3, pp. 399–400.

98. "Andrew Jackson of Tennessee": Ibid., p. 404.

99. "A strapping young man": Schachner 1961, pp. 407–408; Vidal, p. 357.

99. "Even Robertson's iron will": Robertson, vol. 1, p. 112.

99. "Aaron Burr quietly conferred": Mark Greenough, Virginia State Capitol historian; Lomask, vol. 2, pp. 228–229; Parton, p. 461; Scott, p. 13.

100. "Washington Irving, whose future": P. Irving, vol. 1, pp. 190–191.

100. "'The most indefatigable industry'": Burr 1970, vol. 2, p. 406.

100. "President Jefferson had appropriated": Stites, p. 104; Lomask, vol. 2, pp. 238, 433, end note.

100. "Besides throwing open": Jefferson 1897, vol. 9, pp. 58–59.

100. "'Nothing is left undone'": Burr 1970, vol. 2, p. 406.

101. "The *Virginia Argus*, in its": *Virginia Argus*, April 7, 1807.

101. "A Jefferson biographer": Beirne, pp. 60–61.

101. "Three days later, the *Enquirer*": Richmond *Enquirer*, April 10, 1807, Microfilm 23A.

102. "Unreported by either newspaper": Beirne, p. 58.

102. "The dinner inspired a": Dabney, pp. 71–72.

102. "Seated beside Marshall": Beirne, pp. 68–69.

102. "As everyone knew": Scott, pp. 13–14.

103. "Hay, forty-one, was the": Melton 2002, p. 172; Beirne, pp. 32–33.

103. "Thus, two young Richmond": Melton 2002, p. 172; Lomask, vol. 2, p. 234.

103. "Burr objected to two": Melton 2002, pp. 173–176; Jefferson 1897, vol. 9, pp. 32–33.

103. "Burr objected to Giles": Robertson, vol. 1, p. 39.

104. "Edmund Randolph was John": *Concise Dict.*, pp. 841–842; Elsmere, p. 169.

104. "On the distinguished grand jury": Beveridge, vol. 3, p. 465; Abernethy, p. 235.

104. "Robert Barraud Taylor, another": Beirne, pp. 73–74.

104. "'If there be no bill'": Jefferson 1897, vol. 9, p. 52.

105. "The attorneys' irritation": Beveridge, vol. 3, pp. 413–414.

105. "'It is not easy for'": Burr 1983, vol. 2, p. 1028.

105. "Fearing that Burr, free": Parton, p. 464.

105. "Marshall agreed to hear": Ibid., p. 469.
106. "Prosecutor William Wirt shot back": Ibid., pp. 466–467.
106. "So Hay tried a": Robertson, vol. 1, p. 96.
107. "Hay's first report to": Malone, p. 312.
107. "Burr unexpectedly provided": Robertson, vol. 1, pp. 105–106.

Chapter 7: "The Most Finished Scoundrel"

109. "U.S. Attorney George Hay tried": Beirne, p. 89.
109. "He looked every inch": Vidal, p. 277; Abernethy, p. 15.
109. "The Spanish governor of Louisiana": D. Clark, p. 82 note.
110. "John Randolph, the congressman": McCaleb 1963, p. 124; Bruce, pp. 303–304.
110. ". . . as Senator William Plumer": Abernethy, p. 194.
110. "Wilkinson had pledged allegiance": D. Clark, pp. 15–16.
110. "In return for his": Ibid., pp. 105–107; Lomask, vol. 2, pp. 17–18; Melton 1998, p. 72.
111. "The son of a": Hay and Werner, pp. 1, 4, 25–29, 34–38, 46–51.
111. "When the war ended": Ibid., pp. 55, 59, 78, 83.
111. "Undeterred, Wilkinson loaded tobacco": Abernethy, p. 5.
112. "Over the next years": Hay and Werner, pp. 84–94; James, p. 395.
112. "After Wilkinson had led": Hay and Werner, p. 121; Jacobs, p. 144; Kennedy, pp. 132–133.
112. "Carandolet eagerly reciprocated": James, pp. 372–378.
113. "When the courier was": D. Clark, pp. 37–38 note.
113. "Upon General Wayne's death": Jacobs, p. 137; D. Clark, pp. 40–41, 83 note, 97 note; Hay and Werner, pp. 140, 144, 152, 156.
113. "During the Republic's": James, p. 384; Remini, p. 146.
114. ". . . even Thomas Jefferson looked": Abernethy, p. 4.
114. "Troubled by this very possibility": Beveridge, vol. 3, p. 282 footnote.
114. "'Vrijbuiter,' the Dutch word": Kennedy, p. 111.
114. "Although unsanctioned by": Lomask, vol. 2, p. 8.
115. "Thomas Jefferson, to whom": James, pp. 419–427; J. Ellis, p. 127; Kennedy, p. 134.
115. "The failed plot led": Melton 1998, p. 86.

115. "Four years later": Masterson, pp. 307, 316–326, 331, 339–342; Lomask, vol. 2, p. 20; Melton 1998, p. 106.

116. "The filibusters' dangerous potential": W. Irving, vol. 2, p. 487.

116. "As a Spanish infantry": Lomask, vol. 2, pp. 36–37, 96–98.

116. "Alexander Hamilton volunteered": Schachner 1946, pp. 383–384.

116. "Then, in 1805": Lomask, vol. 2, pp. 36–37, pp. 96–98; Schachner 1961, p. 281.

117. "Burr's only notice of ": Lomask, vol. 2, pp. 15, 27.

117. "The next day, after Wilkinson": Ibid., pp. 26–27.

117. "Burr left that meeting": Burr 1970, vol. 2, p. 287.

119. "At a meeting in the": Wilkinson letter to Marques de Cas Calvo, March 12, 1804, Abernethy, pp. 11–12.

119. "To sweeten his offer": Hay and Werner, pp. 199, 212–213; Schachner 1961, pp. 292–302; Cox, pp. 795–800; Abernethy, p. 13.

119. "In his spare time, the general": Hay and Werner, pp. 217–218.

120. "To Folch and other": Schachner 1961, p. 302.

120. ". . . for Burr, through an": Fleming, p. 280.

120. "Just as the full": Beveridge, vol. 3, p. 316.

121. "Instead of the usual custom": Jefferson 1897, vol. 8, p. 291; H. Adams, vol. 2, pp. 383, 369–375, 378–379.

122. "Williamson, a trusted Burr friend": Fleming, pp. 199, 260, 280.

122. ". . . he wrote to Lord Harrowby": Burr 1983, vol. 2, pp. 891–892.

122. ". . . Burr said he would need": H. Adams, vol. 2, p. 403; Burr 1983, vol. 2, pp. 928–929.

123. "'In New-York I am to be'": Burr 1970, vol. 2, p. 305.

123. "And Burr had already": Burr 1983, vol. 2, pp. 921–925.

123. ". . . Burr bought 'a floating house'": Burr 1970, vol. 2, p. 368.

123. "Below Pittsburgh, Burr by chance": Burr 1983, vol. 2, p. 934.

123. "At Marietta, Ohio, Burr learned": Lomask, vol. 2, pp. 59–64.

124. "Harman and Margaret Blennerhassett": Swick 2000, pp. 4, 15.

124. "He played the violin": Ibid., p. 26; Burr 1983, vol. 2, pp. 949–951; Safford, p. 116; Beirne, pp. 156–157.

124. "There were two reasons": Swick 2000, pp. 2–3; Fitch, p. xi.

125. "Burr reached Blennerhassett Island": Swick 2000, p. 38.

125. "Flattered by Burr's interest": Burr 1983, vol. 2, pp. 949, 951; Safford, pp. 116–119; Lomask, vol. 2, p. 129.

125. "Burr toured a proposed canal": Lomask, vol. 2, pp. 57, 65.

125. "In Nashville, Senator Andrew Jackson": Remini, pp. 147–148; Burr 1970, vol. 2, p. 372.

125. "Then Burr went to": D. Clark, p.158 note; Lomask, vol. 2, p. 73.

126. "Wilkinson's letter to Clark": Schachner 1961, p. 301.

126. "Of these, the Mexican Association": Abernethy, p. 25.

126. "The Mexican Association's leaders": Burr 1983, vol. 2, p. 823; Abernethy, pp. 25–26.

127. "Burr and the nuns": Burr 1970, vol. 2, p. 371.

127. ". . . Burr struck out east": Ibid., vol. 2, p. 373; Beveridge, vol. 3, p. 313.

127. "They 'settled the plan'": Abernethy, p. 32.

127. "Wilkinson began laying": Lomask, vol. 2, p. 82.

128. "Possibly at Yrujo's instigation": Beveridge, vol. 3, p. 296; D. Clark, pp. 140–141 note.

128. "Yrujo added fuel to": Schachner 1961, pp. 304–307; Abernethy, pp. 32–33; Burr 1983, vol. 2, p. 941; McCaleb 1966, p. xiv.

128. "Louis Marie Turreno": Abernethy, p. 24.

128. ". . . to Thomas Ritchie of": Ibid., pp. 32–35.

128. "In a report to his superiors": Schachner 1961, pp. 290–291; McCaleb 1966, pp. 40–41.

129. "'My views have been'": Kennedy, p. 268.

129. "France, which was arbitrating": Burr 1983, vol. 2, p. 948.

129. ". . . Jefferson, in his Fifth Annual Message": Jefferson 1897, vol. 8, pp. 390–391.

129. "'You admit him at'": Abernethy, pp. 38–39.

Chapter 8: The Burr Expedition, And Ruin

131. "Burr hit upon a": Burr 1983, vol. 2, pp. 971, 993.

131. "He envisioned 336-acre": Kennedy, p. 243.

132. "Felip Neri, the Baron de Bastrop": Burr 1983, vol. 2, pp. 993–995; Lomask, vol. 2, pp. 111–112; Abernethy, pp. 73–74.

132. "By the fall of": McCaleb 1966, p. 156.

132. "Acting in concert with Burr": Lomask, vol. 2, pp. 102–104.

133. ". . . With a volunteer army": Burr 1983, vol. 2, p. 946.

133. "'He [Burr] observed, what I'": McCaleb 1966, p. 47.

134. "Jefferson's apathy toward the": DeConde, pp. 217, 231–234, 222–225; H. Adams, vol. 2, pp. 249, 257, 301–315.

134. "He bid for a": Lomask, vol. 2, p. 106.

134. "After their meeting on March 22, 1806": Jefferson, 1903, pp. 237–238.

135. "Burr attempted to enlist": Burr 1970, vol. 2, p. 386; Richmond *Enquirer*, February 24, 1807, Microfilm 23A.

135. ". . . William Eaton, who had led": Wheelan, pp, 253–280, 316.

135. "According to Eaton's dubious": Beirne, p. 39; Beveridge, vol. 3, pp. 304–305.

136. "Kentucky U.S. Attorney Joseph Daviess": D. Clark, pp. 146, 178 notes; Abernethy, p. 90.

136. "Frustrated, Daviess and his": Stites, pp. 98–99.

136. "By the spring of 1806": Lomask, vol. 2, p. 151.

136. "When this news": McCaleb 1966, pp. 106–107; Burr 1970, vol. 2, p. 380.

137. "They studied Burr's maps": Abernethy, p. 62; McCaleb 1966, p. 78.

137. "Tyler arranged for the": Abernethy, p. 101.

138. "Pike and his twenty-two men": Ubbelohde, Benson, and Smith, pp. 20–22; Hollon, pp. 101–102.

138. "Any lingering doubts": Hollon, p. 160.

139. "Against the backdrop of": Ibid., pp. 101–102; Ubbelohde, Benson, and Smith pp. 20–23.

139. "For agreeing to a": Lomask, vol. 2, p. 193.

139. "While at Morganza": Burr 1983, vol. 2, p. 1039; Lomask, vol. 2, pp. 124–125; Jefferson 1897, vol. 8, p. 473.

140. "He signed contracts for": Interview with Blennerhassett Island State Park historian Ray Swick; Abernethy, p. 66.

140. "Jackson was recuperating": Remini, pp. 148, 136–143, 147.

140. "Jackson, happy to see Burr": Lomask, vol. 2, pp. 134–135.

140. *"The Western World* was trumpeting"*: Richmond *Enquirer,* November 18, 1806, Microfilm 23A; Lomask, vol. 2, p. 130; Abernethy, p. 68.

141. "Morgan's letter reached Jefferson": Abernethy, pp. 82, 84–85.

141. "Burr made Lexington the": Schachner 1961, pp. 327–328.

141. "At a public meeting": Lomask, pp. 139–141.

142. "Ohio Senator John Smith": McCaleb 1966, pp. 78, 80; Burr 1983, vol. 2, pp. 998–999.

142. "'I never harbored or'": Abernethy, pp. 81, 86.

142. "... but Gideon Granger's letter": Jefferson 1897, vol. 9, p. 456.

142. "Jefferson and his advisers reviewed": Jefferson memos of October 22, 24, and 25, 1806, in his own hand, in McCaleb 1966, p. 90.

143. "Granger sent an agent": Jefferson 1897, vol. 9, p. 456.

143. "In August, seven hundred Spanish troops": DeConde, p. 236; McCaleb 1966, pp. 106–107.

144. "'Jefferson will affect to yield'": *Amer. State Papers,* X, vol. 1, p. 558.

144. "At the Natchez plantation": DeConde, p. 236; Lomask, vol. 2, pp. 156–158.

145. "... Wilkinson laboriously deciphered": Burr 1983, vol. 2, pp. 973–984.

145. "The bombastic letter, so": Lomask, vol. 2, pp. 116–118. Also see Mary Jo Kline's analysis in Aaron Burr's political correspondence. It convincingly shows that the enciphered letter delivered to General Wilkinson was not written by Aaron Burr, but by Senator Jonathan Dayton.

145. "'Your letter postmarked 13th May'": Burr 1983, vol. 2, pp. 986–987.

146. "Summoning Colonel Cushing": Lomask, vol. 2, pp. 167–169; DeConde, p. 236.

146. "The general devoted several": Lomask, vol. 2, p. 167.

146. "... Wilkinson's first letter": McCaleb 1966, pp. 122–123.

147. "'The desperation of the plan'": Ibid., pp. 123–126.

148. "Moreover, Southern Republicans disliked": Kennedy, p. 281.

148. "Convening his cabinet": Jefferson 1903, pp. 248–249.

148. ". . . the president's carefully worded proclamation": Jefferson 1897, vol. 8, pp. 481–482.

148. "Nor did Jefferson's Sixth": Ibid., p. 489.

148. "The reason was Jefferson knew": Malone, p. 253.

149. "U.S. Attorney Joseph Daviess": Burr 1983, vol. 2, pp. 999–1000; Beveridge, vol. 3, pp. 291–292; Abernethy, p. 99.

149. "Jefferson was so disgusted": Abernethy, p. 89.

149. "In early December 1806": Lomask, vol. 2, pp. 186–187; Abernethy, pp. 184, 105; Malone, pp. 244–245, 259.

149. "On the night of": McCaleb 1966, pp. 205–207.

150. "They drank up the wine": Swick 2000, p. 43.

150. "Jackson, to their surprise": McCaleb 1963, p. 77; McCaleb 1966, p. 212; Jackson, vol. 2, p. 148; Remini, pp. 149–153; Lomask, vol. 2, pp. 135–136.

151. "In Nashville, Burr learned": McCaleb 1966, pp. 222–223.

151. "With a small party": Ibid., p. 218.

151. "Stopping at an army fort": *Amer. State Papers*, X, vol. 1, pp. 610–611; Abernethy, pp. 115–117.

151. "Against this aptly forbidding": Lomask, vol. 2, pp. 213–217; McCaleb 1966, p. 232.

151. "After two days' deliberation": Lomask, vol. 2, pp. 217–218; McCaleb 1966, p. 228.

152. "After placing a $5,000 bounty": Abernethy, pp. 218–219; McCaleb 1966, p. 230.

152. "As he explained": Burr 1983, vol. 2, p. 1022.

152. "Governor Claiborne later wrote": McCaleb 1966, p. 234.

Chapter 9: A Landmark Subpoena and Indictments

153. "'We are now enjoying'": P. Irving, vol. 1, p. 191.

154. "In the same calm": Robertson, vol. 1, pp. 113–114, Beveridge, vol. 3, pp. 445–446.

154. "No subpoena was necessary": Schachner 1961, p. 416; Robertson, vol. 1, p. 122.

154. "Once before, in 1806": Beveridge, vol. 3, p. 436 footnote.

155. "Arguably the best courtroom": Melton 2002, p. 178.

155. "Middle-aged and bibulous": Malone, p. 312; Fitch, p. 150.

155. "Like Jefferson and Marshall": Elsmere, p. 203; Beirne, pp. 92–93.

155. "'Mr. Hay makes, I think'": Robertson, vol. 1, p. 118.

156. "The defense, said Martin": Ibid., pp. 128–129.

156. "As a private individual": Ibid., pp. 130–131.

157. "He would send the Wilkinson letter": Jefferson 1897, vol. 9, pp. 55–56.

157. "The president could be subpoenaed": Robertson, vol. 1, pp. 181–188.

158. "The chief justice's implication": Ibid., p. 189.

158. "The chief justice later": Beveridge, vol. 3, pp. 449–450; Malone, p. 319.

158. "Outraged that the president": Robertson, vol. 1, p. 191.

159. "The subpoenas were delivered": Malone, p. 321.

159. "He asked Dearborn": Jefferson 1897, vol. 9, pp. 55–57.

159. "'As to our personal'": Ibid., pp. 56–57.

160. "Luther Martin, he suggested": Malone, pp. 348–349.

160. "'Graybell will fix upon him'": Jefferson, vol. 9, pp. 58–60.

160. "How would Marshall like it": Ibid.

161. "'But would the executive'": Ibid.

161. "'His erect attitude'": Malone, p. 326.

161. "Impeccably turned out": Beirne, p. 121.

161. "'Wilkinson strutted into court'": P. Irving, vol. 1, p. 194.

162. "'In spite of myself'": Wilkinson to Jefferson, June 17, 1807, *Letters in Relation to Burr's Conspiracy*, Library of Congress.

162. "'On appearance of the'": Robertson, vol. 1, p. 197 footnote.

162. "Eaton, the hero of Derna": McCaleb 1963, p. 108.

163. "No sooner had Wilkinson": Abernethy, p. 239.

163. "'Wilkinson is now before'": P. Irving, vol. 1, pp. 194–195.

163. "Lacking the authority to impose": Abernethy, pp. 160, 166; Burr 1983, vol. 2, p. 980; McCaleb 1966, pp. 173–175, 193–195, 197–198.

164. "He jailed men without": Schachner 1961, pp. 370–371; McCaleb 1966, p. 193.

164. "He jailed Dr. Justus Bollman": Beveridge, vol. 3, pp. 314, 332–333.

164. "James Alexander, a New Orleans": McCaleb 1966, pp. 248–249.

165. "In a petition to Congress": Beveridge, vol. 3, p. 364.

165. "In Washington, Federalists complained": Malone, p. 281.

165. "So loud was the outcry": Ibid., p. 279.

165. "'Although I may be able'": McCaleb 1966, pp. 139–140.

165. "In his reply, the president": Jefferson 1897, vol. 9, pp. 3–6.

166. "... Wilkinson was quietly replaced": Malone, pp. 287, 278.

166. "Even as Burr was descending": McCaleb 1963, pp. 47, 52.

166. "'He has laid before me'": *Amer. Hist. Rev.*, Vol. X, 1904–1905, pp. 832–839.

166. "In a remarkable analysis": Beveridge, vol. 3, p. 320; H. Adams, vol. 3, pp. 342–343.

167. "... a Wilkinson emissary, Walter Burling": Burr 1970, vol. 2, p. 403; McCaleb 1966, pp. 121, 141–145.

167. "In March, as Iturrigaray": McCaleb 1966, p. 146.

168. "... the brilliant, erratic Randolph": Hay and Werner, p. 255.

168. "'Such a countenance'": Bruce, p. 304.

168. "Wilkinson had omitted": Lomask, pp. 116–117 (from Mary-Jo Kline, editor of Aaron Burr's papers).

168. "When asked about this letter": Robertson, vol. 1, pp. 327–328; Abernethy, pp. 240–241.

168. "Another alteration, designed": Lomask, vol. 2, pp. 116–117 (from Kline).

169. "'The mammoth of iniquity'": Bruce, pp. 302–304.

169. "Burr took pleasure": Burr 1970, vol. 2, pp. 406–407.

169. "'Merciful God what a Spectacle'": Beveridge, vol. 3, p. 472.

169. "While in Wilkinson's custody": Brunson, pp. 12–13; D. Clark, p. 162 note.

169. "'The very frank and candid'": Beveridge, vol. 3, p. 465 note.

170. "... Jackson was now under indictment": Jackson, vol. 2, pp. 168, 172.

170. "Burr asked Chief Justice Marshall": Robertson, vol. 1, p. 356; Beveridge, vol. 3, pp. 473–475.

170. "Later, when George Hay": Beveridge, vol. 3, pp. 483–484.

170. "... the pro-Republican Richmond *Enquirer*": Parton, p. 476.

171. "Blennerhassett wasn't present": Fitch, p. xii.

171. "Five Burr associates were indicted": Beveridge, vol. 3, p. 466; Robertson, vol. 1, pp. 330–350.

171. "'Fallen, proscribed, prejudged'": P. Irving, vol. 1, pp. 200–201.

171. "'Aaron Burr . . . being . . . under'": Robertson, vol. 1, pp. 368–375.

172. "The indictment said the 'overt act'": Ibid.

172. "The indictments were based": *Richmond Enquirer,* June 27, 1807, Microfilm 23A.

172. ". . . Burr coolly analyzed the grand jury's findings": Burr 1970, vol. 2, p. 408.

172. "'. . . if war be actually levied'": Marshall, vol. 6, p. 488.

173. "He nervously solicited the opinions": Marshall letter to Associate Justice William Cushing, Ibid., vol. 7, pp. 60–62.

CHAPTER 10: EYE OF THE STORM

175. "The victim was hanged": Melton 2002, pp. 161–162.

175. "Treason was codified": Ibid., p. 163.

176. "'. . . stained the English records with blood'": From Judge Francis M. Finch, Beveridge, vol. 3, pp. 401–402.

176. "'Treason against the United States'": *Constitution,* p. 54.

176. "Unhappy with a new federal tax": Elsmere, pp. 98–101.

177. "At the outset of Fries's treason trial": Ibid., pp. 107–112.

177. "The jail was not just unhealthful": Robertson, vol. 1, pp. 350–351; Beirne, p. 129; Burr 1970, vol. 2, p. 409; Malone, p. 330; Parton, p. 477.

178. "Catherine Gratton Gamble": Beirne, p. 138.

178. "Oranges, lemons, pineapples": Burr 1970, vol. 2, p. 409; Lomask, vol. 2, p. 257.

178. ". . . Burr had so many visitors": P. Irving, vol. 1, p. 202.

178. "Even Burr's jailer": Burr 1970, vol. 2, p. 409; Vidal, p. 371.

179. "On June 22, the 50-gun": Wheelan, pp. 334–335.

179. "Judge Spencer Roane of the": Beirne, p. 133.

179. ". . . Winfield Scott, the strapping": Scott, p. 19.

179. ". . . Richmond's Fourth of July": Beirne, pp. 134–135.

180. "'Aaron Burr—may his'": Parton, p. 478.

180. "As war fever spread": Jefferson 1903, p. 255.

180. "But after General of the Army Wilkinson": Beveridge, vol. 3, p. 477.

180. "During the summer of 1807": Richmond *Enquirer,* Microfilm 23A; Beirne, pp. 141–143.

181. "Young, single, well-to-do men and women": Vidal, p. 355; P. Irving, vol. 1, pp. 200–201.

181. "Supposedly at the instigation": Beveridge, vol. 3, p. 471; Schachner 1961, p. 422.

181. "William Eaton caroused": Beveridge, vol. 3, p. 429.

181. "In one of his harangues": McCaleb 1963, pp. 116–117.

182. "Chief Justice Marshall passed the hot days": Stanard, pp. 92–96; Mordecai, p. 117.

182. "'Altho' there is not a man'": Jefferson 1897, vol. 9, pp. 111–112.

183. "The president promised George Hay": Ibid., pp. 60–61.

183. "'... he very early saw'": Ibid., p. 41.

184. "In December 1806, Jefferson": Ibid., vol. 8, p. 501.

185. "When Jefferson learned of": Jefferson 1897, vol. 9, pp. 62–63.

185. "The situation agreed with Martin": Minnigerode, pp. 135–136.

185. "'Our little family circle'": Parton, p. 509.

185. "... Alston had strenuously disavowed": Safford, pp. 227–230.

186. "Since her son Aaron Burr Alston's birth": Minnigerode, pp. 115, 119.

186. "'I beg and expect it of you'"; Burr 1970, vol. 2, p. 408.

186. "'I want an independent'": Ibid., p. 410.

186. "The scholarly landowner and his captors": Fitch, pp. xii, 3–4.

187. "'Burr lives in great style'": Ibid., p. 22.

187. "Blennerhassett could not forget": Safford, pp. 119–221.

187. "He was now deeply in debt": Fitch, pp. 31, 49, 83–84, 221.

187. "One of Burr's attorneys, Benjamin Botts": Ibid., pp. 5–6.

CHAPTER 11: THE TRIAL OF THE CENTURY BEGINS

189. "... Aaron Burr walked the few blocks": Parton, p. 483.

190. "Hay requested a delay": Robertson, vol. 1, pp. 359–360.

190. "For the literary-minded": *Virginia Argus*, August 5, 1807.

190. "On the news pages inside": Richmond *Enquirer*, August 21, 1807.

190. "But his lawyers were as unprepared": Fitch, pp. 16–17.

190. "Blennerhassett walked the": Ibid., pp. 44–47, 7, 12, 28, 62, 67.

191. "Unlike the other 130": Ibid., pp. 7, 17, 40, 47.

191. "An inmate barber": Safford, p. 326.

191. "An anonymous woman left soups": Beirne, p. 172.

191. "Each letter from his wife": Fitch, p. 123.

191. "Jefferson had escaped Washington's": Hay and Werner, pp. 278–280; Beirne, p. 243.

192. "'General Wilkinson has been'": Malone, pp. 361–362.

192. "Not only had Marshall dared": Loth, p. 229.

192. "Marshall himself would later": Stites, p. 96; Malone, p. 356.

192. "'. . . From the citadel of the law'": Jefferson 1897, vol. 9, p. 68.

192. "Marshall was not insensible": Safford, p. 465.

193. "De Pestre's brother-in-law": Fitch, p. 26.

193. ". . . William Duane, the editor of": Ibid., pp. 51–52.

193. "When asked whether he had": Robertson, vol. 1, pp. 370, 383, 380.

194. "The numerous challenges exhausted": Beveridge, vol. 3, p. 483; Malone, p. 335.

194. "He drafted a letter": Jefferson 1897, vol. 9, p. 62.

194. "But then Burr surprised everyone": Robertson, vol. 1, pp. 423–424.

194. "The haphazard jury selection": Lomask, vol. 2, p. 262.

195. "'There is but one chance'": Beveridge, vol. 3, p. 484.

195. "The government, he said, would prove": Robertson, vol. 1, pp. 433–451.

196. "Edmund Randolph, the senior attorney": Fitch, p. 36.

196. "'Law and reason support us'": Robertson, vol. 1, pp. 452–459, 469–472.

197. "'I should have thought it my duty'": Parton, pp. 486–488.

197. "He had located the deposed brother": Wheelan, pp. 280–305.

197. "Eaton testified that he had pretended": Robertson, vol. 1, pp. 475–484.

198. "Eaton was offered 'the second command'": Ibid.
199. "When Eaton reached the end": Ibid.
199. "Eaton's ceremonious departure": Safford, p. 343; Fitch, p. 14.
200. "Jurors and spectators": Beirne, pp. 173, 190.
200. "'I am more convinced than ever'": Jackson letter to W. P. Anderson, June 16, 1807, Remini, p. 157; Beveridge, vol. 3, p. 405.
200. "'He is as far from a fool'": Lomask, vol. 2, p. 151.
200. "... an apocryphal, oft-repeated": Beveridge, vol. 3, p. 499 footnote.
200. "Truxtun testified that Burr": Robertson, vol. 1, pp. 487–491.
201. "The Blennerhassetts' gardener, Peter Taylor": Ibid., pp. 494–496.
202. "Colonel George Morgan and his sons": Ibid., pp. 497–498.
202. "Late on December 10, 1806, Allbright testified": Ibid., pp. 509–514; Beirne, p. 184–185.
203. "When informed of Allbright's testimony": Fitch, pp. 29–30.
203. "If prosecutors were 'now done'": Robertson, vol. 1, p. 514.
203. "Simeon Poole, sent by the Ohio governor": Ibid., pp. 515–518, 526–527.
204. "Of even less consequence": Ibid., pp. 526–529.
204. "Dudley Woodbridge, Blennerhassett's business partner": Ibid., pp. 518–521; on Blennerhassett's extreme nearsightedness, Swick 2000, p. 25.
205. "Prosecutors said John Wickham": Robertson, vol. 1, p. 530.
205. "'No doubt ... that the court'": Ibid., pp. 530–532.

CHAPTER 12: EDEN AND THE SERPENT

208. "George Hay and his lawyers": Melton 2002, pp. 206–207.
208. "Treason, the Constitution clearly stated": Constitution, p. 54.
209. "Burr, 'a crooked gun'": Jefferson 1897, vol. 9, pp. 42–43.
209. "'Before an impartial jury'": Ibid., pp. 62–63.
209. "One of them, Chief Justice Marshall": Stites, p. 103.
209. "Wickham was the only American": Beirne, p. 34.
209. "As Burr watched hyper-alertly": Lomask, vol. 2, p. 270.
210. "Throwing down the gauntlet": Robertson, vol. 1, pp. 533–534.
210. "'no person can be punished'": Ibid., pp. 549–550.

210. "What overt act had been proved?": Ibid., p. 594.
211. "Marshall interrupted Wickham": Ibid., p. 584.
211. "It was the court's *duty*": Ibid.
211. "But Israel Miller, a member": Ibid., vol. 2, pp. 1–2.
211. "Defense attorney Edmund Randolph": Ibid., pp. 3–4; Morison, vol. 2, p. 67; Beirne, p. 33.
211. "Randolph and Hay had been": Reardon, pp. 349–350.
212. "The Constitution's framers, said Randolph": Robertson, vol. 2, pp. 3–4.
212. "'What were Bollman and Swartwout'": Ibid., p. 5.
212. "When Randolph had finished": Ibid., pp. 26–27.
213. "The acid-tongued Scotsman": Parton, p. 460; Alexander, vol. 2, p. 28; Robertson, vol. 2, pp. 28, 39.
213. "Orphaned as a boy, Wirt": Beirne, pp. 67–68.
214. "The Bollman decision, Wirt now said": Robertson, vol. 2, pp. 55–56.
214. "'If treason ought to be repressed'": Ibid., p. 66.
215. "'Who is Blennerhassett?'": Ibid., pp. 96–97.
216. "'The conquest was not difficult'": Ibid., p. 97.
216. "'His imagination has been dazzled'": Ibid.
216. "For the next century": Beveridge, vol. 3, p. 497; Parton, p. 497.
216. ". . . except Burr and his defense team": Parton, p. 506.
217. "'I cannot promise you, sir'": Robertson, vol. 2, pp. 123–124.
217. "He scoffed at government's assertion": Ibid., p. 124.
217. "And what did the force": Ibid., p. 125.
218. "'If I run away and hide'": Ibid., p. 130.
218. "'They were so stupid'": Ibid., pp. 135–136.
219. "Botts condemned the government's attempts": Ibid., pp. 168–169.
219. "'I will say,' Botts said mockingly": Ibid., p. 169.

CHAPTER 13: "WILL O' THE WISP TREASON"

221. "Although it was generally believed": Lomask, vol. 2, p. 276.
221. "Regarded by his peers": Beirne, pp. 222–223.
222. "'I cannot instruct you by my learning'": Robertson, vol. 2, p. 192.

222. "In discussing the treason trial": Ibid., p. 193.
222. "Hay had everyone's attention": Ibid.
223. "'Well, sire, what is the thing'": Ibid., p. 194.
223. "It was 'a most dangerous'": Ibid., pp. 200, 205.
223. "Hay quoted to Marshall": Ibid., p. 233.
224. "'If the assemblage on Blennerhassett's Island'": Ibid., p. 210.
224. "In closing, he warned": Ibid., p. 235.
224. "'It was very kind'": Ibid., pp. 238–239.
225. "Having made his point": Ibid., pp. 242–243.
225. "But Martin was not in the courtroom": Ibid., p. 260.
225. "During a recent visit to Blennerhassett's prison": Fitch, p. 68.
226. "The following day, Luther Martin": Robertson, vol. 2, p. 260.
226. "It is the duty of the court'": Ibid., pp. 260, 262.
227. "He then began his frontal assault": Ibid., pp. 275, 324.
227. "'We see what a system of oppression'": Ibid., p. 348.
227. ". . . saved from hoarseness by frequent sips": Schachner 1961, p. 436.
227. "'there was no proof'": Robertson, vol. 2, pp. 333–334.
228. "All other issues addressed": Ibid., pp. 334–335.
228. "Levying war, he said, 'must'": Ibid, p. 336.
228. "'If I were to name this'": Ibid., p. 337.
228. "'If open deeds, notorious facts'": Ibid., p. 319.
229. "'We say that there is no evidence'": Ibid., pp. 362–363.
229. "'We labor against great prejudices'": Ibid., pp. 377–378.

CHAPTER 14: MARSHALL'S RULING FOR THE AGES

231. "Working until late Saturday night": Simon, p. 252; Stites, p. 98.
232. "Although composed rapidly": Beveridge, vol. 3, p. 504; Simon, p. 252.
232. "Catholics went to a Mass": Beirne, p. 235.
232. "An eye-catching advertisment": Ibid., p. 232.
233. "He began by praising the attorneys": Robertson, vol. 2, p. 401.
234. "And the English doctrine": Ibid., p. 405.
234. "'If a body of men be actually assembled'": Marshall, vol. 6, p. 488.
234. "Bollman's and Swartwout's participation": Robertson, vol. 2, p. 405.

234. "While four of the seven justices": Ibid., p. 406.
235. "This issue, the chief justice said": Ibid., pp. 407, 413–414.
235. "'that an opinion which is to overrule'": Ibid., p. 415.
235. "The point of the Bollman ruling": Ibid., pp. 415–416.
236. "'It is then the opinion of the court'": Ibid., p. 439.
236. "If this were a statutory felony": Ibid., p. 440.
236. "'The legal guilt of the person'": Ibid., p. 441.
237. "'The law of the case'": Ibid. pp. 442–443.
237. "If that was not clear enough": Ibid., p. 445.
237. "'That this court dares not usurp'": Ibid., pp. 444–445.
238. "Until World War II": Stites, p. 101.
238. "Turning to the jurors": Ibid., p. 445.
238. "Hay's parsing of Marshall's decision": Malone, p. 337.
238. "On Tuesday, September 1": Robertson, vol. 2, pp. 446–447; Beirne, p. 242.
239. ". . . the treason charges against the remaining": Robertson, vol. 2, p. 448.
239. "Davis Floyd, the seventh defendant": Lomask, vol. 2, p. 381; Abernethy, p. 263.
240. ". . . Hay requested a new treason trial": Robertson, vol. 2, pp. 452, 455.
240. "Burr enjoyed his liberty": Fitch, p. 78; Minnigerode, pp. 137–138.
240. ". . . lawsuits against him totaled $36,000": Safford, p. 466.
240. "'We could now new-model them'": Fitch, pp. 87–88.
241. ". . . he attended a concert": Ibid., pp. 81–85.
241. "He made the acquaintance": Beirne, p. 57.
241. "'From this lady, the near relation'": Fitch, pp. 134–135.
241. "'I suspect . . . Mr. Marshall early perceived'": Ibid., p. 77.
241. "Blennerhassett's delight with again being at liberty": Schachner 1961, p. 440; Minnigerode, pp. 139–140; Fitch, p. 168.

CHAPTER 15: "A SORT OF DRAWN BATTLE"

243. "'The event has been what'": Jefferson 1897, vol. 9, p. 63.
244. "Hay stoked the president's anger": Schachner 1961, p. 438.

244. "'It is now, therefore, more than ever'": McCaleb 1966, p. 293.

244. "The president and Secretary of State James Madison": Jefferson 1897, vol. 9, p. 63; McCaleb 1966, pp. 293–294.

245. "'As I do not believe'": Jefferson 1897, vol. 9, p. 63.

245. "But upon cooler reflection": Ibid., pp. 63–64.

245. "Burr had somehow managed": Fitch, p. 100.

246. "When five days of testimony": Robertson, vol. 2, p. 539; Schachner 1961, p. 441.

246. "'The scenes which have been'": Jefferson 1897, vol. 9, pp. 142–143.

247. "'The disgraceful and dishonorable scenes'": Beirne, p. 248.

247. "'Impeachment is a farce'": Jefferson 1897, vol. 9, pp. 42–43, 46, 142.

248. "'Removal by address'": Elsmere, p. 193.

248. "'The period has arrived'": Malone, p. 353.

248. "A Blennerhassett neighbor, Alexander Henderson": *Amer. State Papers*, X, vol. 1, pp. 525–526.

249. "William Eaton testified that Burr": Ibid., pp. 537–538.

249. "During his cross-examination of Eaton": Ibid., pp. 602–605.

250. "Littleton Tazewell testified that": Ibid., p. 587.

250. "Major James Bruff, an Army": Ibid., pp. 571–578; Beirne, p. 118.

251. "Wilkinson indignantly denied": Ibid., pp. 571, 579–580.

251. "'We wish to show that General Wilkinson'": Ibid., pp. 704–705.

252. "But on the witness stand, Power refused": Ibid., pp. 608–610.

252. "He admitted having written": Ibid., pp. 579–580.

253. "He had sent Jefferson": Ibid., pp. 542–543, 560.

253. "Wilkinson's long correspondence with Carondelet": Ibid., pp. 545–546.

253. "Samuel Swartwout, who had delivered": Brunson, pp. 27–28.

254. "John Wickham's withering cross-examination": Fitch, p. 111.

254. "'General Wilkinson exhibited the manner'": Ibid., p. 105.

254. "'My confidence in him [Wilkinson]'": McCaleb 1963, p. 124; Hay and Werner, p. 281.

254. "Federalist newspapers acidly suggested": Malone, p. 347; *Virginia Gazette*, October 17 and September 30, 1807.

254. "'And is Mr. Jefferson to be the judge'": Beirne, p. 256.

255. "Blennerhassett deplored the government's": Fitch, pp. 93–94.

255. "'a host of enemies whetted'": Richmond *Enquirer*, October 27, 1807; D. Clark, notes 2–6.

255. Prosecutor William Wirt lampooned Luther Martin's": *Amer. State Papers*, X, vol. 1, p. 554.

256. "'Weighing the whole of this testimony'": Ibid., pp. 644–645.

256. "... Blennerhassett sarcastically noted": Fitch, p. 136.

256. "After all, this is a sort'": Burr 1970, vol. 2, p. 411.

256. "William Duane's Philadelphia *Aurora*": Beveridge, vol. 3, pp. 531–533, 535.

257. "'This opinion was a matter'": Burr 1970, vol. 2, p. 412.

257. "'He [Marshall] is a good man'": Safford, p. 301.

257. "'... the most unpleasant case'": Marshall, vol. 7, p. 165.

258. "Joseph Hamilton Daviess": Beveridge, vol. 3, p. 525; Malone, p. 355; D. Clark, p. 146.

258. "... while Jefferson had once been": Malone, p. 356.

258. "Blennerhassett described the pamphlet": Safford, pp. 465–467.

258. "'From the whole you will be'": Jefferson 1897, vol. 9, p. 163.

259. "Excised from an early draft": Ibid.

259. "Blennerhassett, for one, understood": Fitch, p. 140.

259. "Jefferson asked Congressman John Randolph": Malone, pp. 368–369; Beveridge, vol. 3, pp. 540–543.

259. "Ohio Senator Edwin Tiffin proposed": Schachner 1951, p. 858.

259. "The committee concluded that even though": Malone, p. 360; *Amer. State Papers*, X, vol. 1, pp. 701–703.

260. "Wickham, whom Wilkinson accused": Abernethy, p. 244.

260. "The general then called out Randolph": McCaleb 1966, pp. 276–277; Bruce, vol. 1, pp. 313–314.

260. "Rather than duel Wilkinson, Randolph": Abernethy, pp. 265–266; Malone, pp. 364–365.

260. "In a letter to Congress, Vicente Folch": Cox, *Amer. Hist. Rev.*, No. 19, pp. 806–807.

261. "Jefferson headed off Randolph's": Hay and Werner, p. 289; Malone, p. 366.

EPILOGUE

263. "Burr asked Harman Blennerhassett": Lomask, vol. 2, p. 291; Safford, pp. 451–452.

264. "In Baltimore, fifteen hundred angry citizens": Beveridge, vol. 3, pp. 535–539.

264. "Blennerhassett and Burr argued": Ibid.; Safford, p. 517.

264. ". . . Attorney General Caesar Rodney's description": *Examination,* pp. 25–26.

264. ". . . Blennerhassett remembered that acting Mississippi": Fitch, pp. 147, 114.

265. "His friend Charles Biddle": Lomask, vol. 2, p. 293.

265. "On June 9, the packet *Clarissa Ana*": Schachner 1961, p. 449.

265. "During the early 1790s, Jefferson and Madison": Malone, p. 475.

266. "The Embargo Act of December 1807": Ibid., pp. 488–489.

266. "Deprived of imports and foreign markets": Boyer, p. 224.

266. "Burr made a lifelong friend of": Schachner 1961, pp. 452–453.

266. "Burr blamed 'Mr. Jefferson'": Burr 1983, vol. 2, p. 1091.

266. "At one point, Burr, hoping to avoid": Schachner 1961, pp. 456–461.

266. "He sailed to Sweden, then": Ibid., pp. 461–471.

267. "(Napoleon Bonaparte only dreamed": Gilbert, pp. 1085–1086.

267. "Burr also advanced other proposals": Schachner 1961, pp. 475–477; McCaleb 1966, p. 139.

267. "Louis Roux, a French functionary": Burr 1983, vol. 2, p. 1105.

267. "Burr was ready to go home, but"; Lomask, vol. 2, p. 344; McCaleb 1966, pp. 154–156.

268. ". . . Burr shivered in a freezing": Schachner 1961, pp. 482–485.

268. "His shorthand for this was *muse*": Lomask, vol. 2, p. 301.

268. "'Tell me that you are engaged'": Ibid., p. 306.

268. "To Treasury Secretary Albert Gallatin": Ibid., p. 324.

269. "'Why . . . is my father banished'": Schachner 1961, p. 479.

269. "'She expresses great affection for me'": Swick 1975, p. 503.

269. "'My windows look over the ocean'": Burr 1970, vol. 2, pp. 244–245.

269. "... a British privateer captured": Schachner 1961, pp. 491–495.
269. "... a fire had destroyed the new Richmond Theatre": Stanard, pp. 104–107; Duke and Jordan, p. 51.
270. "In 1813, Wilkinson's surprise seizure": Hay and Werner, p. 312–322.
270. "Eight hundred British troops": Heidler and Heidler, pp. 554–555.
271. "... Scott was a lieutenant colonel": Ibid., pp. 464–465.
271. "President Madison remembered Andrew Jackson's": Remini, p. 158.
271. "But Tennessee chose Jackson": Heidler and Heidler, pp. 260–262.
272. "The time had come, said Burr, to break up": Burr 1970, vol. 2, pp. 434–436; Parton, p. 607.
272. "In the meantime, General Jackson would": *Funk & Wagnalls* vol. 10, p. 283; Boyer, p. 8.
272. "Hay was appointed": Beirne, p. 278.
272. "Of Burr's attorneys, only": Virginia Historical Society, Historic Richmond Foundation, John Wickham biography.
272. "Benjamin Botts perished in the": Beirne, p. 278; Schachner 1961, p. 505.
272. "In 1821, Marshall and the Judiciary could still": Beirne, p. 278; Jefferson 1897, vol. 10, p. 189.
273. "... great Lama of the mountains'": Stites, p. 136.
274. "He [Jefferson] is among the most ambitious'": Marshall, vol. 9, p. 179.
274. "Marshall presided over the Supreme Court": Stites, pp. 109, 167.
274. "Marshall was pessimistic about": Ibid., pp. 152–153.
274. "Harman Blennerhassett rejoined his family": Swick 2000, p. 45.
275. "In a desperate attempt": Minnigerode, pp. 139–140, 144–145.
275. "The Blennerhassetts sold La Cache": Safford, pp. 641–649; Swick 2000, p. 45; Lomask, vol. 2, p. 387.
275. "Margaret was left penniless": Beirne, pp. 284–285.
275. "'There rose the seat, where once'": M. Blennerhassett, "The Desert Isle," from *The Widow of the Rock*, p. 119. In the 1990s, the remains of Mrs. Blennerhassett and one of her sons, Harman Jr., were found in New York City in an unmarked underground

mausoleum that held the intermingled remains of more than a dozen other people. Those of the mother and son were transported to Blennerhassett Island and reinterred in a funeral ceremony on June 29, 1996, four years after the commencement of the exhaustive effort to recover them, which was privately funded and supported by Parkersburg, W.Va.-area citizens. Today, black granite monuments mark the two gravesites near the reconstructed Blennerhassett Mansion.

276. "... Aaron Burr reopened his law practice": Schachner 1961, p. 497.

276. "Two letters arrived": Parton, p. 597.

277. "Twenty-nine-year-old Theodosia's constitution": Côté, pp. 259–260.

277. "Theodosia was bringing her father": Burr 1983, vol. 1, p. xxx.

277. "But Dr. Timothy Greene": Burr 1970, vol. 2, p. 428.

278. "For weeks, Burr": Parton, p. 599; Lomask, vol. 2, p. 362.

278. "The most enduring, which launched": Côté, pp. 280–281.

278. "The wrecker story was revived": Ibid, pp. 307–313.

279. "His avocation as a guardian": Schachner 1961, p. 503; Parton, pp. 608–610; Lomask, vol. 2, pp. 384–388.

280. "... Burr was enjoying 'a green old age'": Lomask, vol. 2, pp. 372–373.

280. "When he was seventy-seven, Burr married": Ibid., vol. 3, pp. 399–401.

280. "Months later, Burr suffered": Schachner 1961, p. 514; Lomask, vol. 2, p. 405.

280. "'There! You see? I was right!'": Parton, p. 670.

280. "Aaron Burr was buried with honors": Burr 1970, vol. 2, pp. 447–449.

281. "Today, yellowwood and white pine": Author's visit to gravesite.

281. "The men removed their hats": McCaleb 1963, p. 310.

281. "The New York Review of 1838": Lomask, vol. 2, pp. 364–365.

281. "'There never was a greater villain'": Parton, p. 641.

282. "Yet he was prone to a singular weakness": Burr 1983, vol. 2, pp. 920–925.

282. "'No, I would as soon have'": Burr 1970, vol. 2, p. 378 note, 379.

283. "Yet reputation appeared to matter little": Parton, pp. 626–627.

284. "'A great man, and perhaps as'": Lomask, vol. 2, pp. 372–373.

285. "In his *History of the United States*": H. Adams, vol. 1, p. 332.

286. "But the trial and its aftermath": Stites, pp. 108–109.

287. "'No man's history proves better'": Jefferson 1900, vol. 1, p. 111.

Acknowledgments

I am grateful to Philip Turner, editor of Carroll & Graf Publishers, for having suggested this book to me, as well as for his support and suggestions during the project's embryonic stages.

Dr. Ray Swick, the historian for Blennerhassett Island State Historical Park, in Parkersburg, W. Va., devoted hours of his valuable time to assisting me in gathering information on that tragic émigré couple, Harman and Margaret Blennerhassett. Dr. Swick also shared some extremely useful facts about Theodosia Burr Alston, and about Aaron Burr himself, and provided an informative guided tour of the reconstructed Blennerhassett mansion.

Mark Greenough, supervisor of tours and historian at the Virginia State Capitol, set me straight on how the Virginia House of Delegates probably appeared in 1807, and generously shared his knowledge about early-nineteenth-century Richmond.

I wish to thank the staffs of Davis Library at the University of North Carolina-Chapel Hill, D.H. Hill Library at North Carolina State University, and the Library of Virginia, in Richmond. In helping me rummage through their institutions' impressive resources, these librarians made my research enjoyable and productive.

I am indebted to my literary agent, Edward Knappman of New England Publishing Associates, for his unvarnished advice on projects past, present, and future.

And I wish to thank my wife, Dr. Pat Wheelan, for her unstinting support down through the years.

Index